Karateka

Nik Forster

First published in 2017 on Amazon Kindle by Ex-L-Ence Publishing a
division of Winghigh Limited, England, www.ex-l-ence.com

This paperback edition published in 2023

ISBN 978-0-645-55640-7

Printed and bound by Ingram Spark

5 Star Review

Bought the ebook at 10:00am today and just finished reading the whole thing at 4:00pm. It was so good that I didn't leave the computer all that time. Nicely interwoven story and very well written. From martial arts details to human relationships and mistakes we're all capable of making, and then hoping to find a way out of them. Try it, you won't be sorry!

Ron Richmond

4th dan senior Instructor
Shotokan Karate

Dedicated to the memory of Shihan Frank Novak. Also, thanks to Sensei Kora Novak, 6th dan Shotokan Karate, for all those years of training.

Preface

I have set Karateka in the early eighties when Karate was seen as the ultimate form of combat and used my experience as a Karateka to convey my knowledge and endeavour to relate a story that may interest those who practice the art and hopefully those who don't.

All characters are fictitious as well as the events.

I spent three years in Japan and although times have changed, Karate is still practiced worldwide, albeit in different styles.

Chapter One

One - Hardship and a fatal error

Bulldozer's first attack caused me to sidestep and dance out of reach. The fear, the apprehension, the nervousness left me as I concentrated on the man opposite; his intention to put me on my back. In his haste to nail me his guard dropped and gave me an opportunity to drive a hard mae geri (front kick) into the space provided just above his groin and below his naval. The kick took him off his feet and sent him to the floor. The crowd shouted their approval. I stepped back and waited.

After a few seconds he heaved himself up and staggered to his feet. I looked at the toothless tattooed man, his bleary eyes and laboured breath. I don't know why but it seemed as soon as I'd knocked an opponent down, I felt sympathetic. I shot a glance at the ref to see if he wanted us to continue the fight.

It was the 20th of April, the year 1983; I will always remember that day.

My name is Tony Mason; I was twenty-three years of age when I fought Bulldozer, I am not exactly tall, lean with dark hair, what's left of it, blue eyes, and an avid practitioner of the martial arts.

Perhaps, if you'll bear with me, it may be more informative if I start and recount the early days of my life from childhood up until this day, to give you some idea of my background, and why I was fighting Bulldozer.

My interest in Karate had initially been kindled by the spate of films that appeared in my youth illustrating this stylised art of combat.

At eight years of age, I watched a Japanese film called Yojimbo which starred Toshiro Mifune and included a fight that demonstrated martial arts; screened some time before the athletic and theatrical Bruce Lee burst onto the scene to inspire young martial artists throughout the world, or the letters MMA, (Mixed Martial Arts), held any meaning.

The choreographed violence and balletic disposal of villains as well as the philosophy, sewed the seed in my mind to follow a career devoted to learning more about this method of fighting.

My first practical experience of my chosen path took place one year later. My father escorted me to a rundown dusty church hall in East Malvern, a suburb of Melbourne close to where we lived.

The cracked windows and graffiti on the outside walls did nothing to dampen my enthusiasm to join the first class, or for the total commitment I felt needed to be given to the sport if I was to be any good; I couldn't wait to wear the "white pyjamas" like the other students.

The instructor, a young Sho (first) dan, pronounced dun, considered I had potential and gave me encouragement; after only a few classes he spent extra time with me to go through Kata (the form of Karate) and practice techniques; but it was sparring that I enjoyed most of all and without the label of "tickets on myself," meaning I thought I was something special, I did extremely well in all the competitions I entered.

I had quick reactions and timing, but also put in a lot of hard work.

In my first junior tournament as a yellow belt, I carried off first prize in my age group for both Kumite (fighting) and Kata (form).

An accumulation of trophies and cups adorned my bedroom as I approached manhood. I still endeavoured to train as many days a week as possible.

My prowess as a fighter developed and I was proud of my ability although my father told me that, "Modesty and humility were virtues to be cherished and not to lose sight of things in life that were important."

Both my parents had been supportive but initially took my ambition to become a professional martial artist with scepticism and although perhaps disappointed with their son's chosen career, did not stand in my way.

It was at the age of eighteen as a first dan karateka that my life changed dramatically and not for the last time.

My father was a salesman for a Japanese car company and, although not a wealthy man, earned enough to feed his family and educate his children: me, my brother, and my small sister. My mother had been a schoolteacher and worked part time at a local primary school to bring in extra money for a holiday or something that would help the family budget.

It was a Sunday afternoon in July; the weather cool even for Melbourne and had drizzled persistently from early morning.

I didn't train on Sundays, not for any religious reason, more to rest my body. That day I tinkered about in the garage to replace a gasket on my car, an old Holden I'd bought from a mate of mine several months before. I could have gone to university when I finished school but chose to work for a garage as a pump attendant to save money so I could go to live and train in Japan.

I would rise early each morning even before the cock cleared his throat, train before I started work, and then don my Karate Gi (Karate suit) again in the evening.

I had been granted a cultural visa by the Japanese embassy and was set to go to Tokyo in January of the following year.

"God willing," as my mother used to say when things were certain but with the chance uncertain ways of the world could prevail.

I was about to clean up some oil from the garage floor when my father's head popped around the door.

'Are you gonna come with us mate?'

The idea didn't exactly fill me with excitement.

'No, I'll finish this dad. How long will you be?'

My father drew in an audible breath and his mind made mental calculations of the time it took to go and return from Heidelberg, a suburb several kilometres away from where we lived.

'About a couple of hours or so.'

I looked at my dad and decided,

'No, I won't come, I'd get bored.'

'That's not nice son, it's yer aunt.'

He seemed stern for a moment, and I thought maybe I shouldn't have said that, but after a second or two his expression softened, and he gave a nod of agreement.

'But yer right, she does go on, see yer later son.'

'I smiled at my dad's last remark and returned to wipe up the spilled oil.

I remember every detail of that day.

The banter as the family made preparation to leave, heard my sister instruct the cat to behave itself and tell him she would be back as soon as possible, my twelve-year old brother ask my mother if John, our cousin, a boy of similar age would be there; my father as he told the family,

"For God's sake hurry up and get organised or we'll never get out.'

They loaded the car and clambered in.

Doors slammed, belts were fastened and after the occupants had fidgeted and arranged things internally to their satisfaction, dad eventually turned the ignition key and they set off.

I arrived back at my house around ten o'clock, I had visited Kevin, a close friend of mine, at his parent's place and although it continued to drizzle, walked the two kilometres that separated our homes deep in thought about the future, the girls I'd liked at school, and how without any conscious effort I had dedicated myself to martial arts.

I'd never considered myself to be an aggressive person, parental guidance and my own ambition had given me, so I was told, a well–balanced attitude towards life.

I'd experienced the usual hormonal changes in my early teens and the frustrations that this transition sometimes brings, but overall reached the age of eighteen with comparatively few of life's bruises.

The lights weren't on in the house as I pushed open the gate to be greeted by the cat who rubbed himself excitedly between my legs.

'Hey, hold it puss, just relax.'

This display of friendship meant only one thing, Tiddles had not been fed.

'Alright, alright, I'll feed you.' I muttered.

I thought it strange that my parents were so late but dismissed it as probably due to my aunt's enthusiastic verbal diarrhoea. I turned the key and went inside, the cat continued to rub himself affectionately against my legs accompanied by pathetic miaows. I switched on the light and headed for the kitchen.

'Ok, ok let's get your little guts sorted out.' The cat gave a soulful wail of hunger, stretched up to me and extended his two front paws.

I ignored his plaintiff cries, went to the fridge got his food out and spooned a couple of dollops of coagulated fish from the tin into his bowl. The flash of a small green light caught my eye.

The answer machine in the kitchen blinked on and off.

I wiped my fingers on a nearby tea towel and pressed the button. The machine rewound and clicked on.

'Where are you? It's four thirty. I thought you were coming over today?'

I recognised the voice as that of my verbose aunt.

The machine clicked off; there was the sound of an elongated bleep, then silence, followed by a voice which lasted just a second before the clatter of the receiver.

I decided to shut the cat up first before I attended to the answer machine and placed the now prepared dish of food onto the floor. Tiddles raced over to the offered bowl.

As I straightened up into the vertical position the machine again registered the sound of a voice just for a second and then repeated the clatter of the replaced receiver. This procedure occurred several times before the long bleep announced that this was the final call.

I was puzzled, who could have called so frequently? Was it my aunt? If so, what did she want? In the first call she had enquired about my family's arrival but after that there was no indication as to who the caller had been. I decided to call her.

The silence of my contemplation was interrupted by the loud ring of the doorbell. The suddenness startled me momentarily; I went and answered it.

A police officer stood in the doorway.

'Tony Mason?' he enquired.

I nodded; I knew something bad had happened by his sombre tone and expression.

'May I come in sir?' He asked.

'What's happened?' I began to understand the continual calls and my family's lateness. I felt a rush of blood go to my head and my knees weaken.

The cop informed me my family had been killed in a car accident. He went on to explain the situation, two young boys under the influence of alcohol had stolen a car, the police had given chase and my family had been in a head on collision with the police car. One cop had also been killed and the other was in intensive care, the youths had been apprehended an hour later when they crashed into a road sign.

I couldn't speak.

The thought of my family incarcerated in metal like filing cabinets or laid out on slabs with tags on their toes, covered with sheets, filled me with horror.

The shock of the news caused me to feel as though I had been kicked in the guts. Despair, sadness, anger, and grief welled up inside me, images of my little sister, my mother, my kind gentle mother, a woman who was always ready to help anyone, any time; my younger brother, a fun-loving rebel with his life before him, and my father, the symbol of my security, the man I could always turn to in moments of stress for advice. All of them now locked away in some dark morgue mutilated and bruised; my imagination caused me to wince involuntarily, the realisation that it was true and not some awful nightmare seeped into my stunned consciousness.

'NO! NO!' I gave a yell of frustration, but I couldn't expel the pain, hurt and emptiness that I felt.

'Surely this hasn't happened please tell me it's not real!'

I stood clenched fisted, hunched over in mental torment. The police officer tried to calm me 'No-o-o-o!!' the scream caused the cat to abandon its meal and run through the cat door into the yard. I fell to my knees.

Several weeks passed, I'd gone from occupant of a happy, supportive family home to a young man bereft by the loss of those held most precious.

My father had not been rich but had paid off the mortgage on the house and saved for him and my mother's retirement. This would now be mine.

'Dad wanted me to go to Uni and do a degree in physical education,' I remarked to my friend Kevin on a bright August day as we sat in the park and watched the movement of the Melbourne traffic.

'What about Japan?'

'I dunno, I can always go to Japan, but I guess I won't always have the chance to go to Uni.'

'Yeah,' Kevin agreed as he shifted on the bench and gazed up into the cloudless blue sky.

'I think that's what I'll do. Go to Uni and then go to Japan with the money Dad left me and if I sell the house, I should be OK.'

'Dead right you'll be OK. No worries; go for it.'

I followed Kevin's upward gaze.

'What are yer lookin' at?'

'I was listening to you, but I was thinking about that crow up there circling. Free, free, can do as he likes, go where he wants. You're a bit like that now you can go anywhere, do anything yer like.'

I looked at Kev.

'Yeah, as long as nobody shoots yer down.'

Kev looked back at me.

'Nobody'll shoot yer down Tone. You're too tough for that.'

'I'm not tough, Kev. Sure, I can fight but that's not tough. Toughness comes from inside you. It's having control, being in control, not giving in to panic and fear. No, I'm not tough, I'm worried about the future. I've lost a big chunk of me and know I'll never get it back.'

'Course yer will. It takes time. What happened was terrible; the most terrible thing that could have happened. But that's in the past now, your mum and dad would want you to make something of yer life, to do good things, to be a success or whatever.'

My eyes began to become misty, and I suppressed the urge to give in to my emotions, switched my thoughts and tried not to betray my feelings to Kevin.

Kevin sensed my state of mind and patted me affectionately on my shoulder.

'Go to Uni, get yer degree. Do it for yourself and yer dad. Come on, let's walk, I'm getting hungry.'

I nodded; we left the bench and made our way through the park neither one of us spoke.

·········

Despite my aunt's penchant for lengthy conversation, I accepted her generous offer to allow me to move in with my cousins whilst I was at university. This was obviously more economically viable for me and enabled me to save my inheritance for Japan.

All the while I continued to improve my martial arts skills.

Each day except for Sundays I would go for a five-kilometre run and then practice Kata and techniques for an hour; at lunchtime I would train with weights, and then spar in the evening.

I had a single-mindedness of purpose that motivated me, to fight in Japan.

My university years had been my most competitive in the martial arts and as second dan I won all the major national tournaments and began to build a reputation for myself as a competent martial artist. My timing and skill had improved over the years, but I put my skills down to hard work and the luck of my genes and refused to be thought of as any one special.

My style of Karate was non-contact; well, competitions were supposedly so, although I had watched many teeth separate from a few gums in the early days of these so-called non-contact matches.

I watched the full contact tournaments with a mixture of curiosity and admiration. I often thought how I would survive against the onslaught of someone whose sole purpose, without restraint, was to flatten me. Maybe I should put it to the test. I put my name down for a full contact bout with mixed feelings, perhaps because although it may sound strange at this stage in my life, I didn't like to hit people, or for that matter be hit, but mainly because my idea of Karate was that it should be lethal, and as much as possible the concept of ippon, one strike finish. In non-contact competitions points are awarded for the perceived theoretical damage to one's opponent if the strike or kick had not been pulled at the last moment; or a punch to the body had scored over a punch to the head because it would have made contact a second sooner; I have witnessed many blows or kicks that would not incapacitate my grandmother but were given the flag by the corner judges as worthy of points.

Not far from where I lived there was a boxing gym, I was curious and decided to look in the next time I passed. It was a small building and one had to climb to the second floor to reach it.

I entered, there was a full-sized ring in the centre of the room in which two fighters, wearing headgear and gloves, threw punches at each other. There were also many bags, speed balls, and floor to ceilings; a device which consisted of a leather ball in the centre of a strong rubber support anchored to the floor and attached to the ceiling.

Several young men and a couple of women skipped or worked on the available apparatus.

It had an ambience of no-nonsense hard work, sweat and dedication.

I took in the scene and was approached by Joe Callan, a typical boxing coach; grey hair, lived in face, around sixty years of age.

'Can I help you son?' He asked.

I explained I'd entered a contest and wanted to get some experience of boxing techniques and if possible, do some sparring. He listened but I gathered from his manner that he was not impressed with karate. He agreed but, on the condition, I trained for a couple of weeks as he wouldn't put me in the ring without the knowledge that I could fight. I said OK.

It was strange at first, my fighting stance had to adapt, and I needed to keep my hands up to protect my face; instructed to move my head more, weave and duck. With gloves it was a totally different experience and seemed to make punches from the hip impractical, far weaker and left your jaw exposed.

After two weeks I'd trained twelve times and sensed that Joe, after watching me, considered me ready to spar. I'd finished on the speed ball when the trainer beckoned to Jacob to jump into the ring with me to go a couple of rounds. He was a young boxer about my age, with a fight booked for the next week.

We faced each other dressed in headgear, mouth, and groin guards.

The bell rang; I'd always been good with my kicks and felt disadvantaged I now had to rely solely on my hands. Jacob danced around and threw several jabs, I could see that he meant business, I parried and countered with a right cross which landed squarely on his jaw, he tottered back then regained his balance.

Whilst we fought, Jimmy Winston, another trainer, a boxing coach from Sydney entered the gym. He stood and watched outside the ring next to Joe.

Jacob again came in hard, and I threw a left body rip and another right cross to his head, this time he went down. I felt several mixed emotions and went to help him up.

Joe chastised him.

'Bloody hell man, how many times do I need to tell you keep yer bleedin' guard up, you walked straight into that cross.' Jimmy nodded approvingly and turned to Joe.

'Could have been luck,' he said.

Joe looked around the gym, a small nuggety pugilist hammered away on a heavy bag close to one of the walls.

'Sammy! Joe yelled. get some gear on and come and do a couple of rounds.'

Joe didn't want to put Jacob back in the ring in case he got concussed and would not be able to fight for a few months, in accordance with amateur boxing rules.

Sammy, headgear, and mouth guard in place, jumped into the ring.

He nodded, we touched gloves. Sammy was experienced, I found out later, a title holder in two different weight divisions. I'd watched him train and had a lot of respect for him.

He threw a few punches in my direction to suss me out and moved well, obviously fit. As the round progressed, he got busier, several combinations forced me back onto the ropes. I managed to defend against most of his attack but copped a left hook. I was fortunate to bring up my right arm close to my head and wore most of the blow on my bicep and forearm; I felt the sting in my ear for some time.

I knew Sammy was a skilled boxer and had to get with it or suffer the consequences. He moved his head a fraction to the left before he threw a punch, an almost indiscernible twitch and I waited for his next attack. He did it again and I threw a right hook, he lifted his left arm to protect his face and I drove a left uppercut to his jaw, he brought his shoulder up and dropped his chin to ward off the blow, I followed with an overhead right as he lowered his shoulder and hit him between the eyes. He staggered.

I could have finished him but chose to give him time to recover. He looked at me through glazed eyes and nodded; Jimmy and Joe exchanged glances from the other side of the ropes; several of the gym's patrons had stopped to watch.

In the second round Sammy was more cautious and I went in for the attack, I landed several jabs in the early stage and Sammy's nose and right eye wore proof of my contact. My strategy was to attack when opportune and then retreat and I saw him become more agitated as his failed efforts to land a knockout punch only frustrated him more. I got through with a solid left hook followed by a body rip which winded him and sent him down onto one knee for a count of eight; again, I could have finished him but chose not to. Joe called time.

Jimmy came over to me as I climbed through the ropes.

'Not bad son, not bad at all, ever thought about going pro?'

'Not really I'm sort of into Karate more than boxing.'

'Mate, take it from me you could have a future in the ring, chance to make some good money.' Jimmy turned to Joe.

'How long have you been keeping this guy under wraps?' Jimmy enquired.

'He's been with me for a couple of weeks' Joe responded.

'Where have you fought before son?' Jimmy asked.

'I've never boxed before; I'm going in for a full contact tournament and I wanted to get the feel of things; of someone trying to get through my defence.'

'You've never boxed before, two fuckin' weeks? Well, you're a bloody quick learner that's all I can say. Joe, try and get this kid to change his mind; he's a natural.' Turning to me he said, 'I've got a gym in Sydney, if yer do change yer mind and if you are up that way call me.' He took a card from his wallet.

'I'll leave this in the office, and you can pick it up when you leave.'

I thanked Joe for his help and for allowing me to train at his gym, I didn't go back as the tournament was in a couple of days but felt far more confident to compete and was grateful for the opportunity to box.

·········

The full contact tournament lacked observation of etiquette prominent in traditional karate and was an open style contest with Tae Kwando, Kung Fu, Kick boxing and any fight style that utilised kicks and punches. It was fought under similar rules to Kick boxing no grappling or throws, kicks below the waist permitted.

I had been learning boxing and was confident that I had enough control to refrain from any infringement of the rules and could give a good account of myself on the mat. I filled in my form and went through all the formalities, signed the disclaimer of responsibility by the promoters and was allocated a number and opponent after I had paid my insurance fees.

The tournament was held at the Dallas Brookes Hall in Melbourne, a large, impressive building built in 1969, that resembled from the outside a huge library and played host to many varied sports, musical and theatrical events throughout its existence. It was scheduled for demolition in 2005 but still stands.

The day arrived. Bag in hand I walked through to the interior that had the capacity to hold two thousand spectators.

There were a good few people gathered inside, several dozen seats were aligned and set-in rows that faced a raised matted area in the centre. I felt like a gladiator and imagined myself as one about to enter an arena and fight for the entertainment of the crowd, which I suppose had some ring of truth to it. Usually when I took part in a competition, I experienced slight anxiety but that was negligible to what I now felt in an area so vast and impressive.

I was directed to a red-faced man in blue jacket and grey flannel trousers, seated at a desk with a sheet of paper in front of him. He ticked my name off a list and pointed to a door.

'Over there, that door there. Be ready in half an hour. There's a short opening ceremony.'

He turned his attention to another young man who had come up beside me.

"Maybe I shouldn't have done this. Maybe I shouldn't have been so hasty." I entered the "dressing rooms" and caught sight of some of the contestants.

"Gee, they're big blokes, I wonder is there a weight category?" I placed my bag on a nearby bench. In the early days, many full contact matches had no weight division and big men would invariably dominate.

A cropped haired man in his mid–twenties, with tattoos and a musculature like Sammy, the man I'd fought as a boxer, proceeded to get changed. I noted that he had hardly any neck and two front teeth missing.

'G'day,' I said in a gesture of friendship.

The man glanced at me as he hoisted his gi trousers up; he nodded condescendingly in my direction but said nothing.

I shot a quick look at his hands; his knuckles were gnarled and the first two at the base of his index and digital fingers were large and hardened and gave the appearance of growths on either hand.

You can generally tell a Karate man by his exaggerated knuckles. Well, one who practises on the Makiwara (striking pad traditionally made from bound rice straw). I looked at my own knuckles as I took off my shirt and fished in my bag for my gi, they were somewhat smaller but equally adept to send vibrations through the Makiwara.

"I mustn't be intimidated by appearances. Things are not what they seem. Never overestimate or underestimate the enemy." Advice given to me by my first instructor gave me comfort. The butterflies in my stomach fluttered uneasily as I drew my belt tightly around my waist.

"Well, here we go. Let's do it." I placed my clothes and valuables in the locker provided, secured the combination, and memorised the numbers as I did so.

Mostly men and a few women, clad in an assortment of uniforms of different styles, had filed out of the separate dressing rooms and into the raised arena, their numbers spilled over into the spectator area.

The audience were seated and waited expectantly as the contestants took their place. A microphone squealed and the voice of the red–faced man, who'd given me directions earlier, filled the hall. He said something about the importance of the event, how nice it was to see so many people and the usual platitudes that roll off the tongues of MC's and persons who prepare audiences for things to come and slip in the odd commercial plug.

The contestants ranged in age mostly from eighteen to late thirties and came from every walk of life, some with pleasant unscathed features, and others with downright battered faces like a bag of chisels.

After a few more martial arts dignitaries had stepped onto the mat and praised the various organisers for making this much anticipated event possible, the contestants vacated the arena and the fights commenced.

I was listed as event number eighteen on the programme and although I had recognised a few faces from among the other exponents it was relatively few by comparison to the non–contact or semi–contact contests of my previous tournaments. Usually, I knew almost everybody and had fought against the same opponent more than once.

I watched the first bout from the open door of the waiting area. The two men were of similar build, both stocky and about five foot eight inches tall, one wore a black Kung Fu outfit, the other a Tae Kwando gi. Both wore twelve ounce gloves a requisite for the competition.

The referee called the two opponents together and gave them a brief lecture on what was allowed and what was not: no elbows to the head or kicks to the groin, no biting or eye gauging. Although with gloves this could prove difficult especially as there was no grappling.

He then stood between them for a second, dropped his arm down, stepped back and ordered them to begin.

Both fighters began to dance around each other, the Kung Fu man made artistic cinematic style gestures whilst the Tae Kwando player released a fast mawashi geri, (roundhouse kick) from off his front foot and caught the Kung Fu man in the ribs. The sound of the contact elicited an audible gasp from the audience and the recipient winced from the impact. The Tae Kwando man sensed his advantage and followed with a series of body punches that slammed into the black gi of his opponent and missed with a cross that could have finished the fight if it had connected, he advanced forward. The referee darted around the combatants to keep pace as they exchanged blows.

After a while the Kung Fu man, recovered from the recent onslaught, planted a powerful front kick that took the wind completely out of his antagonist and sent him to his knees. The referee stepped in and checked the recipient of the planted foot as he knelt on the mat and strove to regain his breath.

The fighter rose to his feet and walked unsteadily to the line in the centre of the mat. He was asked if he was alright to continue. The man nodded. Once more the referee restarted the fray with a downward sweep of his arm and an indistinguishable sound emitted from his throat, like some Neanderthal grunt.

The two were evenly matched and exchanged many spectacular techniques which had little or no effect on each other. The Tae Kwando man was still a little shaky from the kick to his solar plexus but managed to survive the two rounds and both players finished the contest standing up. The Kung Fu fighter was awarded the match and was loudly cheered by his supporters.

Although excited I felt nervous and began to stretch to warm up; I surveyed the following fights. Most of the contests were slug fests with hardly any attempts to block and little or no technique. This was not to deny that the fighters were tough, but perhaps either courageous or foolish to stand toe to toe and hammer it out with someone of often superior power and strength. As mentioned before, in the early days there were seldom weight divisions and when good techniques were executed by a smaller contestant against a heavier, the crowd would show their appreciation. After several bouts two contestants had been carried out feet first and one of the girl competitors had broken her big toe.

It was my turn to step onto the mat. The sight of a limp body being "helped" from the arena didn't add anything positive to my other than strong mental disposition. The last fight had been a pure brawl and both fighters, one a kick boxer the other a Kyokushin fighter, punished each other until the weaker man fell. Both had received bruises from leg sweeps and leg kicks and as they inspected their broken blood vessels and wondered why their knees felt painful in later life, would stimulate their memory to recall the events of their youth on this day.

I was called and knew how a professional boxer felt when entering the ring but had no seconds to rub me down with towels or a corner man to retreat to.

My opponent was a tad taller than me and showed the scars of previous encounters on his face. He tried to psyche me out, but I turned away and continued to circle my shoulders and stretch. The referee called us together. He mumbled the rules and stepped back; his arm raised in readiness.

As soon as the limb of the referee prescribed the arc to indicate that the fight had begun, I took the initiative, I feinted with a left jab and punched with my right, contracted my muscles, and focused all the force of my body into that one blow. It crashed into my opponent's ribs.

A look of astonishment and then pain registered on his face; he was lifted from the ground and propelled several feet across the mat. I took two steps forward and shadowed his progress ready to deliver another blow but there was no need, the would–be antagonist collapsed in a crumpled heap, the fight knocked out of him.

He sat, clutched his stomach, and groaned. I felt sorry for him and hoped I hadn't broken his ribs. I threw the punch more from the adrenalin rush than a desire to hurt him, which in retrospect was the whole idea.

I was declared the winner and went back to the dressing room, sat on a bench, and mulled over the events of the last few moments. I had been advised by many of my friends that it was different from semi contact combat and that the techniques were quite difficult to execute, but my speed and timing, plus my recent boxing experience, had proved that in this case maybe they were wrong. Perhaps it was just a lucky blow. I sat and pondered; my reverie was interrupted by the voice of someone behind me.

'Good punch mate, although he must have been a bit of a wimp to fold up so easy!'

I turned to see the man with the two front teeth missing.

'Oh, yeah, I reckon,' I replied.

The cropped headed man threw a couple of punches into the air bobbed and weaved, whether to impress me or just to loosen up for his next fight I didn't know, but I expressed no emotion.

'I'm on next. See yer later,' the man added and disappeared through the dressing room door.

'Yeah, good luck.' I remained seated but my curiosity got the better of me; I got up to follow him along a corridor and peer through into the fight area.

Two gi clad Karate men came through as I watched and went to their respective lockers.

On the mat, the man with tattoos and minus two front teeth, affectionately called by his mates Bulldozer, played to the crowd, kicked and punched the air and threw several side– thrust kicks with well–timed proficiency.

The two fighters came together summoned by the ref. The now well recognisable grunt of the referee signalled the battle should begin. The fight started in a flurry of kicks and punches from both fighters; Bulldozer turned and charged the man opposite him and delivered a series of potent head punches that sent his opponent back off the mat. He followed with a strong mawashi geri to the lower leg and slammed his opponent below the knee, the man went down. In a real situation the fighter would have finished his task and followed through, but this was a sport, albeit a brutal one, but still a sport with rules. Bulldozer stepped back and waited for the man to rise. No sooner had he regained his feet when another powerful mawashi geri to the man's head sent him down again like a sack of potatoes. Bulldozer danced around the mat, an arm extended jubilantly to the crowd, elated by his victory. He was reprimanded by the referee for his lack of etiquette toward his opponent and the sport. He cared little, bowed reluctantly, and swaggered off the mat.

I returned to the bench I'd occupied earlier prior to Bulldozer's exit. Seconds later he came through the door. I looked up.

'Well done,' I said as he went to his locker and produced a can of Coke.

'Yeah, I hope we get to have a go, eh?'

I confess I gave a less than enthusiastic smile and nodded. Bulldozer laughed loudly, slammed the locker door, turned on his heel and walked from the room.

I remained where I sat for a moment, then returned to my vigil from the door. Most of the other combatants had stayed in the hall but I found a strange inexplicable sense of security in the locker room.

I won both my next fights without much effort.

I don't wish to sound cocky or above myself, but I felt I had superior skills, or perhaps I should say I had trained the hardest. Whether that would be the case when it came to a fight with Bulldozer, remained to be seen.

The crowd had taken little notice of me when I first stepped onto the mat but now, on this fourth occasion, I could feel they were solidly behind me. It was good to have the crowd's support as the day had been long and this was the final bout.

Bulldozer had also survived and grinned at me from across the room, although there was just the slightest hint that his face muscles generated most of the effort to display the teeth that remained in his head, whilst his true state of mind was perhaps a little uneasy. At least that's what I liked to think.

It wasn't long before I stood opposite him ready for combat. The referee once again emitted his guttural grunt, and the match was on.

Bulldozer took the initiative; he had previously witnessed my fights with earlier opponents.

I was told the crowd went totally silent although I don't think either of us noticed.

···•••••···

This is where we came in.

The ref had watched Bulldozer's effort to elevate himself from the crumpled heap that he had been a few seconds earlier, the crowd again roared its approval. He tottered to the line and raised his fists as the referee walked over to him; Bulldozer stubbornly insisted that he was fine to continue but I had a feeling there was something wrong.

'I'm right. I'll be right,' he muttered as he regained his composure. The man was obviously in pain, and I felt apprehensive about hitting him as the referee's arm came down between us.

I held back. I could have felled him several times in the moments that followed but chose instead to avoid his now less than lethal attacks.

The crowd, like a mob of Romans at the amphitheatre, cried for blood, they sensed they could be cheated out of their "kill;" their reaction surprised me.

I ignored their demands and continued to avoid my opponent's attacks without a great deal of effort.

Bulldozer began to get angry.

'Keep still yer little fucker!' he admonished.

His blows became wilder and his techniques non–existent. The fight continued and the crowd became restless, a chant of 'Kill 'im, kill 'im.' rang out.

The referee stepped in between us and called me over.

'If yer don't fight back you'll be disqualified.' I nodded and returned to the fight. There were twenty seconds left on the clock.

Bulldozer got his second wind, a Yoko Geri (side kick) shot out that narrowly missed my head, followed by a Mawashi Geri to the same location. Sidekicks, whilst effective, are often easy to read and I again stepped back. As the crowd readied itself to express its collective frustration, they gave an enthusiastic roar as I turned and released my own side kick that sent Bulldozer across the mat. Immediately I released the kick I regretted it. I thrust out my hip and let it go with full force, muscle contraction on impact. I saw Bulldozer wince with pain. He was pushed backwards and sank slowly to the mat. I walked quickly across to where he fell; the crowd was wild with enthusiasm as I knelt beside Bulldozer. The referee took my arm and pulled me away,

'Stand on the other side of the mat.'

I looked down at the injured man, saddened by what I saw. Blood seeped from the corner of his mouth. A doctor was called.

The referee approached me and again took my arm, but this time led me to the centre of the mat and raised it in victory. The crowd showed their approval by their applause. I was their gladiatorial hero for the night. People stepped onto the mat and suddenly, I had many more friends at the end of the day than when it began. But my elation as the winner of the tournament was marred by the injury I had inflicted on my opponent.

I'd won the all styles full–contact cup and was heartily congratulated by several eminent martial arts masters. For the latter part of the evening, before the presentation of trophies, I watched a demonstration by a fourth dan Kyokushin karateka eventually break a baseball bat after the third attempt with his shin and noted a pained expression accompanied him as he left the mat.

Chapter Two

Two - Self discovery

The tournament had lasted from ten o'clock in the morning until nine in the evening and finished reasonably early by comparison with some events that I had attended in the past; many had dragged on until midnight, the participants and audiences often dwindled as the night progressed, but this day's event had seen the majority of spectators eagerly await the final to witness me, now in their eyes some kind of hero, go up against Bulldozer, as I found out later the previous three times undefeated champion.

After I changed from my gi and taken a shower I was invited to celebrate at the nearby Chinese restaurant by my fellow contestants for persons involved in the tournament. I felt pleased with myself in one way but uneasy in another but couldn't fathom out why this sensation clouded my mood.

I sat at the top of the table, people on either side chatted enthusiastically, some demonstrated with hand movements or emulated punches and gestures of the contest; laughter and noise filled the restaurant as waiters scuttled to and from the kitchen with bowls of oriental dishes. Perhaps it was Bulldozer's condition, now in some hospital, that gave me this inner sense of anxiety; the thought I'd seriously injured another person. I searched deeper into the recesses of my mind and found something that I did not want; not that I had inflicted the injury, nor I should have exercised more control; what disturbed me, and this frightened me, was I'd enjoyed the sensation when I connected people with the mat. I tried to fight the conclusion my mind presented me but each time it returned.

I hadn't held back in my effort to demolish Bulldozer because of the morality of the situation. I had genuine thoughts of pity for the man but deep inside, which unsettled me, was I harboured the desire to lay into him until he was totally and utterly beaten, regardless of the consequences. I felt ashamed of how I could possibly entertain such conduct.

The party had broken up around midnight, a few people wanted to carry on at other venues of less reputable nature than the restaurant; I declined the offer, I felt tired and had to study for a midterm exam the next day.

I shared an apartment with another student, Rochester, who was at the same Uni but studying for a degree in business studies.

His name often elicited comment and sometimes guffaws from persons introduced to him for the first time. He was tall, wore glasses, and his appearance and character befitted that of someone from the nineteen thirties. He always wore a suit and a bow tie whenever he attended lectures, another eccentricity that earned him the reputation of being odd. It was as though his conformity with the conservative idea of dress seemed to appear more diverse on campus than some of the outrageously clad, Rastafarian hair styled youths that plodded the academic halls.

It was Rochester who greeted me as I entered the flat. He was propped up in an armchair with an adequate cushion behind him, his long legs stretched out supported by a stool.

'Ah, the Samurai returns. Did you beat shit out of them? Metaphorically speaking of course.'

I threw my bag on the floor and collapsed into the chair opposite him.

'You're up late' I commented.

'Yeah, little bit of revision and Sherlock Holmes. Well, how was it?'

'I did OK.'

'Ah, there's that modesty creeping out again. Tell me, how did it go?'

'Yeah, I, er.'

'You won?'

'Yes.'

'Congratulations. Why are you so fucking modest? You win a tournament and you're reluctant to proclaim your victory. This attitude will not serve you well in life.'

I gave a half-hearted smile. I really felt embarrassed when people praised me.

Rochester regarded me and then spoke. 'Well?'

'Well, what?' I replied.

'Well, tell me what happened? Why are you so gloomy, for want of a better word?'

'I hit someone too hard. He didn't look too good.'

Rochester closed his book and bent down to scratch his leg; his long fingers moved rhythmically over the exposed part of his shin.

'Bloody mosquitoes! Oh, I see, how bad was he?'

'Pretty bad. I think I'll phone the hospital in a minute to find out.'

'Hospital? Hmn. Look you can't blame yourself I mean, that's what you went there for, to beat someone senseless or get thumped and kicked yourself. I thought that was the whole idea. You fought fairly I presume.'

I glanced at my friend. 'Yeah of course, but something else worries me.'

Rochester stretched his legs once more. 'Oh, what?'

'Well,' I took a slow intake of breath. 'I found out something about myself tonight I didn't particularly like.'

'You mean you're disgusting habit of getting up at five o'clock in the morning and going for a run. You mean you've realised that this kind of behaviour gives your friends and colleagues a bad taste in their mouths and feelings of guilt?'

'No, something more.'

'Please tell me about this amazing self-discovery whilst kicking faecal matter out of someone. People usually get revelations and personal insights in monasteries or Himalayan temples or shrines in India; maybe you could start a new cult or method of self-realisation.'

I had grown used to Rochester's somewhat forthright manner over the two years I'd known him and treated his comments with a wry smile.

'No, I'm serious. I realised tonight that I actually enjoyed punching people, that something clicks when I'm faced with aggression and it's as if it stimulates me.'

'Remind me not to be aggressive,' Rochester stated. 'I thought martial arts made a person non-violent and well adjusted, please ignore all previous remarks they were not intended for offence. What you're saying is you're likely to embark on a violent rampage of destruction if provoked?'

'Listen to me. What I'm saying is, what can I do?'

'You think you have psychopathic tendencies?'

'No. I know I have control in normal situations. It's just when I got on that mat tonight it was all systems go. I felt a sense of fear and then elation and then freedom if you can understand.'

'Not really but surely it's called the killer instinct for want of a better expression. The desire to win, to overcome the odds, and the person opposing you either bears the brunt of your endeavours or sees to it that you don't achieve your goal.'

'Yes, I know but where do you draw the line. There's a difference between protecting yourself and actually enjoying the sensation.'

'Just relax and accept the fact that you have a particular talent for maiming people. It's a much sought-after characteristic. Boxers lose or win fortunes because of it.'

Rochester turned to me, a slight hint of humour in his voice. 'Why didn't you become a professional pugilist? Then you could have really enjoyed your work.'

'I think boxing is great and I admire the hands of a good boxer, but I like to use my kicks. There's something... I dunno boxing sort of falls short of what I want.'

'You prefer a more sophisticated artistic all-encompassing form of inflicting damage on an opponent?' Rochester stated. 'Boxing is never usually described as a martial art, but I fail to see the difference.' He continued.

'Hours of disciplined repetitive training and many top fighters are "artistic" in their movement.

'Yeah, you're right, I suppose.' I answered but felt too tired to enter lengthy discourse on the subject.

'Anyway, I'm off to my bed.' stated Rochester and hoisted himself out of the chair. 'The bewitching hour has long since passed and I'm dropping off.'

'What did you do today?' I asked him as he was about to disappear into his room.

'I studied. Oh, I forgot. Sally someone called about half ten.'

'What did she say?' I immediately felt a warm flush of pleasure at the mention of her name.

'Nothing, said she'd call back tomorrow.'

'Is that all she said?' I asked.

There was a moment's pause.

'No, she also said she wants to have sexual intercourse with you at the first opportunity. Goodnight.'

I shrugged with a gesture that indicated I would get no more sense out of Rochester until the morning and reached for the telephone directory.

I was devastated by the news that Bulldozer had died of internal injuries from a ruptured bladder. I'd killed a man, had taken the life of another human being, the most terrible of deeds.

Evidently the first kick had damaged his bladder and the second finished him. If he had perhaps urinated before the fight, he could well have survived.

There was to be no sleep for me that night. I tossed and turned, tortured by images of Bulldozer prostrate on the mat at my feet.

"Was there something I could have done?" I kept asking myself. "Could I have held back on the kick and still won the fight?"

About three o'clock I left the tangled sheets of my bed and went to the kitchen to make a hot drink. Perhaps that would help me sleep. It had no effect. At one point I wished I had lost the fight; the thought even entered my mind that it would be better I had died rather than Bulldozer. I lay staring at the ceiling until dawn crept into my room. I got up threw on my running clothes and went out into the cold morning to punish my body by completing treble my normal training distance. But no matter how much I sweated I couldn't wash away the feeling of guilt I would carry for the rest of my life.

At the inquest, death by accidental causes was officially judged and duly recorded but it was clear that the adjudicator who presided over the inquiry had little sympathy with the practitioners of full contact martial arts when he gave his judgement.

Chapter Three

Three - Forget the past

Sally Hackett was an Anglo Chinese girl of twenty-one. She studied English with the desire to teach after university. Her mother had come over from Hong Kong and met Ron, her father, and after a whirlwind romance married within two months.

She was their only child, a gentle, good-natured girl who was fifteen when her mother died of throat cancer.

After her mother's death Sally drew closer to her father and helped him to run an English conversation school for foreign students in Sydney, before she went to Melbourne University.

It was Sally who listened to me as I sat opposite her in the university cafeteria. I had liked her from the very first time I'd seen her. She was petite, with a hint of Asian blood visible in her dark eyes, although her hair was naturally quite fair.

I observed her long slim neck and clearly defined jaw in profile when she turned for a moment to locate some person in the cafeteria that'd dropped a teacup. She was indeed beautiful; her presence radiated a sense of warmth and comfort. If this had been under different circumstances I would have normally been elated, and no doubt behaved in a manner designed to try and impress her, but because of the events of the last few days my mood was a deep shade of blue.

I'd explained to Sally the reason I'd entered the tournament and my emotions whilst I participated. The event was now common knowledge at the university and had made the national press. There was a campaign to ban boxing and the pro ban–element seized on the unfortunate death of Bulldozer to strengthen their case, arguing that while it was not the same as boxing, it was still a competition in a way more violent, to defeat the opponent. Sheer brutality, albeit skilfully executed to render them either incapable to continue or unconscious.

The general reaction of the university was that it was just one of those things, tragic, but an unforeseeable result. A few of the more pugilistic sorts admired my prowess and held me in no way to blame for what had occurred; it even elevated me in their esteem.

For myself I held no doubt in my mind that the result could have been avoided if I had used more restraint and the vision of Bulldozer prostrate on the mat continually haunted me.

Sally brought my attention back to the conversation.

'So, what will you do now?'

'I really don't feel like training now. I don't know where to go from here.'

'But what about your career and your plans?'

I turned to her and looked into her eyes.

'I won't jack it in, I know that, but it's just that I have to come to terms with what I've done. I'll stick to teaching; no more competitions.'

'You'll still go to Japan?' she enquired.

I toyed with the paper wrapper that had earlier contained my straw and now stood erect in my glass, the end chewed.

'I think so, yeah, it's always been something I've wanted to do, so yeah I'll go.'

Sally smiled, reached across the table to touch my hand, and gave it a gentle squeeze.

'Then you must go otherwise you'll always regret it.'

She understood and by her genuine concern stirred something within me that was never to be extinguished. I wanted to take her in my arms and kiss her.

There was a moment of eye contact that communicated to her how I felt but I looked away, guilty to feel so good after what had recently happened.

I'd had several girlfriends but my obsession with training had always held top priority in my life and from the start I made it quite clear to any girl that I would not be available for a normal relationship. But with Sally I thought that maybe I could combine the two.

I reasoned that because she understood my ambition, she wouldn't fight against it but help me achieve it, although with the death of Bulldozer my desire to be the World Champion no longer burned with the same intensity. She didn't show it, but I sensed she now regarded me in a different light; possibly not a favourable one.

With my degree in Physical Education, I could teach at a high school or private school and maybe at some later stage take a master's degree to teach at one of the Universities. But whatever I did I had an almost prophetic intuition that Sally would be involved.

The months rolled by, and I threw myself wholeheartedly into my studies, I continued to train but concentrated more on my technique; I began to relax and take time off to spend with Sally. Our relationship settled into a comfortable partnership that once more afforded me both stability and affection in my life.

After graduation she and I took a big step and moved to Sydney into a terraced house in Ultimo; one of many built for the dock workers of the late nineteenth century with two rooms up and two down. A small garden was accessed from the kitchen and the proximity to the city centre made it a good location. I' d opened my own dojo in Sydney in a large room in Sally's fathers building, affiliated to my original style, and whilst still active on the martial arts scene had not taken part in any competitions, contact or non-contact since I had lived in Victoria.

I also took up a position as a temp in one of the local schools and instructed physical education to boys between eleven and eighteen.

Although I was not unhappy and it was an easy life, I still felt restless and unfulfilled. Sally sensed it and broached the subject. Our relationship was at times somewhat tense, primarily my fault.

After a long talk one night after dinner, it was agreed that I would go ahead with my plan to travel to Japan the next February and continue my study of martial arts.

We knew that if I didn't go, I would always have at the back of my mind the feeling that I should have.

I was apprehensive about leaving her, a year is a long time to be apart, Sally was of the same opinion. She said she would move back in with her father as it was silly paying a high rent for one and didn't want to take on a flat mate.

We decided to play it by ear and a break could be a good thing perhaps for us both and whatever way our lives evolved we would always be friends.

The day of my departure to Japan finally arrived; I was of mixed emotions. I wanted to go and yet had reservations. Sally helped me get organised for my trip and accompanied me to the airport. There had been moments of hesitation and emotion from both of us when I hugged her and kissed her farewell. I felt a lump in my throat as I walked through into the restricted access area but consoled myself that it would only be a year. Besides, I would write and call regularly and try and get back before Christmas.

The headmaster at the school where I taught was sorry to see me go and said that he'd give me the best references for me to find a job when I got back.

Prior to my departure I'd been given a reference by my Karate instructor in Victoria, an introduction to the Japanese chief instructor in Tokyo. This was considered essential if I were to become a student of the Honbu (head) dojo and train with senior Japanese Karateka.

Once on the plane I felt more relaxed than I'd done for many years. I was finally on the first step to achieving my ambition, the one I'd had since I was a young teenager; to train in Japan. I felt a sense of excitement well up inside me, I was about to experience something totally different in my life, the unknown.

One piece of good fortune and another reason why I'd chosen to go to Japan in February was because of my good friend Rochester. When he left University, he had completed a teacher's training course and then, like me, taught at a local high school, after one year he'd grown decidedly bored with the effort to teach mathematics to adolescent "maladjusted youth" as he called them, all they wanted to do was bugger about; he decided to go to Japan and teach English, a remunerative profession and one that afforded a change of culture and the experience of something less stressful.

He had lived in Japan for over two years and invited me to stay with him. Over that time, he had become proficient in Japanese and familiarised himself with the culture.

His small apartment, I learned, was in Nerima–Ku close to central Tokyo, convenient for most locations but according to him big enough for the two of us and considered large by Japanese standards.

It was a cold six degrees when I stepped from the plane and made my way, along with other passengers, towards immigration. Although only nine hours travel time from Sydney it was in a different hemisphere with a totally different climate at this time of year, Australia in

February was decidedly warmer; a pleasant twenty–six degrees when I left.

After I'd grabbed my suitcase from the luggage carousel, found a trolley and been through customs and immigration, I walked through to the arrivals area and caught sight of Rochester. He beamed from ear to ear; his attire had not changed over the years although his hair was longer, and he'd put on weight around the face.

He stretched out his hand and shook mine warmly.

'How was the flight? How are you? Long–time no see.'

It was good to see him. It had been three years since we'd last met although we'd kept up a regular correspondence.

'Good, no problems. You're looking well.' I commented.

'Yes, I feel OK, although all this Japanese food is not agreeing with me. It's too good; I eat too much. Anyway, let's get you back home. You must feel a bit tired.'

'No, I'm fine. I'm good,' I replied.

'We'll go back by train. It's the best way, by far the quickest and we can have a chat.'

'Suits me,' I took hold of the trolley and pushed it ahead of me.

'Let's go.'

We left the airport, caught the "Skyline" back to Tokyo, changed at Ueno for Ikebukuro and then onto the Seibu line to Nerima, the journey took altogether about two hours fifteen minutes. The trains from Ueno were packed with hundreds of commuters jammed against each other and I desperately tried to keep my suitcases out of people's way as we boarded and left the tightly packed compartment. I was impressed by the punctuality and cleanliness of the trains, the neatness of the Japanese people and the beauty of the Japanese women. I saw a few Western faces but mostly, as expected, it was a sea of oriental features that moved up and down the escalators and through the subway. The language was difficult for me, and I was reprimanded by Rochester for not being fluent as it had been a lifelong ambition of mine for me to get to Japan.

I had a smattering of Japanese, but I would have been utterly lost if it had not been for Rochester. He was eager to point out the cultural differences, the dos, and don'ts of the culture. I was surprised that men didn't offer their seats to women on the train, often a man would sit comfortably and talk to his wife or female companion whilst she hung on to an overhead strap.

To say the least I was taken aback by the size of Rochester's apartment and couldn't imagine what other people's places were like if this was considered large. It had two bedrooms, a kitchen, and a tiny toilet where the occupant had to sit almost at an angle to take the seated position, along with a bath which I couldn't imagine Rochester being able to fit in unless his knees were tucked under his chin. He told me the Japanese generally have a shower before they get into the tub so, if shared, the water is not "polluted" for the next occupant. I thought if that was the case then "bags I go first."

Before we'd arrived at the flat, we stopped off at the local Denny's, a popular American café franchise. Rochester ordered for us both and then continued to speak.

'So, what's the plan?'

'Well, I'll spend most of my time training and then go back when I run out of cash.'

'As I mentioned in my letter, why not take a part-time job before that happens, working maybe a few hours a day and then you don't have to worry? There is a paper called The Japan Times. It comes out every Monday and lists all sorts of employment. I'll make a few enquiries where I am, see if they need anybody.'

'Yeah, I could do. It would make life a little more interesting I suppose.'

'Good. Variety is the spice of life.'

I agreed and returned to my meal.

After completing the necessary legalities, I obtained my Gaijin Card, a small square document similar in size and shape to a Bankcard but with one thumb print and photograph as identification. It is an indignity imposed by the Japanese Government on any foreigner who intends to reside for more than three months. I took out health insurance and registered as a resident of Nerima.

I was keen to train as soon as possible so decided to visit the dojo of the chief instructor.

Rochester had given me instructions where to get the train and where to get off.

'The inner Tokyo stations are all bilingually marked and the English version of the train map clearly legible, my dear friend, so you shouldn't get lost.' Rochester remarked as he patted me on the back and wished me luck.

Chapter Four

Four - Tokyo Dojo

After a comparatively easy journey, thanks to Rochester, I arrived around midday; with gi in my bag I entered the dojo.

The building itself was three stories high and entertained various businesses in the upper rooms, the dojo was poorly marked and after I had enquired with my limited knowledge of Japanese, managed to locate it on the lower ground floor. I descended some steps; from within came the sound of a loud Kiai, (The vocal expression of physical effort or, literally, a shout), followed by the snap of a Karate gi. I noticed several pairs of shoes just below the last step and added my own to the neatly placed row of footwear on the rack provided.

I entered the dojo, bowed, and gave the customary 'Osu' as I did so.

The dojo was a small square room with pictures of the chief instructor, along with various photographs of several exponents depicted in different poses, each one designed to illustrate their expertise in chosen techniques. The floor was covered with a kind of hard matted material called tatami and a punch bag and makiwara occupied some space in two corners of the room. A distinctive smell pervaded the place, not unpleasant, probably from the disinfectant used to clean the floor.

The author of the sound I heard as I descended the stairs ignored me, completed his Kata, expelled his breath with an audible hiss, composed himself, adjusted his gi and then turned toward me. I again bowed as he approached.

'What? 'He enquired in Japanese.

I pulled out the letter of introduction and handed it to him. He virtually snatched it from me and tore it open. I looked at him as he read. He was about thirty years of age, powerfully built with short, cropped hair and broad flat features. His gi was torn in two places although otherwise immaculate, an almost white frayed "black belt" hung from his waist.

He folded the note and waved it at me.

'I give Sensei here tomorrow, come. Sensei here then.'

I understood from his words in broken English that the person to whom the letter was addressed would be here tomorrow and I may be allowed to train. I took the note grasped in the extended hand and thanked him.

The man turned away and carried on where he had left off. I bowed once more, exited from the dojo, replaced my shoes, ascended the stairs, and left the building.

The man I had spoken with was Daiki Yamada, the chief instructor's right-hand man, a particularly aggressive fourth dan whom I'd seen on film in a couple of competitions. He had an arrogant manner and was renowned for his hard, old fashioned approach to Karate. I was unafraid of his reputation and felt confident I could handle anything that he dished out and would give it all I had.

I had come to Japan to train with the Japanese; to learn as much as I could from them. A lot of dojos in Japan had watered down their methods to accommodate the influx of foreigners in order not to frighten them away. Much of the brutality had gone but on the negative side so had the spirit of Budo.

I took time for the rest of the afternoon to explore the city. I visited Ginza and walked around the big department store, Mitsukoshi, totally awed by the presentation of their goods and stimulated by the variety of aromas that assaulted my senses. I wandered around the food department. The lift girls in their immaculate uniforms complete with gloves, relayed information to shoppers as to the destiny of their vertical chariot.

I was thoroughly taken by this new and exciting experience of another culture, with all its many varied and interesting facets.

I arrived back at Rochester's apartment, the walk from the station past the Yakitori stand, particularly enjoyable because of the delicious smells that came from the stallholder's hotplate. I also dodged the numerous bicycles that raced along the narrow streets; looked curiously at the many stalls and shops that arrayed the line painted area designated for pedestrians.

'You made it OK?' Rochester enquired as I came through the door.

'I did, although I nearly got lost. I crossed over the bridge at the station before recognising where I was then had to go back again

'I got lost a few times when I first came. Don't worry, just stand around looking stupid and I guarantee someone will approach you to give you a hand. If not, just ask. Most people in Tokyo can speak a little English.'

'I'll remember, although the hard part will be for me to look stupid,' I replied.

'Oh no, you'll have no problem,' Rochester retorted with a slight smile.

'Here, I'd like you to meet Satchiko.'

A young Japanese girl appeared from Rochester's bedroom. I stretched out my hand.

'How are you? Pleased to meet you.'

The girl gave a broad smile and inclined her head forward with a slight bow.

'Pleased to meet you,' she exclaimed, took my extended hand, and shook it demurely.

I believed she felt awkward, possibly because it was not her customary way to greet someone.

'Satchiko just popped over for a private lesson,' Rochester explained, 'and we've decided to go and see a film together. Good practice for her. Be a good man and chat to her while I get ready.'

'Of course, go and get ready.'

Rochester excused himself and departed with long strides into the bedroom. The sound of his cheery whistle broke the momentary silence.

'So, do you live in Tokyo?' I asked.

The girl nodded.

'In Chiba prefecture.'

'Oh, is that Tokyo?' I responded, somewhat bewildered.

'Yes, but quite far from Ikebukuro station.'

I looked at Satchiko and felt myself attracted to her. Her softness and the gentle way she spoke reminded me of Sally, the way her mouth turned up at each corner as though she wore continually the faint trace of a smile, her raven hair, dark eyes, and smooth ivory coloured skin exercised an almost hypnotic effect over me. At one point I just stared at her. She must have asked a question and been waiting for an answer from me a puzzled frown on her face brought me back to the moment.

'Er, oh, I'm sorry,' I said. 'Yes,' although I had forgotten the question the answer seemed to cause no problem, Satchiko turned to greet Rochester as he re-entered the room, he looked no different from when he departed, except that he had changed his socks.

'Right, let's go.'

Satchiko turned to me.

'It was nice meeting you. I hope we meet again.'

I nodded. 'I hope so too.'

'I'm sure you will,' Rochester added.

'Satchiko comes here every week for a lesson, so you'll meet again.'

I felt pleased

'Do you want to come with us?' Rochester asked. We're going to see a French film in Ginza.'

Satchiko smiled. 'Please come with us.'

I thought for a moment and then spoke. 'I won't. I can't speak French and the subtitles would be in Japanese so I wouldn't understand it, maybe next time. Besides, I want to do a few things, but thanks for the invitation.'

Rochester guided Satchiko to the door and they slipped into their outdoor shoes.

'Enjoy yourself, there's a video shop down the road. I'll leave you my card, be back later.'

The main reason I didn't go was that I thought two's company and three's a crowd. I was not sure as to the extent of Rochester's affection for Satchiko but reckoned that any man who could not feel attracted to such a beautiful creature must be made of stone, or gay, and I knew Rochester was neither of the two. Perhaps his interpretation of "lesson" meant something entirely different to my assumption

The door closed and the sound of footsteps gradually diminished until I could hear them no more. I picked up my bag, went into my bedroom grabbed a book, "Contemporary Japanese," from a bookcase next to the bed and started to read.

The next morning, I got up for my usual five thirty jaunts to a nearby park. I was surprised to see so many people, mostly elderly, who exercised in a somewhat untidy semi-circle to the strains of a portable radio-cassette player set at full volume that belted out Japanese music.

I was originally concerned that if I exercised in a public park, I would appear out of place, but now at the sight of all the various activities I felt no embarrassment as I secreted myself in a corner to practise Kata.

From where I stood, I could see a man with a cassette player execute dance steps with an imaginary partner, a football team put through an exercise routine, a shadow boxer and, of course, the geriatric aerobics class. The place was a hive of activity, everyone, or group carried out their various routines seemingly oblivious to their neighbours' antics. Golfers, runners, skaters, and dog walkers co-habited with the least possible infringement on each other's limited space.

After an hour's practice I ran home, had a quick breakfast, and prepared myself for the dojo. Rochester had been asleep when I left and as I closed the front door and headed for the station I wondered if Satchiko was with him and thought he was indeed a lucky man if she was, although I didn't remember seeing her shoes on the rack.

I arrived at the dojo, took off my shoes and entered. The chief instructor was seated in a small office just inside the entrance and attended to some paperwork. Yamada was on the mat with four students, going through a warmup before the class.

I knocked tentatively on the door of the small office and bowed low. The chief instructor looked up.

'Os Sensei,' I said and bowed once again.'

He bade me enter and smiled. 'Os, Mason San, eh?'

I had seen the chief instructor a few times both on video and in photographs in books and had heard of his legendary feats of strength and fighting prowess over many years. I had also seen his filmed demonstrations, but here he was, in the flesh.

He was about seventy years of age, but a sense of power still radiated from him. Unlike Yamada he was a lot friendlier and nodded as he read the letter.

'So – so – so. Os!' he beamed as he read. 'Please, get changedo.'

'Osu.' I bowed once again and backed out, bag in hand and eager to get changed or "changedo" as he had said.

I acknowledged Yamada as I crossed the floor and made for the changing room; I felt anticipation and excitement and a sense of achievement as I got into my gi.'

The session was routine, a mild warm up that consisted of a few flexibility exercises and then Kihon, (techniques) followed by partner work to practice them. Most of the instruction was given in Japanese but he used many English terms if I looked puzzled, to explain to me when he elaborated on a particular point.'

Yamada also trained with us and paired up with me on one occasion.

The technique was a straight-forward punch with a move forward, followed by a block and counter from the opponent and then another attack from the original instigator. I easily blocked Yamada's first two attacks which stimulated him to pile on the pressure.

His oriental eyes darkened as he powered forward. I deflected his punch and returned my own in a split second. Yamada was surprised, there was a faint trace of a challenge in my face that seemed to antagonise him.

It was a week later Yamada called me to come and spar with him before the class started. I was up for the challenge and would have done so earlier but it is not etiquette to ask a higher grade, it is up to him or her to suggest it. There were a few other people in the dojo that went through their techniques for future grades.

Sensei was in his office speaking on the phone as I bowed to Yamada and took up my stance. I knew that he wanted to test me and see how good I was in combat.

He had no idea of my past and cared little for it anyway, it was the here and now that's all Yamada was concerned with.

The fight began with a mild exchange of blows almost in slow motion.

With all modesty, my skill and timing allowed me to give the impression that my opponent was a touch cumbersome. Yamada again put on the pressure and became more aggressive as I bobbed and weaved and evaded his attack. I countered and knew that I scored, which made him even angrier. Eventually Yamada lashed out with a vicious kick followed by a reverse punch. The kick contacted my elbow and as I stepped back, I sensed his anger and became motivated by the attack; here in the dojo of my much-respected chief instructor, Yamada and I were as far removed from the true spirit of Karate as a couple of brawlers in a pub. Neither of our minds was free of aggression; Yamada's less than mine but now I began to feel the anger rise within me and the desire to lash out with equal venom.

I stepped back and waited for the powerful reverse punch that I knew was coming and as it came, I blocked and unleashed a reverse punch of my own. The blow found its target and Yamada grunted involuntarily as it smacked into his gi. I had not given it one hundred per cent and pulled back at the last fraction of a second. Several of the students had stopped to watch and exchanged glances as they witnessed the punch thud into Yamada's gut. The pain of the blow was far outweighed by the anger and frustration and humiliation that he now felt, and he rushed at me with renewed effort.

As he ran forward, I turned and raised my leg in readiness of a side kick but instead decided against it and chose to block the attack. That was a mistake. He'd switched tactics and instead of a kick or punch grabbed hold of my gi and began to wrestle.

I was unprepared and fought him off as best I could. Yamada was a Brazilian Ju Jitsu and judo player and in a matter of seconds took me to the floor. I felt powerless. I couldn't kick, couldn't punch effectively, and was totally overpowered by this solid mass of muscle that had control of my movement. Yamada knew that he had me and manoeuvred himself for the coup de grace.

I was by no means weak and cursed myself for my hesitation. I learned two lessons that day: valuable ones.

One, he who hesitates is lost and two that kick, and punch techniques alone are not a foolproof method of fighting, however adept or skilled the exponent is.

As I thought about this point Yamada gripped my neck between his forearm and upper arm, took hold of his wrist and expanded his bicep to cut off my air supply.

I slammed the mat with the palm of my almost free hand, but it was too late; I passed into unconsciousness. It was evidently only a few seconds, but I had no idea how long I was out.

As I slowly returned to the real world, I could make out the face of the chief instructor as he looked down on me.

I shook myself, 'Osu' I mumbled as I twisted my neck back into shape.

Sensei smiled.

'So – so, Daijour.' I saw the chief instructor nod once and then disappear back into his office.

Yamada stood in front of the bag in the corner of the room and toyed with it with an expression that said, "That showed you."

I climbed shakily to my feet. Hiro, one of the black belts took my arm to assist me. Yamada shouted across the dojo in Japanese and Hiro stepped away.

'Thanks, I'll be OK.' I said and looked at Yamada still with a faint trace of challenge in my eye, I bowed slightly. He acknowledged my 'Osu' and punched the bag, the chain creaked as it swung violently from side to side.

I knew then that I must learn either Ju Jitsu or grappling defence if I were to be a competent all-round martial artist.

The weeks passed and I continued to train every day. I came to know and like Hiro, a second dan training to be an instructor. His technique was good, and he was full of enthusiasm for the sport. It was an incident involving him that prompted me to rethink my future at the dojo.

I had concluded that Yamada was a bully and an arrogant arsehole; he took the class and instructed us to step into gedan barai, (downward block forward stance). There was an immediate explosive response as the students reacted as one with a loud Kiai.

Hiro was a fraction of a second behind the rest. Yamada glared at him and then lashed out with a front kick to Hiro's mid–section. Then a hard body punch to his stomach. The young Karate student was not prepared for the blow and sank to his knees, badly winded.

I felt the anger rise in me as the class continued; Hiro limped to the side of the dojo and knelt at the edge of the mat.

Yamada glared and shouted at him to get back in line.

Hiro painfully rose to his feet, clutched his side, and limped back to join the class. We continued to train.

"Prick," I thought. I wanted to give the bastard a taste of his own medicine but clung on to reason. We continued to train. Once again Hiro, still obviously not one hundred per cent because of his recent encounter with Yamada, was slow off the mark and again received the ire of the instructor, with another punch and a slap round his head. I stared ahead, gritted my teeth, and dared not catch Yamada's eye because I knew if I did without doubt it would communicate how I felt.

The class finished without further incident and back in the change room I asked him if he was OK.

'Yeah, I'm good,' Hiro replied.

I nodded and continued to get changed. It turned out he had a fractured rib and must have been in extreme pain for the rest of the class.

It was on the way back to Rochester's apartment that I thought about what had happened at the dojo and what I should do. I knew that sooner or later Yamada would do something and go too far, and then what? I understood the need to develop spirit and the value derived from hard work in the dojo. But sadism was not a characteristic I admired.

The fear of a repetition of the incident in Australia haunted me and I involuntarily winced as my mind presented me with a picture of Bulldozer groaning on the mat. I decided my only course of action was to leave the dojo and find somewhere else. I assumed Yamada would think by my absence that I was afraid of him, but I didn't care what he thought.

It was a difficult decision but one I knew I must take.

Rochester was sympathetic but didn't share my dedication to any art and consoled me with the fact that there were many more dojos around and I should be more adventurous. I explained to him that I had trained in one style for more than fifteen or so years to which Rochester concluded that in that case it was about time I had a change.

I listened to his words and thought that maybe he was right. Maybe there was some logic in his reasoning.

He also informed me that Satchiko was purely a student. The news of this gave me a sense of relief and then apprehension. What should I do?

Rochester had worked out that my casual question as to the status of my relationship with Satchiko concealed some ulterior motive.

'You fancy her, don't you?' Rochester stated when I broached the subject.

'No. I just think she's nice.'

'Of course, she is, she's bloody gorgeous,' Rochester exclaimed.

'It's just that...'

'Just that what?' Rochester interjected.

'Well, you know.'

'No, I don't know.'

I hesitated. 'I'm still not sure how I feel about Sal.

'Look, old man, you're in Japan. You're here for one year so you may as well enjoy yourself matey. You could be dead tomorrow. Take each day as it comes, and all that sort of thing.'

I said nothing but mulled over Rochester's words. "No, I've got to be strong. At least for a while anyway," I thought as I looked at my companion.

Rochester continued. 'Your single, I thought you told me you had an agreement to go with the flow.'

'Rochester's face contorted, and he hunched his shoulders to emulate some evil purveyor of temptation. 'Think of those silky-smooth thighs, those soft yielding hips, those tender pouting breasts, those...'

'Knock it off you bastard,' I interrupted as Rochester, now in full poetic flight, entered greater detail of Satchiko's anatomy and what pleasure awaited me if I were to pursue her.

Rochester finished his lurid description and laughed loudly. I looked at my tall companion, his shoulders moving in rhythm with his laughter.

'You're supposed to be my mate.'

'I am,' Rochester retorted. 'I just want you to enjoy your life a little more. You're too serious.   Let's go out and eat. I'll treat you. How do you fancy some sushi?'

'Yeah, why not. Only it's my shout.'

'No, no. I insist. It's my pleasure.' Rochester countered. 'Would you like me to call Satchiko?'

I playfully jabbed him in the ribs. 'No, don't worry, some other time. Let's go.'

I had been in Japan for over three months and to change dojo for me was, whilst a setback in my schedule to train, also a challenge to find another venue.

I decided to visit other dojos and watch classes of the most recognised styles, but while I acknowledged the skills and effort of the students, I didn't feel as though I wanted to join the class. Also, my own style had fitted me comfortably for many years and I had a cultural visa which, when it expired, I had to renew with the help of the dojo where I trained and maybe they wouldn't back my application.

Although I was not too concerned because I knew there were other ways to obtain visas, I was also aware that Japanese bureaucracy was totally incapable of flexibility and would face the problem when it arose.

I set about my task to find a dojo, scanned the English pages directory, and eventually came up with a place to train that looked suitable.

A Japanese friend of Rochester told me of one Kyokushin world champion who had left the organisation and started a small dojo of his own to teach Karate based on Kyokushin but also with other styles that incorporated throws, take downs and free style wrestling techniques. Even better, the location of the club was close to where I lived. A short bicycle ride two days later found me outside the dojo.

It was bigger than the previous place where I'd trained, built later, the exterior newer and was situated on the ground floor visible from the street.

There were ten punch bags of various lengths suspended from different parts of the room and to the left an area designated for the use of weights, the equipment being old and well used. Several students hammered away at the bags and music blared out from a cassette recorder.

I entered and bowed to one of the black belts who came over and spoke to me. I greeted him with the customary "Osu" and informed him that I would like to train with them if that were possible.

The black belt asked me if I had any previous experience and I explained that I had, but if allowed I would wear a white belt as a beginner as I had no experience of his style.

He turned and made his way over to an older man. Sensei Taguchi, the chief instructor.

glanced in my direction and nodded; I could train with them and was cordially invited.

The friendliness and almost casual atmosphere that pervaded the room was impressive, although this supposedly had a reputation as no easy dojo.

It was open all day, but classes were run from ten thirty in the morning until three in the afternoon and then again at five thirty until nine thirty, classes being one and a half hours each, beginners, intermediate and advanced.

The black belt handed me two pieces of paper; a list of times of classes and fees, plus a membership form. To join would cost me Y20,000 and that included fees to train for one month. After that it was Y9,000 for each month and I could train as much as I liked.

I got changed, warmed up and joined the class.

The chief instructor was a man in his early forties, powerfully built, good natured and with an obvious sense of humour. I liked him immediately, as well as the casual atmosphere there was a great deal of respect from the students both for each other and the instructor.

The class went through basic technique and then practised on the bags, finally to pair up and spar for the last half hour of the class, with a change of partner after five or so minutes. It was full contact but there was good control; the chief instructor enthusiastically took part and dished out the odd reminder to any over enthusiastic student that it was to practice technique rather than lay out one's partner.

Anything was allowed and students continued to fight on the mat after being taken down. As a newcomer it was obvious that sooner or later, I would be tested, and I used a lot of restraint with the lower grades.

Eventually Sensei Taguchi, chose me as his partner. We faced each other, bowed, and then began. I was cautious at first but managed to avoid his kicks and punches and refrained from too hard a response. He began to put pressure on me with a stronger attack. I responded and gave it back to him. He was strong and experienced, and I knew that if he got hold of me, I would be tied up and choked out.

I stayed out of range of his attacks to avoid his attempt to grab me and put in two punches to his mid-section which I know must have hurt. He smiled ducked under my defence, grabbed me below the waist and took me down; again, I felt myself hit the mat and an arm bar applied. I tapped out. He jumped up slapped me on the back and nodded.

'Must guard against take down Tony San. Must spread leg if see coming. Yame, he shouted. The class stopped and his students bowed to one another.

Unlike Yamada, sensei Taguchi felt no threat but enthusiastically encouraged me when I had got through his defence and enjoyed the experience of fighting someone with a different style.

In the months that followed I trained hard and rose to the challenge. I learned many effective Ju Jitsu techniques, throws and submissions, all useful in a real combat situation depending on how many attackers.

Against multiple assailants it is vital that one stays on two feet; to be a good striker is more beneficial under these circumstances.

There was no mystique about the martial arts I practised, simply hard work and commitment. I have always believed the mind and body function more efficiently if in harmony. Although I trained with Sensei Taguchi I continued to persevere with my own style of Kata and spent hours of repetition as I went through the many forms.

I felt more relaxed and happier than I had done for a long time; I had a schedule I enjoyed, an instructor I admired and respected, and a part-time job as an English teacher to give me some extra cash.

Rochester had kindly recommended me to the school where he worked, and I'd gone for an interview and been accepted.

The work was easy if repetitive, but it was a change from the dojo and gave me opportunity to meet Japanese people whom I found to be generally pleasant and hospitable.

Sally had written once and told me she now worked with her father. She missed me but made no mention as to when I would return, although she said that things were as normal back home. I had in turn written and told her about my experiences.

It was one evening when I'd finished the letter to Sally; I was disturbed by a tentative knock on the door.

Rochester was otherwise engaged at a nearby school, and I was alone in the flat. I put down my pen and answered the door. It was Satchiko. She was dressed in a white T-shirt with a mid-length black skirt, her hair straight and black, fell about her shoulders; she had two books under her right arm. She looked surprised when she saw me.

'Hello, Rochester in?' she enquired.

'Hi, no, he's teaching. I don't know what time he'll be back. Have you got a class?'

'I er, thought so.'

The telephone rang as we spoke.

'Look, come in – come in – I'll just get the phone – Denwa.' I beckoned her inside and picked up the receiver.

'Moshi, moshi,' Rochester's voice enquired.

'Oh, it's you,' I answered somewhat surprised to hear from him.

'Is Satchiko there?' he asked.

'Yes, she's here now,

I held the receiver and Satchiko took it, the movement gave me a sample of her fragrant perfume. Our proximity prompted me to take a step back as I found myself about to entertain thoughts of a decidedly non-celibate nature.

'Oh, I see no, it's OK, it's OK tomorrow hai hai, no problem.'

Satchiko replaced the receiver down and turned to me.

'Anything wrong?' I asked.

'He can't make tonight. He sorry.'

'Oh, that's a pity. Er, would you like a coffee or tea or anything?'

Satchiko smiled and shook her head. 'No thank you. It's OK. I will go.'

I wanted to say, 'No, please stay,' but found myself guided by my morality and instead answered. 'OK, well, I'll see you tomorrow.'

That would probably have been that had not fate intervened. As I escorted Satchiko to the door the room began to vibrate gently at first, and then more violently until objects fell from the shelves and plates crashed down from the cupboards.

Satchiko had remained calm at the initial tremor but as the earthquake magnitude increased, she became frightened and held on to me. I comforted her with my embrace although I felt the cold grip of fear engulf me but managed to put on a show of bravado as the tremor began to die down.

'It's OK. It's OK,' I whispered, my mouth was close to Satchiko's ear, and I kissed her gently on the top of her head and stroked her hair.

She clung to me long after the last tremor had died away and turned her face toward me. It was too much for my resolve with her mouth so close to mine and her dark eyes that held such appeal. My lips brushed against hers. I had no idea how she would respond but her mouth eagerly received mine. I felt the closeness of her body; and the contours of her breasts against my chest I took her hand and led her to my bedroom.

Earthquakes or tremors were not an uncommon occurrence in Tokyo; it was the second I had experienced and was a sensation I had not enjoyed. The quake was six on the Richter scale and centred one hundred kilometres from Tokyo, but to me, as I made totally uninhibited love to Satchiko that evening, I was pleased to have been in the city and exactly where I was when the quake struck.

It was only afterwards I felt guilt and tried to justify my actions as being purely physical, but I knew my feelings for her went deeper than that.

I took her to the station, it was eleven fifteen; for a city so lively, so abuzz with activity, it struck me as strange that trains didn't run after midnight, until it was pointed out to me by Rochester the taxi industry would suffer if trains ran all night, regardless of the inconvenience to the public. I responded that surely hotels and restaurants must also suffer, but the system had been functioning for many years and I knew my comments would make no difference.

Rochester was home when I arrived back from the station. 'You've been out! I've been creeping around like a bloody mouse thinking you were in bed.'

I explained what had happened and he listened with a look of amusement and the trace of a smirk on his face as I recounted my story.

'Yes', Rochester stated. 'It was a bastard, shook me. Always causes my bowels to contract when I feel those tremors. You realise how vulnerable you are, how puny and how immensely powerful the forces of nature are, speaking of which you succumbed to those very same forces.'

I nodded and mentally recounted the pleasure of Satchiko's company.

'Yeah.'

We talked late into the night and through into the early hours of the morning. There were no secrets between us, and we discussed many issues from the past, present and future before we eventually hit the sack.

I felt as though I had betrayed Sally, although we'd agreed to play it by ear. I thought to myself, "What if she had done the same thing? How would I feel? I concluded that I didn't really mind." Perhaps I didn't love her if I thought like that.

I tried not to see Satchiko whilst I needed to sort out my head and stayed out when Rochester gave her lessons, but she turned up at the flat unexpectedly two weeks later and I succumbed once more. After that first time she had been on my mind constantly however hard I tried not to think of her.

Inevitably I grew fonder of Satchiko as the weeks passed. She lived with her parents, as was the custom for most unmarried girls, but occasionally told them she intended to stay with a girlfriend and spent the night with me.

For me at that time it was an idyllic life of discovery and exploration, a diverse and different culture from my own. I had not previously been a great traveller and had only been out of Australia once on a holiday to Fiji. So, it was with an almost childlike enthusiasm that I explored Japan. I visited Kyoto, the ancient city with its temples of historical interest where the emperor had lived before his move to Tokyo. It was in the Meiji period from 1868 to 1912 when Edo was renamed Tokyo and established as the capital city of Japan; I visited Kyushu, the island south of Tokyo just over an hour's flight from the city; and the Seven Islands, a night's ferry ride from the metropolis, where the seafood and rugged coastline reminded me of parts of Australia. On each occasion Satchiko accompanied me, a guide without whose help I would have been unable to discover the true Japan, as a well as being a companion and lover.

One year became two and then three; to be honest I'd put Sally out of my mind, I had Satchiko, and selfishly disregarded thoughts of my past. I had written to her, and she knew I had a girlfriend and implied that she also had something going.

I stayed in Tokyo for four years and knew that I had to make some decisions. I'd lived a kind of unreal life; like that of the university student who is surrounded by a false sense of security and a future that stretches ahead somewhere in the distance and the actuality of it has no fixed time for its commencement. It was obvious I must decide what to do about Satchiko.

·····•·•·····

I was told by Sensei Taguchi that my all-round fighting ability had improved, and I was awarded a second dan in his style.

He was disappointed with me because of my refusal to enter competitions and knew that it wasn't because I was afraid. It was this that kept me at second even though he considered my skills were beyond the rank.

I steadfastly refused to fight and took more of an interest as a referee at the tournaments; I also became a club instructor for the lower grades which as a Gaijin was an honour.

I told Sensei Taguchi that I would start a dojo in Australia when I returned and sometime in the future invite him over to grade my students and give seminars.

This pleased him and he said he would look forward to the occasion and would love to visit 'Ostoraria,' as he pronounced it.

My Japanese had improved to the point where I could understand and speak quite well although I could no way read Kanji, comprised of a multitude of different characters, but could understand Hirogana and Katakana, which are less complicated forms of communication. Katakana is used to denote words of Western origin often written on signs or labels.

I had been training with Sensei Taguchi for two and half years, when I paid a visit to the first dojo where I met Yamada the bullying fourth dan.

I descended the stairs and the smell of the area brought back memories of my first few months in Japan. Yamada was in the office reading a magazine: there was nobody else around. He saw me come down the stairs.

He gave me a quick glance followed by a sneer.

'What do you want?' Long-time gone, couldn't take it?

I answered him in Japanese 'Wondered if you wanted to do a bit of sparring.'

He stared up at me in disbelief,

'Oh, Japanese eh. Who do you think you are? You don't come here and say what you want to do.'

'Why, are you scared to have a go?' I asked.

I noticed his features darken and anger surge up within him.

He stood up from the desk, muttered something about Gaijin, and made toward me. I stepped aside and he pushed past.

'Take your shoes off and get on the mat.'

I was aware of my past and had no intention to stand and trade punches and kicks with him.

He was wearing his karate gi, I was wearing a pair of shorts and a sloppy Joe which gave me an advantage as I had more to grab hold of.

I took my shoes off and stepped onto the mat, bowing as I did so.

Yamada gave me a half–hearted nod. Then without any regard to etiquette rushed me,

I didn't trust him and was prepared for his attack. He threw a roundhouse kick to my ribs and followed up with a punch; I grabbed his leg under my right arm and stepped sideways to the left. His punch turned into a wave of his arm as he tried to maintain his balance. Still with his leg gripped by my arm I kicked his supporting leg from under him and he went down. I didn't give him a chance to get up and dropped down with him. I held him from behind, my arm now around his neck. He tried to pull his chin down, but it was too late. I wrapped my legs around his torso and tightened my hold, cutting off his supply of oxygen. After a few seconds he went limp, and I released my grip. I climbed off him and rolled him over on his side.

I stood up, put my shoes back on, turned and bowed as I went out. The last I saw of Yamada was him sitting on the mat with a glazed expression on his face as he regained his senses.

Chapter Five

Five - Phoenix

W hen the time came for me to leave, to say goodbye to Satchiko it was difficult. She wanted to marry me. I told her I was not ready and would come back. She thought I'd take her with me, but I said to her that I wanted to go alone and promised I would contact her, and if things worked out, she could come over. I needed to find a job, a place to live and get set up once again, and if she was with me, it would only give me something else to worry about. Satchiko accepted the situation but could not conceal her sadness.

At the airport she wouldn't let me go and I comforted and assured her that our separation was not forever, only for a short while, and I meant it.

I hadn't heard from Sally for over two years and was surprised to get a letter from her ten days before I left. She wondered if I was still alive and had informed me of life back home and still wanted to be friends. I was happy for her as she hinted that she had found someone else; I hadn't seen her for ages and wrote back and told her of my returning to Australia very soon, but didn't say when, and I'd try and get to see her, that's only if she had time and wanted to.

I felt saddened, guilty, and decidedly miserable when I boarded the plane but the expectation, the excitement at the chance to catch up with old friends and see familiar faces and places, the thought of a juicy Aussie steak, the joy of beautiful beaches and open spaces, the clear blue seas and the warmth of the summer sun lifted my spirits.

I landed at Kingsford Smith airport, Sydney, at seven thirty in the morning; went straight through immigration and customs and was out by seven fifty. I had hardly any luggage, one suitcase and a holdall that was battered and well used.

As I made my way through the "arrivals" exit I caught sight of a familiar face, I took a second look and realised it was Sally. I felt a rush of embarrassment and then a feeling of pleasure at the sight of her. She smiled and waved enthusiastically as she caught sight of me.

Sally hugged me warmly and kissed my cheek. She looked stunning and had obviously taken a great deal of trouble with her appearance. It was worth every second.

She looked older and more mature than when I left, even more lovely than I remembered. She still retained that softness in her eyes and gentleness that had attracted me all those years ago.

'What are you doing here? How did you know I was arriving today?'

'Rochester told me', Sally replied. 'I got a letter from him last week saying the day you were coming back, and I contacted the airport. He was talking about marriage.'

I had written to him myself but hadn't seen him recently as he went to Hokkaido for three months on a job, but I knew he had been keen on a girl called Akiko, obviously very keen.

' Yes. 'I met her once, a lovely girl, she does things on TV.'

'Yes, Rochester said,' Sally looked at me.

'And what about you; and where's Satchiko? I wanted to meet her'

'She's still in Tokyo',

'Is she coming over'?

'No immediate plans, Look, what are you doing now?' I asked.

'Well, I came to meet you, do you want to come and have lunch? Dad would love to see you.' Sally suggested.

I looked at the face of the girl who stood opposite me with her dark hair and slim figure.

'Why not? Yes, that would be good. I'm staying in Wollstonecraft on the North Shore. I'll just dump my stuff and then come over, if I can remember how to get to your place.'

'I'll give you a lift.' Sally offered.

'Oh wow, thanks that would be great.'

I picked up my case and swung the hold all over my shoulder. 'It feels strange to be back.' I said as we walked toward the car park.

'I'm sure it does,' Sally agreed. 'Does it feel good?'

I took in the bright early morning sunshine and clear blue sky and then looked at her.

'It certainly does.'

Sally smiled and took my arm.

'Come on, I'll show you around. A lot has changed in four years.'

"It certainly has." I thought.

After my long absence from Australia, I was like a kid at the seaside.

As Sally drove back from the airport and through the city, I noticed buildings that didn't exist when I left and commented several times, much to Sally's amusement,

'That wasn't there before,' and 'My God, doesn't that look different.'

My immediate intention after I got back from Japan had been to get organised and start my own dojo to teach on a full-time basis. I was well known in Karate circles and although I had been away for a few years my reputation was still intact. I knew that if the worst came to the worst, I could teach Phys Ed in schools as I was qualified and felt sure I could take up my old job again, but it was a last resort, and I didn't really want to go back into education. I turned to Sally,

'I have to go and visit my aunt in Melbourne some time just to say hi. I hear my cousin John is at university now studying philosophy. What he'll do with a degree in philosophy is anybody's guess.'

Sally laughed. 'Well, he can always teach.'

'How is your dad?' I enquired as Sally negotiated a corner and changed gear.

'Oh, he's good, getting older, he would like to retire. I think he wants me to take over the   business.'

'Are you interested in that?' I asked

'Maybe, it's good to work for myself in one way but it's a lot of worry and responsibility in   another.'

I nodded. I wanted to ask about her love life and if she'd had many men in her life since and who was the guy she'd mentioned in her letter. She was young, attractive and with a warm personality. I thought it would be impossible for her to not be involved with someone.

'Have you got anyone, well anyone, special?' I enquired and tried to appear disinterested.

'You mean, is there a man in my life? '

'Yes,' I replied.

'That's for me to know,' she answered with a smile.

I didn't pursue the point. I felt confused. What about Satchiko? I loved her. I was sure of that but here was Sally, being with her made me feel good, I could be myself.

It had been a long time but how I felt when I saw her at the airport awakened something extremely strong within me. I was comfortable with her; we had always been on the same wavelength.

'What's happening with Satchiko?'

The question was direct and again took me by surprise. 'Oh, well, I...'

I didn't know what to say.

I didn't want to lie to her. I took a second or two to answer.

'I don't know, play it by ear I guess.'

Sally seemed satisfied with the answer and as we sat and waited for some traffic lights to change, looked across at me.

'You haven't changed much. Your hair's going a little thin and your face has lost weight but apart from that you look pretty much the same.'

I gave her a quick smile. The reference to my deteriorating follicles didn't exactly fill me with joy but I was aware of the fact and had to face it.

'Rochester was always teasing me and said I could polish my head in five years' time, cheeky bugger.'

'I think bald men are sexy,' Sally remarked, 'and anyway you're hardly bald.'

'No, but it's the thin end of the wedge, Dad was an egghead. It's genetic.'

The conversation continued around baldness and the hormonal implications of such a condition until we arrived at Wollstonecraft, a leafy suburb on the North Shore.

On the journey across the harbour bridge, I had taken in the beauty of the view, the Opera House and the numerous boats that filled the bay, the ferries as they pulled away from Circular Quay.

We were also accompanied by the rattle of a graffiti scarred train on an adjacent track that travelled across the bridge in the same direction. I could clearly make out the faces of the few travellers through the somewhat dirty windows.

The size and scruffy appearance of the metal monster was in stark contrast to the immaculate carriages that wound their way beneath the city of Tokyo, but it was like seeing an old friend.

I felt a sense of satisfaction that I had made the decision to return to Sydney, with its natural harbour and aesthetic beauty.

The place where I was to stay was with a woman named Carol Chandler whom I'd met in Japan. She had married an American, but it hadn't worked out and returned to Australia to rebuild her life. She had a house, bought by her previous husband, and a young son of twenty who worked as a helicopter pilot in the Northern Territory so consequently had plenty of space. I had written to her and asked if she knew of anywhere to stay, and she'd replied that I was more than welcome to stay with her and would be pleased to have my company. The house was big and a little scary at night, she said, by way of an excuse. She was an astrologer and referred to various planetary movements, of which I had no idea, that forecast events about to happen by the study of complicated astral charts.

She was thirty-eight with classical features and experienced in the ways of the world. I had always liked her, but our relationship had been plutonic although I was aware of her obvious charms.

Upon our arrival she hugged me warmly and bade Sally and I to come in. She showed us around, told me to dump my stuff in the room allocated to me and instructed us to feel free to do our own thing. She said she had to rush to give a lecture at a place on the upper North Shore and needed to do some preparation of her subject; she would catch up with us later.

I went into my room, put my case down and turned to Sally.

'I won't unpack, although I'd like to have a shower and get changed. Do you mind, Sal?' I asked.

Sally shook her head. 'Please do, for both our benefits.'

'I'll be about fifteen minutes.'

Carol shouted a farewell and left the house. She had forgotten some item that she needed and had to go to the city to get it.

'I'll be about an hour,' she yelled as she departed hastily.

I acknowledged her retreat, had a shower, came out and stood at the door of the room where Sally was seated. She browsed through an Astrology magazine and looked up at me as I entered.

'I don't know what my Sun sign is. Do you know yours?'

I carefully towelled what remained of my hair. I was naked to the waist and covered by another towel for the rest of my body.

'I think I'm Sagittarius rising, according to Carol.' I responded.

The movement of my arms as I rubbed my head caused the towel around my waist to fall to the ground and left me totally naked. Sally laughed as she looked at me and my attempt to reclaim my modesty.

She stooped from the chair and picked it up.

'Here, cover yourself up,' she said and threw me the recently fallen cloth.

I took it and replaced it around my waist. 'Sorry about that....er'

I came over to her and sat on the arm of the chair and pretended to read the article, her proximity took control of my emotions, and I stroked her hair, she looked up.'

Neither of us spoke slowly our faces moved closer, our lips at first tentatively renewed their acquaintance and gradually increased the pressure with each fresh contact.

She leaned back and looked me in the eyes.

'Are you sure about this?'

'What about your bloke?' I asked my voice betraying my emotions.

She didn't answer.

I pulled her to me; the towel fell to the floor.

Events seemed to move quickly from then on. I stayed at Carol's for a month and rented a room in George Street from Sally's father who had the upper floor and two rooms on the third for his English school.

I worked hard, painted, and fitted mirrors, and hung several bags throughout the area to emulate Sensei Taguchi's dojo in Tokyo. I still had some money left from my father's estate and had managed to save several thousand dollars in Tokyo from my efforts to teach English over the four years I was there.

Sally helped me with the paint jobs along with a couple of my former students who were more than pleased to have their old sensei back. My first classes were barely patronised but gradually the ranks started to swell, and I began to have a healthy turn out. I ran two lunch time classes, an evening class for beginners and advanced from Monday to Friday and an afternoon class on Saturday.

I'd thought about Satchiko many times since I had been back in Australia and eventually after three months made her an audio tape to explain my feelings. Again, I experienced the familiar pangs of guilt and whilst I felt somewhat callous, I made the decision; four weeks later I proposed to Sally, she accepted.

We were married six months later, the ceremony conducted in the Sydney Botanical Gardens on a cloudy day in late October. Ron had spared nothing to provide his only daughter, the light of his life, with a day she'd always remember. When I first returned from Japan, I sensed that he thought I was a fool to have gone in the first place. But after a while he realised that I really did love Sally and she loved me. Deep down he liked me, and I knew him to be a considerate and decent person. He also had one ambition: to have a grandchild. There would be no-one in the world prouder than Ron to take his grand child out on a Sunday afternoon.

She beamed happily throughout the ceremony and assured her father that it would be a day she would cherish and be forever grateful. My garrulous Aunt and the rest of the family on my side had come up from Melbourne and Rochester and his wife had flown over from Tokyo to be there. I really appreciated Rochester's gesture but not enough to rescue him from my aunt who had managed to pin him down at the reception and had almost bent his ear off. Kevin, my mate from childhood, had been my Best Man, now married himself and father of two children.

We spent our honeymoon in the Whitsunday's, an idyllic island paradise away from the trauma of city life, in a luxury hotel close to the beach. It was two weeks of bliss for us both, we ate, drank, swam, danced, and spent hours making love under the tropical stars or in the comfort of our room.

When we reluctantly returned to reality, we rented a two-bedroom terraced house in Pyrmont, the inner suburb next to Ultimo, an easy walk to the city and close to Darling Harbour; an area of deserted wharves and train tracks that was planned for redevelopment.

The house was compact and had a small garden that backed on to an alley which led to Little Mount Street and allowed pedestrian access.

We furnished and decorated the house in the way that suited us both, although it was Sally who exercised the most influence as to how to furnish and the choice of colour schemes; I trusted her judgement.

We had been married for just over a year when Sally announced that she'd seen the doctor and he had confirmed she was pregnant. I was thrilled but Ron was ecstatic and convinced it was a boy. Sally didn't want to know the gender until the birth and told him to just "wait and see."

My school had also taken off. I had several children's classes, and I derived a great sense of satisfaction to see them train in earnest. At first, I had been reluctant to teach kids as I knew their concentration span was of a limited duration, but my experience at schools had taught me a few lessons. I adjusted my method as to how to instruct and changed the topic or exercise if I sensed they were "wandering." We also played games as a reward for their effort.

It kept my classes lively and focused which helped my younger students respect me.

That week had been a good one, with two new private students enrolled for an early afternoon class; I was pleased to accept them as I needed a few more to make life that bit more financially comfortable. I trained first thing in the morning and throughout the day if I had the chance, if only to stretch, perform Kata or punch the Makiwara to harden my knuckles.

If I hadn't stayed back that evening my life would have been totally different.

Chapter Six

Six - All for a cat

I struck my final punch with an expulsion of breath and a loud Kiai, the vocal expression of my physical effort as I concentrated my energy into that last blow. The shaft of the Makiwara bent back and I heard it split at the base. I even surprised myself but assumed after many years of punishment my wooden partner had finally had enough.

I stepped away took a towel from a nearby peg and rubbed myself down. I generally felt weary after my day, but it never seemed like work to me. I enjoyed every minute; it kept my body and mind in perfect harmony by the self-discipline and knowledge of my body's ability and limitations.

I checked around the dojo to make sure the windows were locked and the water in the shower room turned off. Satisfied all was in order, I switched off the lights, pulled the door closed, left the building, and crossed the street. It was a cold miserable night; the wet pavement shimmered from the lights of cars moving down the road.

Pyrmont Bridge had been closed to the public for some time, so I generally walked the long way to my house; because it was raining, I decided to catch the bus that cruised slowly into view from the end of George Street.

The bus's wipers jerked back and forth across the windscreen as it pulled close to the stop. No one else waited and I jumped aboard through the open doors. The engine ticked over as I dug my hand in my pocket and pulled out some change.

'Nice night,' I said. The driver tore off a ticket and passed it to me.

'Yeah. Still, I guess we need the rain,' he cast a quick glance in his mirror and turned the wheel as the doors closed. The movement of the bus's acceleration caused me to grab hold of one of the straps as I moved down the aisle and swung myself into a seat. I delved down into the bag that held my gi and pulled out an old Walkman to which were attached some earphones. I plugged them into my head, sat back and listened to a song from "Pennies from Heaven" whilst I stared out of the rain splashed window. We reached Harris Street; I stood up and jerked the cord above my head to signal to the driver that the next stop was mine.

Jumping from the bus I hastened home, head bent forward to shield my eyes from the rain. Sally would cook dinner if she got home before me and vice versa if I got home first. We would wait for each other so we could sit down together, have a meal, and talk about the day's events. She'd had a day off and the prospect of warm soup and the company of my beautiful wife quickened my pace. The rain began to lessen into a soft drizzle when I arrived on my doorstep; I turned the key in the front door.

The aroma of freshly baked bread greeted me as I caught sight of Sally in the kitchen, her apron stretched across her pregnant stomach. I smiled at the sight of her.

'It's only me.'

'Hi, darling. Are you wet?' She asked as she planted a kiss on my cheek.

'Still raining?' she enquired.

'No, it's virtually stopped,' I looked around the kitchen for any food to steal. 'I'm starving.   What've we got?'

'It's not much, a vegetable soup and some fruit and yoghurt, easy to digest.

'Oh, did you get the milk?'

'Ah!' I clutched my head in a somewhat over dramatic theatrical gesture.

'I forgot. I'll go now.'

'No, it's OK. I'll get some tomorrow.'

'My wife wants milk. My wife shall have milk,'

I hugged her and placed a wet sloppy kiss on her forehead. 'It's good for growing babies.'

'No, Don't worry. It's miserable out and you're probably tired. I can wait.'

'Say no more. I shall be five minutes,' I reassured her and left.

The Milk Bar around the corner was closed. I broke into a run and decided to head for Ultimo where there was another shop. The rain had stopped, and the air seemed cleaner, perhaps because it settled the pollution, if only for a short time. I was about to enter the shop when a small fluffy cat, dampened by the rain, came toward me, and voiced a pleading miaow.

I've always loved animals and this cat was identical to the family pet my sister had doted on. Its marked coat and colour were almost the same. I bent down and stroked it; my thoughts went back to my life in Melbourne and my family.

'Hey, you're a little wet aren't you mate?'

The cat rubbed herself vigorously against my leg as I fondled her damp ear. After a few moments I left her, her tail erect ready for more affection and went into the Milk Bar. I picked out the milk from the display fridge and looked around for something to buy the cat.

'Got anything for cats?' I asked the woman.

She nodded towards one of the aisles.

'Under the bread.'

'Thanks,' I replied and followed the direction of her nod. I purchased a small treat from the rack and left the Milk Bar. The cat seemed to know I had bought her something and sidled up to me. I could hear her purr as her enthusiasm at the prospect of food motivated her friendship. She had a particularly sweet face, and I was captivated by her expression.

'Here you go.' I unwrapped the cat treat and handed it to the excited feline. She butted my hand with her head then patted it with her paw to secure it faster.

'Steady.' I laughed at her frantic attempt to hasten the delivery of my gift, stroked her damp fur, and gave her the treat.

She turned her head to one side, swallowed the mixture of fish and dried meat with enthusiasm and looked eagerly up at me for more.

'There's no more madam,' I picked up my milk, my knee cracked as I did so.

'Geez, I'm getting old, puss. See you later.'

I gave her a final stroke and walked away in the direction of my house.

The cat watched me as I departed and then ran, her body fluffed up and almost side on, tail erect as she passed me.

The animal continued with her playful behaviour until she was several yards in front.

I laughed.

'Silly puss,' I muttered under my breath and looked back over my shoulder; a car approached at high speed. Its over revved engine got louder as it got closer.

Harris Street had always been busy and although a flyover had taken away a lot of the traffic it still had its steady share during the day. I thought before I went into the shop that it was a dangerous place for a cat to live, near a main road, but assumed it was probably street wise by now to have lived to adulthood. The cat seemed to realise my worst fears. It stepped into the road to investigate the flattened remains of a pigeon that had not been quick enough a few days' earlier. A feather, the only remaining part of the bird not firmly adhered to the tarmac, blew in the breeze.

Although soggy it rose and fell with enough regularity to stimulate the cat's interest; I stopped. At the same time the cat halted in her tracks and stared into the headlights as the car approached. I caught a glimpse of the occupants as they raced by, one of them grinned and pointed. They could have avoided her but instead it seemed as though they purposely wanted to hit her.

There was a dull thud and the cat's twisted body lay in the wet road like an old, carelessly discarded glove. I stood where I was in disbelief and regarded the poor creature which only a few moments earlier had been a warm and playful cat.

Meanwhile the car pulled up outside one of the houses not far from where I stood.

The occupants got out. They were obviously under the influence of something and came back to look at their "work." One wore a tee-shirt and jeans, Doc Marten's boots and had a shaved head, with a small tattoo of a flying bird on his neck. The other had straggly long hair tied back with a piece of tatty ribbon and wore a vest and a dirty pair of jeans. His arms muscular, and a scar on his right cheek. They reached the body of the cat and looked down.

'Poor little pussycat,' the long-haired man grinned.

'Yeah, a shame in it.' His shaven headed colleague smirked.

I felt a mixture of hatred and fear. I was now presented with the reality of a situation, what should I do? Two thugs, obviously street wise and no doubt experienced in thuggery of one kind or another, and me never actually tested in real combat, where there are no rules, in a no holds barred confrontation.

I felt uneasy and began to feel my stomach turn over and my limbs involuntarily shake. I took a deep breath, lowered my shoulders, and walked towards the two men.

I was within a few feet of them when the man with the long hair drew his foot back 'Fuckin' cat,' and kicked the animal's corpse into the air. The tail and the head seemed to momentarily meet for a second and the animal's entrails spilled as it fell to earth.

Something inside me snapped and I shouted at the top of my voice a loud 'Oi' which caused the two men to swing around and look in my direction.

'Isn't it enough that you killed it?'

Buzz, the thug with the cropped hair and Louis, his muscular companion, looked at each other and then at me as I drew closer. I suddenly felt very alone. I wished I'd said nothing, but it was too late for that. I knew it was a case of fight or flight. Louis was the first to speak.

'Was it your cat?' he asked.

I said nothing. He went to the dead animal and picked it up by the tail. It was wet and the eyes were closed, its entrails hung from its stomach and blood dripped from its mouth. I recalled my sister's cat and the day I had last seen her, the family killed by drunken thugs, like the two who now leered at me. I seemed to go into a trance and turned my gaze to Louis who swung the cat in readiness to throw at me.

'I hate fuckin' cats, ere you have...' The word never left his mouth. The taunt was stifled with the sound of the back of my right fist as it slammed into his temple and wiped the stupid grin off his face; I followed through with a left hook and saw two teeth spin into the air. His skull snapped back as if he had been struck by a sledgehammer and he folded up like a recently read Sunday broadsheet. I swung round and faced the other thug.

Immediately after I hit Louis, I knew the folly of my act. I'd done it again. I'd killed a man; I could sense it. I knew he would never breathe again as I watched him fall into a twisted position where the cat had lain moments before, now next to her assailant in a macabre deathly embrace, the cat's broken head next to Louis's on the wet cold road.

Buzz was taken by surprise. His colleague was an experienced street fighter but the speed with which he had been demolished changed his attitude. He stared down at Louis's body with a blank expression then knelt to listen to Louis's chest. He stared back at me.

'Youse killed 'im. He's fuckin' dead.'

I said nothing; I just remember being in a state of shock.

'Youse killed him, yer bastard,' the thug yelled at the top of his voice.

A Police car on the opposite lane of traffic switched on its blue light, swung around, and pulled into the kerb. Two cops got out. Buzz looked at the Police as they approached, screamed, and pointed his finger angrily at me. 'He killed me mate,'

One of the officers came over.

'What's going on then?'

His colleague bent over the body of Louis and glanced up at me.

'Yeah, what's been going on?' he echoed.

Chapter Seven

Seven - Life changes

S ally had waited over an hour and was concerned, perhaps more annoyed than worried I'd taken so long. She assumed I was engaged in conversation with somebody or had met an old friend or had even decided to go for a quick run as I'd done in the past. She sighed resignedly, turned on the television and lowered herself into a nearby armchair. She didn't really wish to watch anything, but the cathode ray tube offered some sort of comfort whilst she waited.

I rang Sally from the police station.

'Where are you? Where have you been?' she asked. There was a moment's pause after I explained what had happened.

'I'll come down -- no I'll get a taxi -- I'll phone Dad.' I heard her replace the receiver and imagined her concern.

At the Police station I was questioned. Buzz's version of the story was totally different to mine which; according to him was I had attacked Louis without provocation because he had accidentally killed a cat. The

Police Sergeant had his doubts as to the truth but went through the usual procedures.

I was asked if I required a solicitor to be present but due to my misguided faith in the Australian judicial system I declined.

I was confined to a cell whilst the Police questioned Buzz and sat within the grim four walls. I felt deeply depressed and unsure of the future; just over an hour ago I had been relaxed, happy and had a life to look forward to. Now, as I sat and read the graffiti of former inmates, I was overwhelmed by a sense of gloom. I had never been a defeatist, but things looked bad, and I sensed what lay ahead was none too positive. My thoughts turned to Bulldozer and how bad it seemed, as though I were a killer, I had been responsible for the death of two men and tried to shake the unwanted thought from my head as it danced around my brain to taunt me.

The door opened and gave my mental torment a momentary reprieve. It was the Sergeant.

'This way please, Mr Mason.' There was an air of polite disinterest in his voice. As far as the Sergeant was concerned it was just another brawl, but with serious consequences, that had to be investigated and charges laid if necessary.

The officer was one of those unshockable types. He'd seen it all in his thirty years' experience and took each day as it came whatever arose as just part of the job.

I followed the Policeman through the corridor at the back of the building toward the front desk and was greeted by my wife and father-in-law. Close to them two women stood in what looked like a kind of play pen but was an area designated to secure felons or noisy persons. The two women were indeed the latter and yelled abuse at a female Police Constable who led a colleague of theirs by the arm toward the cells.

I felt concern for Sally, heavily pregnant and involved in circumstances hardly beneficial to her mental state.

In turn, Sally felt concern for me as I followed the large Police Sergeant to the desk. I acknowledged my wife's presence with a half-hearted smile and raised my eyebrows like a naughty boy who had been caught out at school for some misdemeanour.

'What's happened?' Sally asked me as I drew closer.

The Police Sergeant interjected. 'Is this your husband?' Sally nodded. The Police Sergeant continued. 'Your husband will be charged with manslaughter and held in custody until trial.'

Ron stepped forward.

'Is bail possible at all?' he asked.

The Sergeant looked questioningly at Ron.

'I'm his....' His voice was momentarily drowned out by a string of obscenities aimed at the female police constable by one of the women in the "play pen."

'Knock it off Denise, or you'll be in trouble, like your mate,' the Sergeant stated in a strong but clear voice.

The author of the vocal obscenities glowered at the Sergeant and pulled a defiant face but ceased her ovation.

Ron continued. 'I'm his father-in-law.'

The Sergeant nodded. 'You'd better come this way.'

Ron had lived in Sydney all his life and had a circle of friends, both ordinary and influential and managed to secure my freedom with a substantial amount of bail money.

It was with mixed feelings of relief and anxiety that I lay in my bed that night, staring at the ceiling, while Sally lay beside me.

'Sal, if the worst happens and I have to go to prison, then it would be really difficult for you.'

'Don't be so stupid. You won't go to prison,' she replied.

'I don't know what happened. It was like I just sort of lost control. I was scared, I guess. I must be crazy.' I sat up in bed.

'Look, go to sleep. Get some rest. It'll be OK,' she reassured me and gently rubbed my back.

I felt the tears begin to well up in my eyes as fear and desperation fought to take control of my mind. I felt ashamed. What kind of man was I?

'I couldn't stand being in a cage, Sal. I just couldn't stand it.' My lower lip began to quiver. 'God, how things change.' I choked.

'You can't change things. What's done is done. If it's as you say then it'll be OK, you'll be acquitted, don't worry.'

I turned and put my arm around her slim shoulders and took a grip of my emotions. She nuzzled closer. I fought back the tears and the intrusive lump in my throat and took a deep breath.

'You're right. I'll face things as they come.'

'That's better, that's more like it,' she sounded like my mother when I was a child,

'Come on, try and get some sleep,' Sally stroked my hair and kissed my cheek.

I patted her large stomach, returned her kiss lightly on the mouth, took a deep breath, closed my eyes, and tried to clear my mind.

·····•·····

I continued my life as normally as I could under the circumstances and ran my school. My students knew me and ridiculed the newspaper reports and publicity that circulated after the event.

One of the papers that ran the story had dug up from its past records the "Bulldozer" incident and there was the hint or insinuation that perhaps I had indeed used excessive force. My solicitor was outraged on my behalf and various legal documents were issued, but the damage had been done and at the trial the Judge had deemed it necessary to rule that all previous publicity should be disregarded, but the seeds had been planted.

My transition into fatherhood took place a month earlier than expected, due no doubt, to the pressure on our lives that the impending trial and uncertainty of the future placed upon Sally.

I had wanted to be present at the birth and was in the dojo with a class when the telephone rang. It was Ron. He had been on a visit to his daughter when the contractions started, bundled her into the car and raced her off to hospital. He telephoned and told me where they were.

I replaced the receiver and shouted an apology to my students as I quickly pulled on a track suit top and changed my trousers.

'It's my wife. She's giving birth. See you later.'

I asked my most senior student to take over and lock the dojo when he left. I raced down the stairs, into the street and ran as fast as I could to the nearest taxi stand.

I got as far as Wynyard, grabbed a cab, and instructed the driver to put his foot on the gas and head for the hospital.

Ron was there as I flew up the steps to the entrance.

'How is she? Where is she?' I asked impatiently before my father-in-law could answer.

'She's through that door, I think, and I guess she's OK!' Ron stated as I headed for the door he'd indicated.

A nurse came through at the same time as I attempted to go in. 'I'm afraid you can't go in there, sir.'

'I'm Tony Mason. My wife's having a baby. She wanted me to be there. I need to be with her.'

The nurse continued to walk. 'I'm sure you do but she's not in there. She's in Room A at the end of the corridor. Please follow me.'

I did as she said, stopped by a linen cupboard where I was issued with the required mask and gown and followed her through the door marked 'A.'

A doctor and nurse were with Sally as she lay recumbent with her legs in the air. They hardly gave me a second look as I entered.

'This is Mr Mason,' the nurse stated as I approached my wife and wondered where I should stand.

Doctor Chan acknowledged my presence with a nod and gestured for me to position myself beside my wife's head.

'G'day, Mr Mason. Just in time. A few more minutes and you would have been too late to see your baby born.'

I gave Sally's hand a gentle squeeze and did as the doctor instructed.

Sally was encouraged to push; her face contorted indicating spasms of great pain. She let out a scream that confirmed my assumption, I watched as she grimaced in what must have been severe agony; she was told to push as hard as she could; I felt helpless and spoke softly to her; the pressure of her hand on mine grew stronger as the contractions increased.

From my position I could just make out the blood–flecked purple, pink shape that emerged to be that of a child, my child, our child, a girl.

The baby was held for a few seconds by the feet, the umbilical cord cut and tied with the efficiency of a chicken factory worker who dresses fowl; the placenta washed away.

Our new daughter, because she was premature by a month, was immediately taken into special care and Sally and I held her only briefly before she was whisked away.

We named the child Clare, a beautiful healthy little girl doted on by her grandfather and showered with gifts.

The birth of my daughter made me even more aware of my situation and I felt more insecure as the date for my trial drew closer.

I had discussed it with my father–in–law, and he'd assured me that Sally and Clare would be looked after if the worst happened, and I was foolish even to think about such things.

'I feel like the sword of Damocles is about to drop,' I confided to Ron a few days before the court case.

'Don't worry, the defence lawyer is the best,' Ron reiterated.

The lawyer was a well-known Sydney Barrister by the name of Brian Thompson, who'd defended many accused felons in the past and in most cases, had got his clients acquitted or awarded reduced sentences often better than they deserved. He had instructed me to plead guilty to manslaughter with mitigating circumstances. I was reluctant at first, but he told me that I had killed a man although arguably in self-defence and it was my best shot.

There were a few people in the public gallery when I took the stand and swore the oath; I had seen it done in numerous films but had never appeared in Court before except for the inquest on Bulldozer and that was far more informal and not a trial as such. But now I found myself about to face a serious charge with the full weight of the law poised against me.

·····•••····

Buzz sat on one of the benches to the right of the court room; a few relatives of Louis arrayed themselves in one of the pews, as if they attended Church, decked out in their best attire to give some credence to their attempt to portray an image of respectability.

I avoided their glares and scowls and listened to the charges filed against me.

Sally sat with Ron, not far from Louis' relations. Her face didn't betray the anxiety she must have felt. Clare was cared for by my aunt who had come up from Melbourne to give the family support and help. Whilst I teased her about her ability to talk the hind leg off a donkey, I also held her in great affection as she'd been a surrogate mother to me as well as an admirable aunt. I felt a tinge of comfort from the knowledge my family were a hundred per cent behind me.

I'd been instructed to plead guilty, but in my mind, I felt that I was innocent of any intention to kill anyone and much to my Barristers dismay pleaded so.

The Court laboured through its procedures with an air of Victorian melodrama, bewigged officials and legal clerks orated in an almost alien language.

The facts Buzz related made me feel utter contempt and incredulity at such blatant lies.

The judge had been told, I had instigated the whole affair and abused and cursed Louis for his accidental collision with the cat. He then went on to say, under oath that Louis, an avowed cat lover had been deeply distressed at the death of the animal and when he attempted to place the unfortunate creature's body in the side of the road and inspect it for means of identification, he had been viciously attacked by me.

I was allowed to see my wife and father-in-law. Mr Thompson came over to Ron and Sally.

Ron looked serious.

'Not going too well, eh?' Ron said in a somewhat subdued voice away from Sally's earshot.

'It's early days, Mr Hackett, early days and we've yet to hear your son-in-law's testimony and we have a witness, an elderly man who lives in Harris Street, so all is not lost but I wish he'd listened to me and followed my advice.'

I was decidedly pessimistic as I nibbled half-heartedly on the cheese roll that had been provided for me. The idea that the whole system of justice rested on the oratory skills of grossly overpaid legal hawks didn't console me; that really, they had no personal interest in their clients but played a sort of game, the stakes readily provided.

A loss of a case amounted to a loss of kudos and possible future employment, although the prosecution had less to gain from a conviction than the defence from an acquittal. Perhaps this view reflected my pessimism and once again Sally raised my spirits by her rebuttal of my opinion and that it wasn't black and white.

'I guess you're right,' I shrugged. 'I mean it, Sal, I've been thinking. If I go to prison, then you must divorce me.'

Sally registered an expression of surprise and then of hurt.

'Why, for God's sake? Stop being so negative. You won't go to prison.'

'But if I do,' I persisted.

'I don't want to talk about it,' Sally exclaimed.

'I mean it, Sal.'

Sally looked at me and tears began to well in her eyes.

'How can you be so cruel?' She said angrily. 'For God's sake the trial isn't even over and you're being so negative.'

'I don't mean to be cruel, Sal. I love you. I love you more than anything in the world. It's best for you. I'm only thinking of you and Clare. What kind of life would it be for you to be married to a man convicted of murder?'

'Manslaughter,' Sally interjected.

'Manslaughter, murder, what's the difference?'

'I'm not talking about it I can't believe you're saying this.' Sally turned away and hid her face.

I went to her and cast a quick glance at the officer employed to guard me.

He had unavoidably heard our conversation and had become unwillingly involved in our disagreement. He nodded to me and gave me permission to hold my wife and turned away as he did so. I swung her round. Her face was streaked from so many tears and her soft dark eyes were red.

I was overcome with emotion and pulled her to me, kissed her and stroked her cheek.

'I'm sorry, Sal,' I whispered. 'I wouldn't hurt you for the world. I love you.'

I tried to hold back the tears but one escaped and rolled down my cheek before I choked them back and regained my composure. I held her to me.

The Police officer shuffled embarrassedly on his feet and moved closer to the door. He looked through the small window and turned his back on us.

After the recess I was returned to the witness stand and this time cross examined by the prosecution. There were the usual questions that established my identity and occupation, which didn't augur well, and the prosecution continually emphasised my occupation and had a field day when he recounted the years, I spent in Japan solely for the purpose of improving my ability to kill.

I strongly denied this and an objection by the defence was sustained on the grounds that it was a statement that misled regarding my motives for the practice of martial arts.

The Prosecution attempted to paint the picture that I had looked for an excuse to put into practice my "deadly skills," using the Prosecution's own words.

My Defence on the other hand argued that I was not a violent man and several of my students testified as to my character and argued, on the contrary, practitioners of martial arts were less inclined to violent acts and generally more self-disciplined than persons who wish just to perpetrate violence.

The trial continued for three days, and the Jury deliberated for over four hours before they reached a decision.

I watched them file back into the Court room and my stomach turned as if I awaited the result of an examination. Sally smiled to encourage me, and I gave a weak smile back in response. Ron patted his daughter's hand and acknowledged me. I nodded and forced another smile.

The Jury settled themselves and the Judge requested their verdict.

The foreman stood, cleared his throat, and spoke in a clear loud voice.

Chapter Eight

Eight – Despair

'We find the defendant guilty.'

I winced visibly and my head fell forward and hid the suppressed tears. Ron put his arm around Sally's shoulders and comforted her. She stared at me from across the court room and tried to catch my eye. Eventually I returned her look. I could see through my misty eyes her calm courageous face, could feel the inner strength that she had summoned to rebuke me for my silly threats with respect to divorce. I looked away.

Louis' relations nodded approvingly and leered at me with contempt. Buzz concealed a smile of satisfaction, talked to the Prosecution, and cast a triumphant glance at me from time to time.

I was gob smacked. Although pessimistic I had always held some belief that justice would prevail, and I would be acquitted. In my mind I had acted purely in self-defence under extenuating circumstances. If I hadn't struck out Louis would have no doubt attacked me. Like so many situations visited in the cold light of day they sound benign; but the outcome of the moment is totally unpredictable and to gauge how much force is necessary at that instant is not an immediate consideration when you feel you are threatened with the unknown. One of the things taught in karate. Do not instigate a fight, but if you must fight then commit totally to your attack.

The sentence was to be announced in three weeks. In the meantime, I was to be held in custody. In one way I'd been lucky. I had enjoyed the luxury of freedom whilst I awaited trial. Sometimes suspects were interned for months before their case was heard then found to be innocent.

I was escorted downstairs into custody, and it seemed as if my world had come to an end. My life had dramatically changed by the prospect of confinement. All I held most dear would be denied me, the companionship of my wife, to watch my child grow, my freedom, the hopes and dreams we shared together for the future, gone like a bubble that had suddenly burst.

Why? All because of the testimony of some slimy thug.

I felt waves of hatred well up inside me, a sensation I hadn't experienced before, in that moment I felt myself change. I wanted to kill Buzz, to smash his skull with my fist and make him take back every lying word. This vile snake with his twisted truths had totally changed my life with far reaching consequences.

Sally was permitted to see me briefly before I was taken down.

'Don't worry, darling. You haven't been sentenced. Maybe you won't go to prison.'

I listened to her words and her calm logic managed to spark a faint glimmer of hope within me.

The weeks before I was sentenced, I experienced the indignity and curtailment of freedom by confinement. I was taken to a prison outside of Sydney and grew decidedly more dejected as the weeks passed. I had always had a tremendous amount of self-discipline but now it was as if I had given up and couldn't be bothered. I sat away from the other inmates when not required to do other duties and waited for Sally to come and visit.

My response to my fellow prisoners who tried to converse with me was not rude but conveyed without doubt that I wanted to be left alone.

Eventually I was required to appear in Court for the day of sentence. I was summoned, picked up by a prison van and taken to Sydney.

To see the outside world with all its bustle and brightness, with people able to enjoy the freedom to go where they wanted, when they wanted and with whom they wanted, made me even more aware of the possibility that I could lose this for a long time. Three weeks had already seemed like a lifetime. I looked at the guard opposite me and knew from where I sat, I could lay him out before he even knew what had hit him.

But then how would I get out? What would I do? Where would I go? I couldn't go home, that would be the first place they'd look.

The guard turned to me; he was a man of about forty-eight, but the years had not been kind to him, he smiled and revealed a broken tooth.

'It's the big day today, eh son?' he said as if he spoke to one of his own before their wedding, or an event looked forward to for some time. There was no malice or sarcasm in his voice.

'Let's hope it don't go too bad for you.'

The guard's words offered me encouragement and were stated with sincerity. I nodded. 'I hope so too.'

I was escorted into Court and taken to the cell I first occupied. There was an air of familiarity about the place, the same smell, the same subdued light that sharpened my awareness of the situation. I remembered the dojo I first visited and how the sense of smell can stimulate memory.

Sally and Ron were in Court and my best man, Kevin. I wondered where Rochester was and what he was up to, I hadn't heard from him for some time although I knew he was back in Tokyo with Akiko. I had intended to write but somehow couldn't bring myself to do it. After all, what could I say?

"Have murdered someone, am in prison, love T."

The judge entered and the court rose to their feet. Again, there was that air of tense anticipation before the Judge read out the sentence. Sally gripped her father's hand, and I took a deep breath, she looked earnestly at me and gave a faint smile.

The Judge looked down, cleared his throat, and went on.

'Tony Mason, you have been found guilty of manslaughter. It is therefore the duty of this Court to mete out punishment befitting the seriousness of the crime.'

'It doesn't sound good,' Ron muttered to his daughter.

The Judge continued. 'You are a skilled practitioner of a martial art and therefore as such required to exercise responsibility and restraint. You were confronted with a situation and used, in my opinion, unnecessary force. Not only that, but you also took the initiative and instigated an attack on Mr Louis Rissotti, resulting in his death. I therefore have no alternative but to sentence you to eight years' imprisonment with a non-parole period of five years.'

The Judge rose, adding an air of finality to the proceedings. There was a silence in the Courtroom whilst the various parties took in the severity of what had transpired, then a murmur of conversation followed by the shuffle of feet as they prepared to leave the Court. Again, I felt as if another pile of life's dirt had been poured on me and stood in silence until the officer beside me applied pressure to my arm and pulled me from the dock. I looked across at Sally, I could see her weeping whilst Ron offered some comfort.

I didn't know what to do, I looked around the courtroom and thought about escape but there were too many police, and I knew I stood a good chance of recapture before I even made it to the door. My mind raced as I tried to come to terms with what had happened. In some ways I felt less shocked than when I had been accused. I knew there were Appeal Courts, and I also knew Ron would try his best to get my release, but in the meantime, I had to be confined like some battery hen, the thought of which filled me with dread.

I was led to the cell allocated before transportation to the gaol and found myself beneath the Courtroom, thoroughly shocked and in a state of disbelief. The last three weeks had left me tired, stressed, and without any sense of purpose in life.

Sally and Ron escorted by a guard, made their way toward me. It was as though I had decided there and then. Sally no longer wept but her eyes showed signs of her recent tears. She rushed to me and threw her arms around my neck. The guard gently pulled her away. I am ashamed to say I remained cold and impassive and looked down at her tear-filled eyes.

'Well, at least now we know.'

'Know what?' Sally replied and knew full well what I meant.

'What you have to do.'

'Tony I'm your wife for better or worse. Remember?'

I remained resolved. 'I want you to divorce me, Sal. I don't want to see you. I don't want you to visit me. I want you to start a new life.'

'What are you saying? I love you. I can't believe you are saying this. Why are you so selfish, so stubborn? You can't do this I'll wait for you. Besides, there are appeals.'

Ron put his arm around Sally's shoulder as I was led away.

'Listen to me. I'm going to see you Tony,' she shouted after me. 'I'm going to see you.'

I felt as though I wanted to scream and tell her that I loved her more than anything else in the world but instead said nothing. I was convinced I was right to give her the chance of a new life and was determined, however painful it was, to see it through. I went with my escort down the narrow-tiled passage and into the prison van.

I was told Greenacres was built in the early Nineteenth Century, an ugly, badly designed building with green paint as its predominant colour. It had an air of detachment about it as though it was a world of its own; I found myself driven through the heavy barred gates along with a guard and three other men, to our new "home." The guard, a powerfully built man in his late twenties, sat opposite us; stony faced he fingered his baton.

Upon arrival we disembarked and were registered.

'Ave to check in and get the porter to show us our rooms.' Chimed Curly, a bald, somewhat thin man with hardly any teeth; he was one of the three men with me in the van. He smiled and revealed his gums.

'No talking, Curly,' the guard admonished.

A strong smell of cooked food emanated from a building to the right, I assumed it was the canteen. We were "checked in" at a desk and then showered, given a medical and an anal examination for any contraband, then prison attire and shown to our "rooms."

The prison was divided into various levels, and each had several cells in corridor fashion with iron railings and thick wire mesh as guide rails, metal steps connected each level; there were many people moving around.

Designated areas were assigned to the inmates and prisoners were not allowed to inhabit different levels without permission. They could quite freely visit inmates on their own level at certain stated times. I noticed the recreation areas, a large gym, and a television room. Several prisoners worked out and stared at us as we were taken to our respective cells.

I was to share accommodation with Curly and opted for the top bunk. I organised what little stuff I had and climbed up to my new bed, which I would occupy for at least the next five years.

'You can go out, yer know. Have a look round,' Curly said to me.

'No, it's OK. I'll stay here for a while.' I replied. I thought that to walk around would make me feel even more depressed.

Curly shrugged and left the cell.

I sat on the bunk and took in my surroundings, the cracked basin, the makeshift toilet facilities, the army style blankets, absence of colour and the total lack of feminine touch. I placed my head in my hands and rubbed my eyes. Somewhere, from the very depth of my being, I found a spark of courage, of determination to get through this hell and out the other side as best I could. The spirit of Budo had not totally been extinguished within me.

Longbeach, a prison for serious felons, was closer to Sydney but equally as dark and gothic on the exterior as Greenacres. Both prisons were high security and housed inmates for serious offences.

Each operated with a similar system; prisoners could request to be placed in protection if there was any considered threat to their person. Paedophiles, grassers, ex coppers or young pretty boys, were usually among the most frequent inhabitants of protection.

Many of the prisoners there were considered of lower social value than the other inmates, even by the wardens. There was a hierarchy within the prison system and rules to be observed, those who neglected to adhere to these unwritten instructions were brought to account by the enforcers, whether they be "screws" or inmates.

The wardens were aware of "the pecking order" and generally kept out of matters unless they interfered dramatically with the smooth function of the prison or threatened security.

In Longbeach, at the top of the prisoner's hierarchy was a thug named Granston, I later discovered he was an evil, callous, repulsive man with little or no trace of humanity. He was thirty-two years old, six feet tall with lank black hair. He had been in and out of institutions all his life, his first conviction, when at fifteen years old, he killed a fellow pupil from his school. From there his education in crime took off. He had a natural disregard and contempt for the law and was totally fearless. He had been convicted of robbery, assault, and rape; he killed the boyfriend of one of his victims and subjected the girl to hours of torture and humiliation. At the age of twenty-seven he had been involved in a prison riot and had murdered a guard. He was a lifer with no hope of release and consequently had nothing to lose.

In recent years he had played the game and kept out of trouble but still manipulated and pulled strings. He had two unsavoury companions who backed up his demands on his fellow prisoners with muscle: Russell, an ex-boxer convicted of murder whilst involved in a drug deal and Green, equally as physically formidable, an ex-SAS elite soldier, convicted of armed robbery and assault.

Granston had a regular prison visitor, A John Simpson, the father of the girl he'd raped, a man bent on forgiveness who looked for the decency he believed existed in all people. Granston played up to his ideals to give the impression he was repentant; it was in his interest,

Within the prison system it was usual for the ethnic minorities interned to form their own "communities" based on race because of a common interest in language and familiar customs. Longbeach was no different in this respect but ran a trial integration of different racial groups. One of the participants was Deuce, an Aboriginal Elder who had come to reside, along with many others of his race in one of Her Majesty's prisons.

It was whilst he had a smoke in the exercise yard that he caught sight of Granston with his two thugs, Russell, and Green as they moved menacingly through the ranks of inmates like predatory animals hunting for something to kill.

Deuce pulled on his cigarette and watched. He saw Granston nod in the direction of a young man, Alan Munro.

The youth caught sight of the three men; a look of fear crossed his face. He turned and went hurriedly toward a door he thought may afford him some escape.

Deuce continued to watch as Granston and his two gorillas followed through the same exit. Deuce caught the eye of one of the wardens. No words were spoken but in that visual exchange a lot was said. The guard turned away. Deuce gave vent to his contempt, spat on the ground, and drew on his roll up.

Munro had run toward his cell, entered, and closed the door behind him. The rest of the prisoners were in the yard or recreation area, he was alone. He heard the footsteps of the three men approach and stood by the door; he listened.

He'd noticed Granston look at him the first day he arrived but thought little of it. What did he want? He had no idea of what was to follow.

The door flew open as Green's foot contacted the metal, and he extended his leg. The sound of the sudden explosive impact and the sight of the men in the doorway sent a rush of cold fear through Munro; his stomach turned.

'What do you want?' he stammered.

Granston grinned.

'Your little cherry.' He fixed his eyes on the terrified boy.

'Eh?' the boy enquired. He began to understand the lank haired man that leered at him meant exactly what he said.

Granston didn't even bother to reply. He nodded to Green and Russell who grabbed the boy's arms, swung him round and forced him to the floor.

'No,' the boy managed to raise a muffled shout before Green's hand clapped over his mouth.

'Now, now. Let's keep quiet shall we,' the man soothed.

Granston's hands went to his fly, he slowly unzipped himself.

'Feeling horny, are you? Suck on something before lunch you little fucking shit.'

Granston struck the boy across the face with his clenched fist, grabbed his hair and pulled his head back. He moved closer to the now stunned youth.

'Eat this yer dirty little fucker.'

Deuce knew what was going on, he shook his head and tossed the cigarette butt to the ground. 'Bastards.' he muttered under his breath. He looked again at the guard who had conveniently moved to the end of the yard. Ten minutes passed before the three men reappeared. Granston grinned and joked with Russell as they came through the cell door.

The tannoid system announced roll call, several men formed a loose line as Deuce made his way to the cells. He passed the men as he did so and stared at Granston who glared back at him as if he was some inferior creature.

'What's that fucking black cunt giving me the eye for?' he enquired of Green.

'Maybe he fancies you.'

Green and Russel sniggered but Granston's expression remained fixed as he mentally filed a suitable punishment for the impudent Aborigine.

Deuce moved quickly through the corridor and made his way to the cells, he looked inside each one before he finally came upon Munro huddled in a corner. His face was savagely beaten, and he was naked from the waist down; his body hunched up in the foetal position. Deuce placed his hand on the boy's shoulder. He noticed the blood on his face and legs. He shook him gently.

'It's okay son.'

He remained where he was without movement and stared blankly at the wall.

'Come on mate, it's roll call. I gotta go, so have you.'

Again, the boy said nothing. Deuce stood up. He didn't want to leave him but realised that he needed help. He turned to hear the voice of Jones, one of the wardens.

'Come on, Deuce, you should be in the ––' He stopped mid-sentence as he caught sight of Munro.

'What's this?'

Deuce shrugged.

'I dunno. I just happened to be going past and I noticed the kid in 'ere.'

Jones knelt beside the boy; he knew immediately what had happened. He also knew that Deuce knew who was responsible but would get no information from him. The boy maybe would tell but Granston and his colleagues had no doubt threatened him and his family with various unpleasant consequences if he grassed, fear would keep him silent.

'Go to roll call. I'll deal with this. Tell Dr. Rushton on the way down.' Jones ordered.

·····•••••···

The prison Governor sat at his desk and spoke on the telephone as Jones entered. He acknowledged the warden's presence with a nod and continued to talk for a few more minutes before he replaced the receiver.

'Yes, Jones? What is it?'

'The young Munro, sir. He's in the hospital bay. Beaten up and sexually assaulted.'

The Governor shook his head and stared out of the barred window for a second.

'Any idea who's responsible? No, don't tell me. I can guess; Granston.'

Jones nodded.

'But of course, no way to prove it, unless the boy testifies and then it's just his word against Granston and his cohorts.

How is he, savagely beaten up?'

'He'll recover. Just shaken and bruised, still a bit in shock.'

The Governor nodded. 'I'll go and see him, see if we can get anywhere with this. God, I'd love to nail Granston. Short of hanging the bastard not much we can do. That's off the record, Jones. Put Munro in protection.'

Jones gave a half smile. 'Yes sir.'

'Oh, by the way, we've got a new inmate from Greenacres. A bloke called Mason. I don't know why the fuck they're sending him here. He's due for parole in a month.'

'No, I can't see the sense of it; he should be going to a low security prison.' Jones replied.

Who knows the workings of bureaucracy? Anyway, here's his file.'

Jones took the papers from the Governor's extended hand and shuffled through them.

'Animal lover evidently; not in the biblical sense; killed a bloke; martial arts. No problems with him, been a model prisoner for the last five years. It says here he is liked and respected by the guards for watching out for some of the younger blokes.

Jones acknowledged the Governor's words and continued to flick through the pages.

'Pick him up tomorrow morning at eleven thirty,' the Governor stated and rose from behind his desk. Is that okay? Eleven thirty tomorrow?'

'Fine sir, no worries. I'll get Officer Palo to cover for me.'

The Governor extended an arm that indicated Jones should go first.

'Thank you, sir.' The two men exited.

I knew I had changed considerably over the five years I had been behind bars. My physical appearance no longer had that youthful look and I had lost much of my hair on my now shaven head. I was more muscular, more confident in myself and had adjusted to the confinement of prison life, although reluctantly. At first, I spent hours in thought about the past and what might have been, of my daughter and my wife and how I had come to this pass. After six months I came to terms with the situation and used my time to train my body and mind to preserve my sanity; after two years I was scheduled to Library duties which gave me the chance to read and improve my knowledge.

I worked out for as many hours as I could each day on the punch bag, the weights, did hundreds of push ups and practiced my forms. At first several of the prisoners had sneered at me as some "Bruce Lee" of Greenacres but because of my internment due to manslaughter, I had some kudos and was considered not someone to cross lightly. I had no desire for trouble, just to be left alone to listen to my Walkman. At night in my cell, I visualised myself as the singer or fantasised I was in some bizarre situation, whilst the music poured into my ears. It was my escape from the four dark walls and took me from the confines of my "cage" to anywhere I chose to go.

I favoured music from the thirties, but pop to classical would also stimulate my imagination.

Sally had tried to contact me many times and for three years sent me several letters a week. I never read one of them. She had come to the prison, but I declined to see her. In my misguided mind I needed her to have a second chance whether she wanted it or not. It had been the hardest thing for me to do and I was on the brink of giving in when her letters stopped.

I felt that even though I had not seen her or knew how she was, there was still the urge to contact her, to write to her, but I resisted the desire with an almost superhuman effort.

The long, lonely nights and the monotony of the days bored into my soul. The prospect of years of incarceration filled me with such depression that it was only my training that kept me sane.

It was a day like any other; I had worked on the punch bag and taught one of the inmates a few techniques when my name was announced over the tannoid to report to the visiting area. I ignored it.

The prisoner with me said nothing. He knew that I'd heard, and it wasn't his business.

A guard approached me. 'There's a bloke to see yer.'

I looked at the uniformed man. 'A bloke?' I echoed.

'Yeah, a bloke.'

I turned to my companion. 'I'll be back in a minute.'

As I came through the passage and into the visitor's room, I could see a familiar face. It was my old friend Rochester, still elegantly attired with his bow tie but now his suit was better pressed, and he had an air of opulence. It was good to see him.

Rochester caught sight of me and was a taken aback at first by the physical change in me but recovered quickly. He wanted to give me a hug but knew this was not allowed, instead he settled for a nod of his head.

'How are you, old friend?' he asked and broke the awkwardness of the moment.

I sat opposite him.

'I'm okay, surviving.'

I looked across at the tall man seated a few feet from me. 'You look very prosperous. How's your wife?'

'Akiko? Oh, she's well. The kids are fine and, yeah, business is good. You remember I started an import business? We're back in Australia now, in Queensland. Bought a great house in....' Rochester stopped and realised perhaps he painted a too rosy picture and would make me feel uncomfortable.

'Well, but y'know, we're okay.' He continued.

I smiled at him and understood his motive for changing the subject.

'No problem, I understand, you don't have to worry about me mate, you're on the outside. I'm on the inside.

I'd have been surprised if you hadn't have done well; good on yer, it's good to hear.'

Rochester crossed his long legs and looked around him.

'Nice place, eh?' I joked. 'If you saw my cell, it would remind you of your flat in Tokyo, only it's bigger.'

'I'm pleased to know you have retained your sense of humour.' Rochester stated.

'How did you know I was here? I asked.

'I er got it from Sally, I had no idea what. Er'.... and I was in Sydney, and I thought you could probably do with having a visitor. If you need any help when you get out; if I can be of any assistance, please let me know.

What are you going to do?' Rochester asked.

'The only thing I can do I guess, teach martial arts. I learnt a few things in Japan in various styles and I still practice every day.'

'You certainly look stronger.' Rochester commented.

'Yes, I suppose I am, it was martial arts that got me into this mess. Well, no, that's not exactly true. It was me that got me into this mess and it's me that must get me out. I'll survive.'

Rochester looked down at the table and then up at me.

'I saw Sal as I told you, two days ago.'

In a way I didn't want to know.

'Oh, yes,' I said, as I tried to control my emotions. 'How is she?'

'Well, that's one of the reasons I came to see you.'

I felt apprehensive I feared that something was wrong. 'Is she okay?'

Rochester paused before he answered.

'What's the matter with her?' My raised voice with an edge of anxiety betrayed my feelings.

'No, no, she's fine.'

I stared at him.

'It's Clare. She's hurt.' Rochester said.

'Clare? What happened?'

I became more vocal and agitated as I waited for Rochester's reply.

'She's alright. Just listen for a second will you and I'll tell you.'

I managed to control myself and sat back in the chair. 'Well, go on then.'

'There was an accident.'

My mind raced and I fought to keep calm.

'Accident?' I repeated. Memories of the day my parents were killed flashed through my mind.

'A domestic one, Clare was in the kitchen. There was some rice boiling in one of the saucepans and she reached up to look inside and...'

'Oh, my God,' I muttered.

Rochester continued. 'She was badly scalded, and she's lost the sight of both eyes.'

'Both eyes? Oh, Jesus no.' I was stunned.

'The doctors think there's a slim chance she'll get her sight back in one eye.'

I sat motionless as I took in the full implication of what had occurred. 'When did this happen?'

'Two months ago.'

'Why wasn't I told?'

'You were told, Sally wrote and told you.'

'I never opened any of her letters; they're in my cell unopened.'

'You always were a stubborn bastard; you haven't seen Sal or written to her since you've been here and that's nearly five years. Mate you're a real dork.'

I realised how stupid I'd been, selfish in the knowledge that if I saw my wife, I would feel self-pity and maybe not have the strength to survive, feel vulnerable and emotionally exposed, a condition I no longer wanted to experience, without any consideration of my wife.

'She's a brave little kid.' Rochester said.

I took little comfort from those words. I hadn't seen my daughter since she was less than six months old and knew that I wouldn't recognise her.

'She's having plastic surgery and the quacks reckon she'll have hardly any scars on her face. I wish I could be the bearer of better tidings.'

I remained silent, images of Sally, Clare my child, and thoughts that I had pushed aside for these last five years came to mind.

'Sally's become very…. how shall I say? She's a Pentecostal.'

'A born–again Christian?'

'Yes. I suppose it's her way of coping.'

I nodded. 'Yeah, I guess so. How did she get involved with that?'

'I have no idea,' Rochester replied, 'but I have a little bit more, well, maybe bad news. I don't know.'

I said nothing but waited for Rochester to continue.

'She's involved with someone. A member of the Church.' Rochester looked at me and studied my face for any sign of emotion, but there was none.

'Ah I suppose that's why the letters stopped. Don't worry, that's what I wanted for Sal, to have a new life, to meet someone. That's OK.'

'Is that the truth or are you just saying that?' Rochester asked.

'That's the truth. I didn't see her. I didn't read her letters. I'm surprised she waited so long. She's a beautiful woman, or she was five years ago.'

Rochester looked closely at my face as I spoke and searched my features for any betrayal of a contradiction to what my words said. There was none he could discern.

'I thought that's what you wanted, although only you know why you would want such a thing?' He gave a sigh,

'I dunno we have always been good friends and were pretty close in Tokyo remember? I was always straight with you, and I'm going to be straight with you now. Why the fucking hell you did what you did to Sally I'll never understand. Anyway, that's none of my business but I just wanted you to know.'

I acknowledged his remark with a nod of my head, 'Right Ok no problem.' I replied.

There was an awkward pause before Rochester continued.

'Tell me, how did you manage for the last five years? Was it...? I mean, terrible?' He asked.

I looked across at my friend as he stared questioningly and awaited my reply.

'You manage because you know one day, you'll be free. You'll be on the outside. You'll be able to walk in a straight line for miles. You can eat what you want. You can go where you want. You don't have to call out your name three times a day. And you know God willing one day you'll walk out through those gates.'

The tall man seated opposite me nodded as he listened.

We could talk for thirty more minutes, in which time Rochester recounted the events that led up to his return to Australia, his assurance that Clare would be fine and that he would help in any way if he could.

'Oh, I almost forgot I heard from Satchiko recently.' He stated.

Satchiko, the image of her flashed into my head and I experienced a feeling of pleasure and then shame that I had just up and left.

'Akiko hears from her from time to time. She's still in Tokyo. I think she can speak English better now. She went to America for two years. She's OK I think.'

'Good, she was really nice,' I remarked.

Rochester studied my face then recounted the events that led up to his return to Australia, his assurance that Clare would be fine, and he would help in any way if he could.

I bade my friend farewell and told him if I was granted parole, I would get in touch. I returned to my workout.

Chapter Nine

Nine - Longbeach

I lay back on the bench with the weight of the barbell poised above my chest. It was four hundred pounds. I had been training virtually every day for five years and gradually added more weight as I progressed. I had gained inspiration from a sixty-year-old Asian Indian called Sri Chinmoy a popular spiritual cult leader I'd read about in a magazine. He was able to perform amazing feats of strength by concentration and perseverance. He was authenticated by many respected people including world famous body builders, along with photographs and testimonials. I had by no means attained the ability to lift anywhere near the amount of weight he managed but had surpassed my previous limitations twofold.

I pumped out five repetitions with comparative ease and began to slow up on the sixth when one of the wardens arrived. He waited until I had returned the barbell to the rack and then spoke. He had seen me train many times but still seemed impressed.

'Good one.'

I eased myself from under the barbell. 'Thanks.'

'Get your things together. You're moving,' the warden remarked.

I did a double take. 'Moving? What do you mean?'

'You're leaving Greenacres, mate, going over to Longbeach.'

'But I may get paroled in seven weeks.'

'That's right. Don't ask me, I'm just the messenger.'

I said no more but followed the warden to my cell where I collected my few belongings, said a quick farewell to my roommate, a rather overweight man of thirty sentenced for manslaughter, but unlike me his offence was from behind the wheel of a fast car. Curly had long since left, although with his track record would probably show up again sooner or later.

I accompanied the warden to the office and after a few formalities Jones escorted me to the gates; a prison van waited.

The vehicle was like the one I was transported to Greenacres but a more modern version; I felt a sensation of excitement, combined with apprehension to go out of the prison. Why transfer me to another high security gaol for no apparent reason? The machinations of the prison system were a mystery to me.

I had been institutionalised for five years and experienced a strange sense of insecurity as I sat in the van. The gates swung open. From the interior I looked out through a small, barred window as we made our way down a main street.

I saw free, unconfined people, couples talked, elderly ladies pushed trolleys, at traffic lights cars I'd only seen in television commercials drew up alongside the van; I knew somewhere out there in that mass of humanity and urban sprawl were my wife and daughter. I tried to imagine the kind of life they led; what Clare looked like, how she had coped with the loss of her sight. My head filled with uninvited images of the accident, boiling water against her innocent face as her hand reached up to grab the saucepan.

I involuntarily recoiled in horror; my face contorted at the thought.

Jones looked across at me and noticed my pained expression.

'Are you OK?' he enquired.

I realised my behaviour must have seemed odd, like some person I'd once seen on a train who recounted his thoughts aloud, oblivious to the bemused glances of the rest of the passengers.

'I was just thinking of something. I'm OK.'

Jones stared at me to see if I would repeat my previous behaviour but relaxed when he saw I appeared to be normal once again.

The journey to Longbeach was about three hours and for me renewed my desire to be free. A situation I had always desired, obviously, but now as I glimpsed the outside world once more, so close to it, almost breathed the free air, I couldn't wait for the final seven weeks to pass. I had to get parole.

Why had they moved me? What reason? I had gotten used to Greenacres, knew the rest of the inmates, had a regular routine worked out and a job in the prison library where I could take advantage of the many books available.

If ever hell could be comfortable then I had established myself and survived as best I could under the circumstances.

The prison loomed into sight and the driver swung in through the massive gates. We'd arrived; the vehicle halted. The rear door was unlocked, and I stepped out into Longbeach correctional centre. Several men clothed in prison green were in the yard as I was escorted to the Governor's office and told to wait.

Jones accompanied me. He hadn't spoken much but watched me look out of the window of the van on the journey. I later learned that he'd wondered why I had killed someone who accidentally ran over a cat.

As the Governor's door opened Munro came out. He was still bruised, his face swollen. He had undergone a medical examination and been called back into the

Governor's office, but still would not reveal the names of his attacker. He avoided my eyes as he passed; I took little notice of the boy.

'Are you alright, son?' Jones enquired. There was genuine concern in his voice. The boy said nothing but moved awkwardly out of the office, still bruised from the anal rape and sexual abuse he had been subjected to a few days ago.

The Governor was seated behind a large desk, in front of him an open file. He looked up at me as I entered.

'Tony Mason, Hmn, according to this you have been a model prisoner.'

'Yes sir.'

'You are up before the parole board in just under two months. That's not long to go.'

I stood before him, dressed in the dull drab prison green issue uniform, and nodded.

'Yes, boss.'

I was confused as to why I had been transferred and brought to see the Governor, but I had come to accept everything as normal whilst in internment and grown philosophical regarding life's monotonous routine, especially within the confines of one of Her Majesty's prisons.

I couldn't put my finger on it but had a suspicion there was motive for my presence that I was unaware of.

I was taken to my cell and began to arrange the few possessions I owned.

Most of the other prisoners were in the yard or recreation areas when an ebony skinned man in his late fifties appeared in the doorway. I was surprised to see him but nodded in his general direction.

'G'day, my name's Deuce,' the black man smiled.

'Hi,' I retorted.

'I'm yer cell mate.'

I could hardly contain my surprise.

'My cellmate?' I repeated.

'Yeah, sorry about that, mate. Don't yer like blacks?' he asked.

I was caught off guard; my expression betrayed my surprise.

'Never thought much about it mate.' I said and continued to arrange my belongings.

Deuce remained where he was and then beckoned to me. 'Here, come with me.'

I looked at the man as he turned in the doorway.

'Come with me. I'll show yer something.'

I hesitated, and then followed.

Deuce led me up several flights of stairs to a small window. He motioned me to join him.

'See the outside world.'

We had come to a small, barred window through which the street could be seen. I stood on tiptoe and peered through the dirty glass.

'This is the only place in this shit hole yer can see the outside world.' He stood back to allow me better access.

I looked beyond the dirty pane to a narrow tree lined street and renewed my contact with the outside world be it from a distance. Several children played within the grounds of a nearby school, their shouts and laughter clearly audible. I thought of my daughter, she would probably attend a special school; I would try and see her as soon as I got out, even though I had unwillingly renounced her.

'What are yer in for?' Deuce enquired and broke my reverie.

'Manslaughter,' I replied.

The large face of the Aborigine showed no emotion.

'I come up here once a day and have a look out just to remind me what it's like. I'm up for parole in three months and then I'm gonna walk down that road and I tell yer something, I'm not gonna look back at this hell hole for fear I may be turned to salt or shit, or something.'

I continued to look out of the window. I was surprised, I was about to share a cell with an Aboriginal. I didn't give a toss who my cell mate was if he was clean, didn't snore or fart every five minutes and didn't want to shaft me.

He cast a quick glance over his shoulder, 'I can fix you up with things.'

I looked at him. 'Like what?' Although I knew perfectly well what he meant.

'Well, like yer know things.' He gave a wink and revealed his teeth in a broad grin.

I'd managed to keep clean of drugs and however low I sank I didn't want to go down that path.

'No thanks, I'm right.' I answered.

'Things are OK in here. Granston and his two mates are the ones to watch,' Deuce continued. 'Real fuckin' bastard scum. Don't give a shit about anything, a lifer so ...' he shrugged his shoulders and grimaced, his leathery face showing even more lines with the contraction of his facial muscles.

I listened, not particularly interested but remembered the names. I only had a few weeks to go. There was no way I wanted to screw it up.

'Just watch 'im. Keep out of his way.'

'I will,' I replied.

We walked back to our cell; Deuce informed me of what was what and who was who. I didn't care. To me this was just a short stay. I noticed an elderly man dressed in civvies walk toward the visitors' section accompanied by a warden. I wondered who he was.

Deuce noticed my curiosity.

'That's Mr Simpson, he visits prisoners. Fucked if I know why, Granston especially; brings him magazines and things.'

I met Granston for the first time at roll call. Three men whom Deuce had spoken of stood a few feet behind us.

'Looks like we got a new boy,' Granston remarked loud enough for me to hear.

'Yeah,' Russell replied. 'Looks sweet, don't he?'

I stood next to Deuce, turned around and glanced at the three men, I held Granston's eye, and then looked back. He felt the glimpse of a challenge and sneered. I mentally cursed myself and wished I hadn't done it but the temptation to show this vile apparition that I was not afraid of him burned too strongly. I also noted the appearance of Green and Russell, two huge men of obvious physical capability; I answered as my name was called out.

'Here.'

Granston sniggered.

'Mason, eh? Certainly, no Free Mason, 'he remarked.

The thing that distinguished Granston from the usual thug was that he had a little more intelligence but used it in the cause of discomfort to others. He ruled by fear, his appearance alone intimidated, his lank greasy black hair and gaunt face, tattooed arms, and scar on his left cheek, lent a formidable look to his tall frame and arrogant manner.

'I think we've got a real hard man,' Granston hissed to his companions. The three men stared at me, and I could feel their collective gaze bore into my neck.

Deuce picked up on the communication. 'That's Granston,' he murmured as quietly as possible.

'Careful.'

After roll call there was a recreation break, the inmates broke rank and went their separate ways.

I was interested in checking out the weights in the gym and made my way to the area. On arrival I shot a glance around the place; Granston and his entourage were not far behind. I went over to the bench, ducked under the bar, and placed my hands each end in preparation to lift the one hundred kilos. It was not heavy for me, and I lifted it off with ease to do a couple of quick reps.

From my peripheral vision I caught sight of the three men enter and slowed my repetitions to give the impression it was heavy. There was a punch bag suspended to the left and leg machines, along with a universal system in the centre of the area. I replaced the weight on the rack, eased myself slowly out from underneath and ignored Granston and his cronies.

I feigned exhaustion, sat on the bench, and breathed heavily. Russell made his way over to where I sat, picked up another two fifty kilo plates and with Green's help added them to the bar. I stood up. Russell had not asked me if I had finished my session but had just taken the liberty of changing my weights.

Granston watched as Russel manoeuvred his considerable bulk under the equivalent of three hundred and ninety odd pounds. He braced himself and lifted the weight from the rack.

The barbell hovered in the air within the grip of the huge hands and then sank down towards his chest. I could see his pectoral muscles strain as he pushed against the heavy load then repeated the process four times before he replaced the bar. He heaved himself from underneath like some oversized stuffed doll, his arms in a position as if in a western film about to draw both pistols. He shot a glance at me and grinned with an expression that said, "Get that buster."

I thought the man a complete gronk but remembered in seven weeks my date with the parole board and assumed a look of admiration.

'Very strong,' I said.

Russell continued to leer and enhance his anthropoid features which made him look plain ugly instead of repulsive.

The next dickhead to give a display of his prowess was Green, who went to the punch bag and began to pound it with his naked fists. The bag swung under the impact as the man thumped and kicked to demonstrate his undeniable power. I watched and noted the man's posture, his speed and technique, mentally countered and looked for his weaknesses.

Granston swaggered over to me; I stood close to the bench press.

'Think you're a hard case, do you?' he asked as his dark eyes bored into me.

I could feel the intense hatred pour from the man. There was a quality of evil about him, thoughts of ring wraiths from Tolkien's novel sprung to mind as he stared contemptuously down. I didn't answer.

'I'm talking to you, you little prick. Are you fuckin' deaf?'

Again, I said nothing but felt a strong urge to put the evil creature on his back, to flatten him, but the consequences of this action dictated that I remain detached. The thought that I could walk out through those gates in less than two months controlled my urges. I said nothing.

My silence seemed to affect Granston more than if I'd answered.

'The silent type, eh? Let's see if you can yell.'

Several prisoners in the Gym had become aware of the situation and whilst they didn't stare, watched with interest as to the outcome.

Granston nodded to Russell; he made to move close to me. I stiffened and felt my stomach muscles contract as I waited for the attack.

Granston's demeanour took a dramatic change; he smiled and called to Russell in an overly loud voice, 'See if you can do it again, Rus.'

Russell stopped and looked puzzled.

'See if you can press four hundred this time,' Granston remarked and nodded toward the direction of the door.

I remained alert despite the change in Granston's attitude as he now grinned and nodded at me.

'Good press, eh?'

I caught sight of the reason for Granston's instant character change. One of the wardens had come into the gym and observed the group of prisoners gathered around the bench press. I could also see a familiar black face behind the officer.

The warden went over and looked suspiciously at the men. Granston leered at the warden.

'Alright, boss, everything OK?'

The warden, Officer Palo, looked at Granston. He disliked the man intensely, but he was also afraid of him. He knew that one or two officers were "tame" as far as Granston was concerned and that he had got away with more than he should. He addressed Granston.

'Lot of people doing bench press,' he said.

'Sort of competition,' Russell replied.

'Yeah' the warden nodded, 'Hmn'

'Anyway, let's cut outa here. Fancy a smoke?' Granston remarked.'

'See yers later Mazzer.' He turned and looked at Deuce.

'Oh, and we'll definitely see you later.'

The men left. I sensed Deuce felt his intestines move at Granston's remark and knew that they'd try to get him. It wasn't coincidence that the warden had shown up when he did and Granston knew it. I turned to Deuce.

'Why did you do that?'

'Do what?' Deuce replied nervously.

'Call the cavalry.'

'I didn't call the cavalry.'

'Granston thinks you did,' I replied.

'Ah, he don't know for sure,' but Deuce hadn't convinced himself and I could see he felt the cold grip of fear rise within him.

'Anyway, thanks.'

'I didn't do anything,' Deuce again denied.

'Alright,' I remarked and went back to the bench. I lay underneath, took a grip of the bar, and pumped it up and down, did ten reps and replaced it on the rack.

Two green clad prisoners came into the gym and exchanged glances; I replaced the barbell on the rack.

Deuce stared at me as I sat up and his lower jaw began to gape in amazement.

Fuckin' 'ell, 'he mumbled. 'Fuckin' 'ell.'

It was in the lunch queue that Granston demonstrated how he felt towards the Aboriginal. He sauntered in with his thugs and went immediately to the front; nobody challenged him. The last person who did was found in the shower with a serious knife wound.

Even the wardens said nothing, pretended not to notice and turned their attention elsewhere.

Deuce was about to receive a ladle of custard when Granston dug him in the ribs with his knuckle extended from his clenched fist. Deuce winced with pain and the dish he held clattered onto the floor. Although plastic it made a noise as it hit the ground.

As was the custom when a plate of food or cup of liquid is spilled a loud cheer goes up from the rest of the diners seated at the tables.

Deuce was momentarily winded and Granston's arm supported him as the warden came over. 'Are you alright, mate?'

Granston asked, Deuce coughed and held his side.

'What's up?' the warden asked.

'Deucey had a coughing fit or something,' Granston remarked with a false air of concern.

'You OK, Deuce?' the warden asked.

Deuce straightened up. 'Yeah, coughing fit. I'm OK.'

'Well, clean this mess up. Get a mop.'

I was three people behind Deuce when Granston had swaggered in. I'd seen him deliver the blow to Deuce's ribs and felt contempt of the thug, as I had when Hiro was kicked and punched by Yamada in Tokyo; I controlled myself and looked away.

Later that night, in our cell, I heard Deuce mutter Granston's name in his sleep, let out a loud yell and sit bolt upright. He shook and trembled before he regained his composure; looked over at me, I closed my eyes. He remained upright and stared at the blank wall for some time before he sank back in his bunk to sleep.

The next day after slopping out, when buckets of urine and excrement were emptied, prisoners given breakfast, and duties performed before roll call, they had time to themselves. I was on kitchen duty and had to wash down tables. I returned to my cell to listen to music on my Walkman and sat propped up on my uncomfortable bed; the sound of Pavarotti rang in my ears and carried me away from the confines of the prison; but in the back of my mind lurked thoughts of my daughter's condition and how she was coping.

Whilst I experienced the music of Puccini, Deuce was about to experience something quite different. He told me later Granston, Russell, and Green had followed him into the shower room and blocked his exit. Another prisoner using the facilities hastily departed without a look back. Deuce told me he felt sick with fear. He was not young and knew he was about to get beaten up; to be savagely attacked could leave him permanently disabled. He noticed that Granston held something in his right hand and his life passed before him as he felt the powerful grip of Green and Russell on each arm; he was hurled against the shower wall. Officer Palo passed the showers and glanced in as he went by. Granston concealed what he held in his hand and began to whistle.

Palo continued down the passage and Green stuck his head round the door to make sure he'd gone. Deuce said he was convinced he was as good as dead anyway and let out a loud scream. Green slammed his fist into his stomach and the scream turned into a gasp of pain. Green followed up his attack and clamped his hand over the man's mouth.

'Shut up yer black bastard,' Green scowled.

Granston swaggered across the tiled floor.

'Strip him,' he commanded.

'You ain't gonna fuck him are yer?' Green looked surprised.

'Don't be stupid. I wouldn't touch him with yours. I wanna see if that dirty brown shit colour washes off. Better make it hot,' Granston muttered.

Deuce rolled his eyes under the pressure of Green's hand. He said he knew the hot water system was hot. He tried in vain to struggle free from the powerful grip, but it was no use.

I'd left my former position on my bunk and leant on the rail outside my cell.

The music from La Boheme still in my ears, a prisoner hurried past almost knocking me over.

I took the earphones off and yelled at him,

'Hey what's the hurry mate?'

He turned. 'Sorry mate. Keep out of the showers. The showers keep away from the showers,' he repeated and strode off.

I looked in the direction that he'd gone and wondered what he meant. Another prisoner walked by my cell and muttered out of the corner of his mouth as he passed.

'In the showers. Your cell mate's coppin' a hidin'.'

I got the message. I knew that Granston had got Deuce. I went back to my bunk.

What should I do? I only had a few weeks to go before my non–parole period terminated and besides, I owed nothing to Deuce. He was an Aborigine and there were many Aborigines in Longbeach. Why couldn't they help him?

Then I thought about Granston and his repulsive features and of Deuce being beaten and possibly killed.

"The man tried to help me when he thought I was in trouble. Damn it!"

I left my cell bunk and made towards the showers. I saw Russell's head peer from the doorway and could hear sounds of a scuffle from within.

Russell barred my entrance.

'Fuck off Mason.'

Granston heard Russell mention my name and called across to him.

'No, let him in.'

Russell stepped aside and I entered the shower area. Deuce was naked and constrained by Green about to turn on the hot water.

'We're gonna wash the black bastard and then play doctors.' Granston sneered, his face twisted in cruel expectation.

Deuce struggled feebly and I read terror in his eyes as Green's hand roughly gripped his mouth like some reptile coiled around its victim, his features were squashed and contorted under the pressure.'

I did a quick mental calculation. There were three of them and I knew Granston had allowed my entry to teach me a lesson; I was on the punishment list. I felt the tentacles of fear claw at my stomach and the adrenalin rush through my veins.

Granston nodded to Russell.

'Get the fucker,' he scowled, a smile of satisfaction crossed his face as he envisaged Russell's demolition of this recent upstart that had dared stare back at him in roll call with such arrogance.

Russell rubbed his hands together almost gleefully as he stepped forward. He made a bad mistake and underestimated his opponent. To him I was small, not overly bulky, muscular but scrawny by comparison to himself.

He came toward me and didn't even bother or expect to have to defend himself.

I took a step back and calculated the weakest parts of his anatomy available; his groin would have been my first choice, but he moved in such a way I couldn't execute a clean shot. I turned sideways toward his advance and with all my force stamped with a side kick (Yoko Geri) to his left kneecap. I gave it all the power I could; I had trained on hard wooden boards and on heavy sand filled bags, so consequently developed some considerable force. I felt the kneecap dislocate and the joint of his leg

give way, he collapsed to the floor. It was not a
fancy technique or a complicated one but extremely
effective.

Russell screamed in agony and clutched his knee,
I looked down at him.

'Hey.'

Russell turned, his face twisted with hatred and
pain toward me. I stared back at him, I no longer
had any compassion; gone were the days when I was
reluctant to hurt my opponent, all I saw was a thug
and a bully who would without any conscience beat
an elderly man to death, He scowled up at me.

'You cunt, you filthy little prick, you're dead I'm
gonna.........'

He didn't finish his sentence; I lashed out with
a roundhouse kick. My shin contacted his face and
spun his head round, drops of saliva left his open
mouth and he collapsed, this time unconscious, onto
the tiled floor of the shower.

Granston witnessed the turn of events and
screamed manically to Green.

'Get him, Kill the cunt. Kill 'im. Tear 'is fuckin head
off!'

Green threw Deuce aside and made towards me.
The black man staggered away from the shower,
snatched up his trousers and looked for a way out.

Granston blocked his exit; I braced myself for
Green's attack.

The shower area consisted of ten shower units;
there was a space in which to change to the left of
where I stood and from there an exit point. I assessed
that I had maybe a metre of space to my right and a
metre behind me.

Russell, semi–conscious, lay to my left; Granston
began to circle closer to me.

I figured he'd wait for Green to attack then either
join in or await the outcome if it seemed to be going
in Green's favour.

I didn't want to come to grips with the man whom I knew, from what Deuce had told me, to be an ex–SAS man and capable of a few dirty tricks, but in a fight situation in a limited space it's not always easy to dictate terms. Green slowed his advance then put his head down and charged like a Rugby forward in a scrum. From years of experience, I knew when someone was about to attack, the tell-tale sign of a slight movement, a shift of weight or change of expression, an intake of breath, a contraction of the muscles. I had faced too many opponents to be taken off guard and sidestepped his charge. At the same time, I grabbed hold of his outstretched arm and placed my foot in his path.

The momentum and power of his attack along with the assistance of my hand caused Green to hurtle into the wall with a hefty thud. He reeled for a second and turned, dazed.

Granston took the opportunity whilst I was occupied to attack. He lunged at me from the side just as I heard Deuce yell to warn me. Deuce stood close to Granston as the action took place and noticed what the lank haired man held in his hand. It was a syringe. He had a good idea what it contained.

'Watch 'im he's got a fit in his right hand.' Deuce yelled.

I had been aware of the movement, spun around and grabbed Granston's right arm at the wrist stepped past him and brought my knee up hard onto the outstretched limb directly against the joint of Granston's elbow. It snapped and became disjointed. He screamed with pain; I then wrenched the limp broken arm downwards, still controlling the wrist and stabbed Granston in the knee with the syringe, I helped the contents of the crude device into his blood stream by a downward pressure on the plunger with the palm of my hand. He continued to scream and writhed with agony, his face one of pain and horror as he realised, he had been the recipient of the contaminated blood.

'Yer fucker!' he shouted at the top of his voice.

From my peripheral vision I saw Green move toward me and knew I had to disentangle myself from Granston. I could smell his foul breath and his cry of agony was uncomfortably close to my ears and caused them to ring. I let go of the man's hand and brought my elbow up into Granston's jaw. He was out before he hit the ground.

I prepared for Green who was still somewhat dazed from the recent contact with the wall. He moved more cautiously towards me now. Deuce had watched the events and now shot his head around the shower doorway to see if all was clear. He could see Palo coming down the corridor.

'Screw!' he shouted across to me.

Green was so filled with rage and hatred and his intention to kill me he cared little for anything else. I, on the other hand, wanted to be out of it and in no way caught in a position that would compromise my chance of release; I had no choice and concentrated on the powerfully built man before me.

I again looked for his weakest point, but this time it was different. I wanted to finish it quickly and took the initiative. I feinted with a punch.

He lifted his guard and at the same time I delivered a groin kick with all my force into the man's crutch. Green buckled up and clutched his now severely bruised testicles, I waited until he was at the correct height before I hit him with a left hook to his neck with the palm of my hand and a right cross to his face.

He flushed, momentarily turned white, and sank to the ground unconscious.

'Let's go,' Deuce called.

I looked at the three men. Granston had begun to recover and from where he lay mumbled something about killing me, although his broken jaw distorted the message. Neither of us bothered to stay to decipher the injured man's garbled words but left via the changing room exit. Palo came through as we were about to leave.

We both froze. I knew I'd been caught. I felt my heart sink and that familiar sensation in my stomach I'd experienced so many times throughout my life.

Deuce broke the silence as the three of us stood and faced each other.

'Looks like Granston fell out with his mates, boss.'

Palo looked past us and went through without comment. Deuce, still half naked, and myself with two or three blood stains on my tee shirt headed back to the cell block. I was shaking when I walked into my cell and sat on the bunk, Deuce sat opposite, neither of us spoke, my mind raced. "Now what will happen?"

There would be an inquiry. I could be charged with assault and most certainly lose my parole as well as get a few years added to my sentence. "But why didn't Palo say anything?"

Deuce put his shirt back on and adjusted his trousers. His hasty exit from the scene had given him little time to complete his attire.

'What was in that syringe?' I asked.

Deuce jerked up his trousers. There was no belt or cord, just very weak elastic that would break under comparatively little strain.

'Bloody trousers,' Deuce muttered, 'never keep 'em up. What did you say?'

'What was in the syringe?' I repeated.

'Domino's blood I guess,' Deuce answered as he continued to attend to the problem of his trousers.

'Domino's blood?'

'Yeah, HIV positive. Granston's done it before. Stuck a bloke a year ago.

'What happened?

'He got away with it?'

'Who?'

'Granston,' Deuce replied.

'The bloke knew he'd be dead for sure if he grassed on him, so it just meant if he kept his mouth shut, he'd live longer.,

'Did he contract it?'

'I dunno. Domino, that was the bloke, got out about six months ago.'

Deuce ceased to fiddle with his trousers and looked across at me.

'I owe you one. I would have been done bad for sure. You handle yerself pretty good. I'm impressed.'

I nodded as a response and looked at the Aboriginal.

'Why do you think Palo just let us go?'

'Palo hates Granston's guts, you did 'im a favour, he probably wanted you to sort out Granston. I know the governor's not too keen on him either.'

'What do you reckon will happen now?' I enquired.

'I don't reckon anything will 'appen. Well, I dunno for sure, but I tell you this; if Granston had stuck that needle in me I'd 'ave sung like a fucking bird no matter what he did. But he'll be after yer for sure now. He'll try and kill yer if he can.'

'I get out of here in a few weeks. Well, maybe I do, and if I have to stay in here because of Granston then if he doesn't kill me, I'll kill him.'

Deuce looked across at me. 'Yeah, I reckon you would too.'

'How come you're not with your mob and how did you end up here?' I asked.

Deuce thought for a moment.

'Fuck mate it's a long time ago, there was a blue in the "London," a pub in Redfern, the cops come along and all 'ell broke loose; mate it escalated into a riot. I was off me brain mate. Bloke's chucking bottles and everything..'

Deuce's forehead creased as he recounted the events. He shrugged his shoulders.

'Some cunt handed me a fuckin' brick and said chuck it. So, I chucked it, I didn't aim at anyone I just tossed it. and hit this girl cop on the head, she died in hospital. The cops had
me tagged and I was dragged into the back of a paddy wagon; they beat the shit out of'

me, went to court and got ten years. I've been here eight.' I looked at the old man as he recounted his story. I knew that Deuce wasn't a bad man and was accepted by the wardens and prisoners of all races who considered him neutral; sometimes acting as a go between; he kept out of trouble. Earlier on in his sentence he told me he had "betrayed" his people by association with a white man and took his part in an argument. He copped a few bashings from his own people and at one time was considered an "Uncle Tom," but re-established his acceptance when he failed to "grass" on his attackers. He had acquired a certain amount of wisdom gleaned from his years behind bars and was part of an experiment to integrate prisoners by mixing races where it was possible; thus, his sharing with a whitey.

That afternoon at roll call Granston and his two thugs were obvious by their absence, but no-one said anything or treated it as out of the ordinary. Everybody knew what had happened. Their names were not even called. I was treated with a new respect by my fellow inmates at the line up for the evening meal and Palo, who was on duty at the door, didn't bat an eyelid when I joined the queue. It was as though Granston, and his two gorillas had never existed.

They'd been taken to a public hospital with a guard posted twenty-four hours, Granston with a broken arm, a broken jaw, and a badly lacerated tongue; Russell, with a broken leg, was still concussed; Green had badly swollen testicles and was under observation.

Most of the prisoners had little time for Granston, he was feared and hated by many, but such was his power that no one had up until now successfully challenged him. I had unintentionally done them and most of the wardens; a big favour. As for myself I hadn't entered the situation for a fight and hoped that I could've possibly reasoned with Granston. But I'd had confidence in my ability to handle myself if necessary.

The one thing that concerned me most was I may have lost my freedom and when I came face to face with Palo in the changing rooms, I was convinced I had.

The silence, the total continuation of normal prison life, had me puzzled but I left it at that and certainly wasn't going to broach the subject. But I couldn't believe that I had been transferred to deliberately come up against Granston. It was too ludicrous. How would they know that I would conflict with Granston? We could have become good mates as far as the prison authorities knew. Granston and his thugs could have killed me. I shrugged it off as mere fantasy and prayed that my parole would go as anticipated. Fortunately, or otherwise the story that Deuce and I related, that Granston must have had an altercation with his lackeys was accepted, Palo said nothing to contradict it.

The weeks passed comparatively quickly; the prison took on a more relaxed atmosphere with the absence of Granston. It was obvious that the authorities were also relieved not to have to contend with the undercurrent of evil that Granston radiated. But no doubt another "top dog" would take his place. There were plenty to choose from; life goes on.

It was on the day I was due to go before the parole board that Deuce entered the cell and told me that Granston and Green would be out of hospital in a week or so and probably back in Longbeach.

'He'll be out to getcha, that's for sure.'

'Maybe.' I shrugged.

'He knows you're up for parole and stand a bloody good chance of getting out. Just watch yer back.'

I listened to the man's words and felt apprehensive. The idea of having to look over my shoulder for the rest of my time in jail was not what I wanted and dismissed the thought as negative. To worry about a thing sometimes brought about the condition one tried to avoid. I'll face that when I come to it, I thought.

The day to meet the Parole Board arrived. There were five men and two women along with the Governor to hear my application. Palo was stationed by the door. I looked at him and searched his face for any indication of his intentions.

He stared straight ahead and avoided eye contact.

'Please sit down,' one of the women on the panel requested. I did as I was bid and looked across at the board about to appraise me for my eligibility to be released. One of the men wrote something down on a piece of paper and asked me if my name was Tony Mason.

I thought it was a bloody stupid question but answered as politely as I could. My mind kept returning to the shower area as further questions were asked.

How many of the programs had I taken and what progress had I made? What would I do if I were granted parole? How would I support myself? Why should I be given parole? Did I have a place to live? That was a prerequisite for all prisoners who sought parole.

The Governor handed a piece of paper to the woman next to him; she read it and then passed it to her companion. I wondered what the hell it said. It reminded of when I was at school and heard the joke about the man smashing into a parked car. When the owner of the vehicle came out some time later to discover the damaged vehicle, he read the note on the windscreen, it said, "Passers-by" and people on the bus opposite think I'm writing down my name and address and contact number. Sorry, but I'm not.'

I smiled to myself, then realised where I was and the seriousness of the situation.

Information, mostly from Greenacres, about my behaviour and conduct throughout my internment was predominant and I knew whilst I was there, I'd given no reason to jeopardise my chances of release. It was my short stay in Long beach that had the possibility to ruin my chances.

The hearing ended and no mention was made of the shower incident, much to my relief. I was instructed to leave and return to my cell while the board deliberated. After twenty minutes or so I was returned to the room and sat down.

The woman who appeared to oversee the proceedings addressed me.

'We see no reason why your application should not be approved.'

I heard the words and could hardly believe my ears. It was like I had been given the best present I could possibly hope for. Christmas, the day I got my black belt, my degree, and birthdays all rolled into one and then one better.

I sat back in the chair and hardly took any notice of what the woman said as she outlined the conditions and requirements of my parole. Whatever she said I would agree with. I wanted to rush across the room and kiss her.

I was led out and glanced at Palo, who nodded as I passed. I nodded back with relief and gratitude. Palo had remained silent, and I was soon to be a free man, although if he had wanted to drop me in it, he had ample opportunity at the inquiry immediately after the incident.

It was as if a great burden had been lifted, within a day or two, I would walk through those gates to freedom in the clean fresh air, to visit parks and restaurants, to do simple things: drive a car, sit on a bus or train, go to bed, and get up when I chose, to jog, to do all the things I had been denied for the last five years.

Deuce could see by my expression that it had gone well.

'Fuckin' stroll on man.' He beamed and held out his hand, 'stroll on.'

I shook it vigorously. 'Thanks, you'll be next.'

'I hope so. Geez, I hope so.'

'No worries,' I replied. 'I'll buy you a drink at the Rocks when you get out, or that pub you go to wherever it is.'

'You're on,' Deuce replied and slapped me heartily on the back.

·····•·••···

On the day of my release, I said goodbye to Deuce and gave him my ex-father in law's address and told him he could contact me there. Russel came past us from his cell.

'Swapping addresses, are we? Don't forget to write.' Russel said sarcastically; I ignored his remark, collected my stuff, and went into the Governor's office, wished good luck and given the usual discourse on the benefit of the corrective system and why I should avoid a return visit.

I shook the Governor's hand and left with my Parole certificate. The place somehow seemed different. I'd spent my last night in gaol and now I was on my way to freedom. I had a different perspective on things. I met Palo on his way to the office,

'Good luck.' Palo offered his hand.

I took it and looked the man in the eyes.

'Thanks,' I said, the intonation in my voice could have held many meanings.

Don't come back,' Palo added and turned to enter the Governor's office.

Chapter Ten

Ten – Time to move on

T he moment I had thought about for the last five years finally materialised.

The side gate swung open and, dressed in the same clothes that I had worn five years' ago and with my battered shoulder bag that contained my worldly possessions, I stepped out to freedom.

It was August and the weather was cool, a blustery south wind tossed a few leaves around outside the prison walls and a pigeon fought his way against a strong gust to alight on the gutter of the prison building. I had often watched birds fly over the prison or peck about the yard and thought how lucky they were to be free, and now I was like them, no longer confined to a cage. I gave a last look at the prison in all its stark severity and headed towards the bus stop. I had two hundred dollars in my wallet and an outdated bankcard. My plans, to go into the city to renew it then visit the Social Security and job centre were put aside; the first thing I wanted was to have breakfast and a cup of tea as a free man.

I caught the bus into the city and walked down from Town Hall to Kings Cross. It was as though I had been out of the country for five years, so much had changed since my imprisonment. It reminded me of when I came back from Japan and toured the city with Sally. The thought of her played on my mind, her, and Clare; I was curious to know about her condition.

The wind carried tiny droplets of rain and the clouds scudded across the sky as I entered the small cafe in the Cross and took a seat in the corner.

The waiter took my order: scrambled eggs, tomatoes, mushrooms with six rounds of toast and a pot of tea. It tasted as I'd imagined, and each mouthful savoured and chewed slowly to prolong the sensation for as long as possible.

After my meal I sat back and read the newspaper, bought from a news stand next to the station. When I entered the café, I'd noticed a telephone by the door, it took all my powers of restraint not to call Sally.'

The meal had made me relaxed, and I remained where I sat to experience the sensation of freedom.

I paid the bill and headed for my bank in George Street. My account had a balance of three thousand dollars, diminished from my savings by solicitor's fees five years previously. It would help, but I knew I must find work, and soon. I wondered what my chances would be to teach again in the high school system but dismissed the thought; with my record nobody would employ me.

I made my way to my father-in-law at Ron's English conversation school and noticed the plaque that advertised courses; interested parties to enquire within. There was a torn piece of a poster I recognised as my advert for Karate classes, a tiny piece of faded green paper under the head of an old rusty nail was all that remained. I picked at it with my finger and released the remnants of my bygone ad to the mercy of the wind blowing down the main street. I hesitated, then stepped through the door into the building. It had a familiar feel and brought back memories of paint and students and laughter and aspirations for the future.

I climbed the stairs to the third floor and entered through the glass doors. There was a reception desk directly in front of me and a door to the side that led to the areas designated for classrooms. I wondered what had become of my dojo and decided to find out; left the reception area and climbed up one more flight of stairs. The door was locked but there was a sign which read Lotus Shoes.

I knocked tentatively and waited. There was no answer. A face peered from one of the rooms further along the corridor.

'There's nothing in there, mate. It's....

The voice stopped and the author came forward, his eyes squinted to clarify the figure that stood before him. I recognised the voice and the man immediately. It was Ron.

He walked along the corridor until he got closer. There was a moment's pause and then he put out his hand.

'Tony,' he exclaimed.

I smiled and clasped the outstretched hand. He looked older, he'd lost a lot of weight but still retained his energetic manner and enthusiasm.

'You look...'

'Rough. I know,' I finished his sentence.

'I wasn't going to say that. I was going to say well.'

'Thanks,' I replied, and looked at the elderly man. He wore a smile on his face.

'Well, don't let's stand here. Come downstairs to the office. When did you...?'

'I got out this morning. I'm on parole.'

'That's good news. What does that mean exactly?'

'Oh, it means I'm free as long as I behave myself and stay out of trouble. I have to report to the local cop shop every so often and I can't leave the country, but apart from that I can work and whatever.'

'Great.' Ron regarded me; I imagined he must have thought how the years had hardened and changed me; not necessarily for the better.

We descended the last few steps in silence and entered Ron's office. 'I use that room upstairs for storing books and files. I let it to that computer company that was interested in it after you went... but they moved out. You remember them, I'm sure.'

'Yeah' Joan something wasn't it?' I recalled.

'Yes, anyway, they moved to Hunter Street. Grab a seat.' Ron gestured towards one of the chairs.

In the office was a desk and two chairs. A bottle of spring water with a dispenser took up a large amount of space in the right-hand corner, a few plastic cups, and a filing cabinet to the left.

I sat on one of the chairs; Ron took the other.

'So, what are your plans?' Ron made himself more comfortable and cleared a space on his desk.

'I'm going to stay at a halfway house for a while but I'm looking for somewhere else to live. Get some source of income and try and start again.'

Ron rubbed his eyes and put on a pair of spectacles that lay on the desk.

'A place to live maybe... hang on a second.'

He pulled a small red book from a drawer in his desk and flicked through the pages; he ran his finger slowly up and down each one.

'Ah, here we are, Konstantin. Maybe I can help. He's got a two-bedroom furnished apartment. I'll call him. The only problem is he just wants someone...' Ron picked up the phone and dialled as he spoke. 'To stay for a couple of months. He's going back to Greece for a holiday. It's over in Marrickville. It's reasonably -- Oh, hi Rick, it's Ron, - Ronnie yes, look, are you fixed up with anybody? Good, because I've got my son-in-law here and he's after a place. Yeah, I know it's only for a couple of months, that's all he wants.'

I listened as Ron continued to talk, my eyes wandered around the small office. He finally finished and replaced the receiver.

'It's fifty bucks a week for three months, fully furnished.'

'What, he lives there now does he?' I enquired.

'No. He lives downstairs. As I said, back to Greece and then his son and daughter in law are coming back here with him and they'll need somewhere to live so the place is vacant for a couple of months.

I nodded. 'Sounds goods.'

'Yeah. I'll give you the address and you can go around and see him. It'll give you a bit of time to find something more permanent. He wasn't going to let it because if someone he didn't know got in maybe he couldn't get 'em out or they could wreck the place.'

'Yeah,' I replied. 'That's OK. As you say it'll give me a bit of breathing space. Thanks, Ron.'

'No worries. Have you...,' Ron looked across at me. 'Now I know it's not my business'

I could feel another lecture coming.

Ron continued,

'Well, that's not exactly true Sally is my daughter. I was mad with you; boy was I mad, I was going to come to the prison and tell you just how much, but Sal begged me not to; sure, it's between you and Sal but I think you could've kept in touch. Not seeing her or writing really cut her up. I know you know about Clare because we saw Rochester and he said he had seen you.'

I looked at the floor.

'You thought you were acting in her best interests but, damn it mate, she was your wife, and nobody could have been more supportive. She needed you and you weren't there. She was wounded Tony, hurt; I was really worried about her. Don't you dare hurt her again.'

'I know Ron. I've been lectured by Rochester and you're right, believe me I regret it, I acted selfishly.'

I thought to myself, now it was too late. Sally had a new relationship and a new life. It's what I wanted and if it wasn't that Clare had had the accident, I would not have asked about her.

In prison I trained every day, to the limits of my physical endurance, punished myself and inflicted pain upon my body as if I wore hair a shirt for my sins; to keep my mind off the woman I loved; to contact her now, it would all seem to have been for nothing.

'I was just worried about Clare. I really would like to see her, but I er...

'Of course, you would. She's your daughter,' Ron exclaimed. 'Sal will let you see her. She's gotta a guy now and is happy, just don't upset that, besides, she's changed quite a bit.'

'What's this bloke like?' I asked tentatively.

'He knows all about what happened. He's a member of the same Church, look it's been five years, and it's all in the past. Little Clare, she's a cracker, a lovely kid. Sal's got back on her feet, and I know she wouldn't deny you the right to see your kid even though you....... Well let's leave it at that.'

'I'll give her a call. Is she still living at...?'

'No. She moved to a place up the road in Ultimo, a terrace house parallel to Harris Street.' Ron picked a pencil from one of the pen racks.

'Here, I'll write it down with the telephone number, give her a call first. Clare goes to a special school.'

'Is there any chance that she'll recover her sight?' I asked.

Ron stroked his chin and looked up thoughtfully.

'Maybe in one eye, she's got to have an operation next month. The poor little kid's feeling a bit upset now.'

'Yeah, I can understand it.'

'No, no. She is a brave kid. She doesn't care about that; no, she had a dog and it got pinched.'

'Pinched? Why, who'd want to pinch a dog?'

'It was an American Staffordshire terrier, a friend of David, that's Sal's bloke, knows a bloke who breeds them and of course Clare always wanted a dog, so David got a pup for her.'

'Why is it valuable?'

'Well, yes and no.'

'I don't understand,' I said.

'Well, I think they cost a few bob to buy for starters but David probably got a good rate as it was his mate, but they look identical to a Pit Bull Terrier, well they're virtually the same breed, think it was pinched for dog fighting.'

'Dog fighting?' I repeated.

'Yeah, there's a racket going on in the western suburbs. Of course, we haven't told Clare. She thinks it's just lost but it's been over a week now and I've advertised extensively, but nothing. Poor kid loved that dog.'

'Wasn't it dangerous? I mean if it was a fighting dog?'

'The biggest softy you could ever meet, a lot of character but a softy.'

I recollected how my younger sister loved our family cat. I stood up.

'I'll call and go and see her.'

'Yeah, do that. Only remember Clare doesn't know yer from Adam. Oh, here's that address and number of the flat. Give him a ring. Let me know how you go. What about work? Are you going to go back into teaching?'

I shook my head. 'I don't think the educational system is liberal minded enough just yet to employ an ex– con.'

'What about Karate or whatever. Are you gonna start another place?'

'I dunno. I'll see what happens, but I need a job, that's for sure.'

Ron smiled. 'The place upstairs is vacant. We could come to some arrangement, like before.'

I looked across at the bespectacled man.

'I thought you might kick me out and tell me to stay away.'

Ron laughed. 'I never thought you deserved to go inside to start with; those two bastards were obviously no good to boot, both got records as long as their arms and you get sent down. I wonder what would have happened if you couldn't have handled yourself.'

Ron stood up and walked with me to the door.

'The older I get the more I take things as they come. They say you get narrower minded, but I think I can handle anything now. Anyway, see how yer go and don't be afraid to call Sally. I know she'd be ... well er...' Ron hesitated, 'pleased to hear from you.'

I wasn't exactly convinced but thanked Ron and set off for Marrickville where the flat was located. It was three o'clock that afternoon when I rang the bell of Rick Konstantin.

It was answered by a large Greek man of about sixty-five.

'My name's Mason. Tony Mason. I'm Ron's son-in-law.'

'Ah, yes, so please come in.' Rick had a heavy Greek accent and was sometimes difficult to understand.

'You call before, eh? Yes, yes, please I show apartment. One moment, I get key.'

Rick shuffled off down the corridor of his flat and disappeared into a room off the hall.

I stood and waited for him to reappear. There was a strong aroma of pipe tobacco mixed with the smell of toast. Several pictures hung on the wall, one of a couple in their early twenties; holding hands and smiling at each other.

A few moments later Rick emerged with a bunch of keys and mumbled to himself whilst he thumbed through them.

'Ah, this one I'm thinkin' is one.' He shuffled back towards me.

'Please this way.'

I followed the elderly man out of the front door and up some stairs to the flat above. We stood for a few moments while Rick tried several keys and continued to mumble as he did so. Eventually he found the right one.

'Ah here.' The door opened and we entered. It was a small apartment with two bedrooms.

I noticed a telephone and a television set; the place had been newly decorated in readiness for his son's arrival.

'It's for three months, this place free. No people here. I go back to Greece for holiday and then come back altogether. So, I just three months person here.'

'Yes, I understand. it's just so I can get on my feet. It's extremely helpful.'

'Through here bathroom, toilet, and here small laundry for wash.'

The man gestured towards the rooms as he spoke.

'Comfortable place. It's good, eh?'

'Yeah, it's good. Thank you, yes, it would be exactly right.'

'But only three months. Because you Ron's son-in-law I let you have. But only three months. For my son.'

'Thanks, I understand. Three months.' I'd got the message.

'When you want place?' the old man asked.

'When can I ...?'

'When you like, up to you.'

'Well, how about tonight?' I answered.

'No problem. Here, I give keys.' The man fumbled about with the key ring, handed me the key, and gave me a few instructions regarding rubbish disposal and locations of various shops in the immediate vicinity. I handed over the agreed amount of money.

'Telephone, please pay this bill. I pay. No-one use for long time, so I show you date starting.'

'Don't worry. Just give me next month's bill or when I leave, I'll pay it.'

'No, I bring up later. I show you. OK?' the old man insisted.

'Yeah, that's fine. No worries,' I replied, not really particularly concerned about it.

'OK. I – er – go now. You stay, eh? If – er – you need something calling me, OK?'

'Yeah, I'll do that,' I responded.

'Don't forget. I downstairs. I go next week. So please ask.'

'I will,' I replied and placed my shoulder bag on one of the chairs.

The man finally left, and I took a closer look at the apartment. It had a small kitchen and was on the first floor. There was a living room and two bedrooms, one of which looked out across a park. A large tree cut out most of the light and was so close to the units that I had the impression that when I stood in front of the window, I was in the branches of a tree house. I wondered why the old man had let it grow so big, but it was a beautiful plant and I guessed that maybe he was a tree lover. I later discovered that his wife had planted the tree when they first came to Australia. It was her pride and joy and when she died, he was reluctant to impede its growth in any way.

The kitchen was particularly clean and the smell of paint strong in all the rooms.

There was a reasonably new suite of furniture and a new bed in the main bedroom, one of those huge affairs with a radio and cassette built into the framework, I smiled and thought how Sal and I used to joke about people who slept in those types of bed.

I was only too grateful to take advantage of this large ostentatious monstrosity and wallow in luxury beneath the sheets.

I looked at it with all its bells and whistles and felt a wave of pleasure go through me at the thought that this night I could sleep in such a bed, look out of an open window, and get up when I chose.

My thoughts dwelt on my immediate future and what I would do for the rest of the day. I had to give notice to the halfway house and inform my parole officer of my new address.

"I'll go and buy some food and a few things I need and then..." My eyes alighted on the telephone. "Shall I or shan't I?" My curiosity got the better of me and my hand went toward the receiver. I pulled out the piece of paper Ron had given me and punched out the numbers with my extended finger. There was a moment's delay and then the sound of the signal indicated that the recipient's telephone had rung. A child's voice answered.

'Hello,' I said, 'is that Clare?'

'Yes,' the small voice replied, 'who's that talking?'

I didn't know what to say. Should I say, Daddy or what?

'It's – er –Tony,' I eventually responded. 'Is Mum there?'

The little girl didn't reply but I heard the clunk of the receiver being laid down and the sound of footsteps followed by a child who announced there was a "Tony on the phone for Mum to talk with." A few seconds passed and I again heard the receiver picked up and adjusted to the speaker's mouth.

'Hello, 'is that you Tony?'

I listened to the voice I had not heard for so long. 'Er, yeah, I saw your dad today.'

'I know. He called and told me you were out.'

'Yeah, I got out today,' I went on. 'I just thought maybe I could... I heard about Clare and the accident. How is she?'

'She's OK. She's managing. There's a strong chance she'll regain the sight in one eye.'

'Oh, great, that's good, er, is there any chance ... I mean, could I...?'

'If you want to see her you know you're quite welcome. I'm sure she'd want to meet you,' Sally stated.

Her voice was calm with no trace of malice.

'I won't screw anything up for you Sal, I just want to see her and then I'll leave you alone.'

'There's no need to be so dramatic. You can see her as many times as you want. We can work something out.'

I felt relieved; unsure how Sally would take to hearing my voice again and worried she might be angry and tell me to leave them alone, but then I thought of Sal and knew that for her to behave like that would be out of character.

'Well, when I've got a bit of time on my hands. Now I'm in Marrickville. Yer dad fixed me up with a place for a few months, so wherever's...'

There was a moment's pause.

'How about tomorrow morning?' Sally suggested.

'Yeah, fine. Er what time?'

'Say eleven o'clock. You know where we are?' she asked.

'Yeah, off Harris Street. I've got the address"

'OK. So, see you tomorrow then.'

I agreed and replaced the receiver.

I looked around the flat and switched a radio on in the kitchen, opened a cupboard and searched for a kettle. The news blared out introductory music followed by the voice of the reader. I happened to catch a familiar name and listened intently.

Granston had escaped; Green with him and although he knew about his partner's condition regarding possible HIV, accompanied him more out of a sense of survival than any loyalty.

Granston burned with a hatred for me that could only be extinguished with his death or mine, he had escaped from custody with help from his brother, an equally unsavoury thug, and a couple of Bikies, by overpowering the guards whilst being transferred back to prison.

His arm had healed as much as the reasonably short time allowed and he could use it in an awkward manner, an occasional twinge of discomfort reminded him that he should show some restraint in certain directions.

After their getaway they headed for the Cross where Granston had a few contacts and ended up at a place inherited by him and his brother, a small, terraced house in Newtown registered under their mother's name from a previous marriage before she died: thus, no connection with the Granston name.

Jason, Granston's brother, hadn't lived at the house for some time and intended to rent it out but never bothered; the place had been neglected.

He lived in a house in the Cross and ran a series of rooms where prostitutes working in the area would take their clients. The girls were charged various rates that depended on how long they used the room, a fee paid before they went in and a further fee if they went over time.

He also acted as a minder and would step in if the girl's clients were overzealous or complained. He cared little for the girls; it was the threat to his source of income that caused him to take the role of Sir Galahad. He was as unsavoury as his brother and just as revolting to look at but lacked that dark evil quality that his older brother possessed.

Granston knew I had been granted parole; Russel was still inside and communicated with Jason from time to time. It was through this communication that Granston learned of my connection with Ron. Russel knew I had given Deuce my details; he'd paid a visit to Deuce's cell whilst he was away and found the paper on which I'd written the address.

'I'm gonna kill that bastard. I'm gonna fuckin' tear his fuckin' bollocks off.' Granston raged as he snorted a line of coke.

Green looked across at his companion.

'Why don't we just fuck off to Brisy?'

'Because I have a score to settle.'

In a small house in Paddington John Simpson, the prison visitor, also heard the news of Granston's escape. He stared thoughtfully at a photograph of his wife and daughter perched on a nearby cabinet before going into his bedroom to fetch a two-way radio from his bedside table. He tuned into the police wavelength.

Chapter Eleven

Eleven – Something to live for

I t was early evening, I sat in front of the television with my feet up having recently returned from a walk around the neighbourhood to familiarise myself with the area, when the doorbell rang.

It was Ron my father-in-law, he had kindly brought a few items of mine Sal had kept; I invited him in. I was curious to know about Sally's new romance.

We talked about the weather and other small talk before I asked.

'You say her new bloke's a nice guy.'

'Yeah, he's nice. Clare really likes him. He's a member of the Church that Sal goes to.'

'Yeah, you mentioned that; is she sort of full on with this religion thing?'

'I'd say she's pretty committed,' Ron replied. 'Every Sunday and sometimes during the week.'

'What do you think about it?' I asked.

'What can I say? It's given her a different perspective on life. She went through a bad patch, and yeah, I helped as best I could. Let's put it this way. I'd rather she hadn't got involved with all this holier-than-thou business, but it's not harming anyone and as I said it's, well, the older you get.' Ron looked across at me. 'If you get my drift.'

'Has she heard any news about the dog?'

'About Bozo? No, not a word. I had a call from some bloke, but it wasn't hers. I ring up the RSPCA every day to see if there's anything, but I think I'm on a losing wicket.'

'You think it's been taken for fighting?' I asked.

'Yeah, either that or for pig hunting. But I reckon dog fighting. There's been a lot of it out west lately, wicked if you ask me. Bastards.'

Ron left an hour later, I sat and thought how I could help find Clare's dog before I eventually roused myself, had an unsupervised shower, and sunk into the folds of the massive bed.

·········

I rose early the next morning and went for a run around the deserted streets. The weather was cool, the southerly wind had picked up.

As my feet moved rhythmically over the paving stones, I thought I must join a gym to keep up with my weight workout. I didn't want to lose the strength I had attained through lack of exercise. I thought of Granston and what Deuce had said about him, that he'd try and get back at me because of his arm and the dose of infected blood I had administered,

I knew he had nothing to lose. The man was not sure that he was HIV positive but lived his life on the assumption that he was with disregard for the future consequences of his actions.

"I'll face that situation when and if it arises" I dismissed him from my thoughts.

It also crossed my mind how Deuce was, and I wondered if he would get parole in the next few weeks. Maybe I should write to him and see if he knew anything about dog fights, and if so, maybe he could give me information. I'd heard him mention pit bulls on occasion but couldn't remember in what context.

After I got home from my run, I carried out my ablutions and put on clean shirt and trousers. I had very few clothes and the ones I had were mostly now too tight.

I ate a bowl of cereal for breakfast with a couple of slices of brown wholemeal toast and an apple, left the apartment at ten fifteen and allowed myself plenty of time to get to Ultimo. I caught a bus to Broadway, walked down Harris Street, and arrived at ten fifty-five.

I felt nervous; the house was newly painted and had a small iron gate which I tentatively opened, I knocked. There was the sound of movement from within and a small face appeared from behind the door.

'Hello,' she enquired.

I looked at her and could see that she was blind by the way that her eyes appeared to be focussed on some distant horizon, there was a trace of a scar on her forehead.

'Hi,' I said. 'You must be Clare.'

'That's right. Are you, my Daddy?'

I was surprised she'd called me Daddy and was unaware of how much Sal had told her about me. 'Yes,' I replied.

'Come in please.' The small girl opened the door to allow me access. I entered the front room. The floors were wooden and well-polished and a couch and a round table with four chairs made up most of the furniture. I could see through into the kitchen and into the small garden beyond where I caught a glimpse of Sally as she hung some clothes out. My heart skipped a beat. After all this time I was about to face her in the flesh and not in my imagination.

Clare fumbled for my hand, located it, squeezed it with her small fingers and clasped it tightly; she led me through into the garden.

There were stairs that went up to the bathroom and bedrooms on the left of the entrance near the kitchen. I noticed a dog's bowl next to the fridge containing a small amount of food. Sally caught sight of me and came from the garden.

Clare called out, 'Mummy, Daddy's here.'

The kitchen was small, and I remembered how in our previous house we'd cook a meal then watch TV from the table. I watched her entry from the yard and noticed how she brushed her hair back with her right hand, her index finger separated from the rest, a movement I had visualised many times in the confinement of my cell.

She stepped into the kitchen. I didn't know what to do. I wanted to give her a hug but held back; instead, I stood and smiled.

Sally came straight to me and gave me a hug. My arms involuntarily responded, and I hugged her. She broke away, smiled at me again and held me at arm's length.

I was not expecting any kind of warmth from her and felt unprepared.

'You've lost a bit more hair, but apart from that you look well. You look very strong,' she said.

'You look well too,' I replied.

The years had shown in Sally's face as well as mine, but she was still a beautiful woman and her eyes still held their gentleness, which enhanced the placid manner that I remembered.

'So, you've met Clare,' Sally said, and took her daughter's hand.

'Yes, but we haven't really got to know each other.'

'Do you want coffee or tea or anything?' Sally enquired.

'Have you any mineral water?'

'I have,' Sally answered.

'Can I have orange juice, Mummy?'

'Please,' Sally corrected.

'Please,' Clare repeated.

She turned once again to me. 'One mineral water coming up.'

'And one orange juice.' Clare added. The little girl laughed, took my hand and led me from the kitchen.

'I'll show you something,' she tugged me gently away.

'Where are you taking ...Daddy?' Sally said.

The word 'Daddy' had an unfamiliar ring in such a context. I hadn't thought of myself as a Daddy.

'I'm going upstairs to show him something,' Clare replied.

I looked at Sally to seek some sort of confirmation that it was alright.

'It's OK' Sally mouthed. 'Don't be too long. I'm making him a drink.'

I followed my daughter up the stairs and into her bedroom. She was totally familiar with the layout and had no trouble negotiating any object in her path.

Her bed was in the corner of the small room and there was a dressing table with a mirror.

On the opposite side several books lined a bookcase and a scruffy Teddy Bear lay on the bed.

'Do you want to see a picture of Bozo, my dog?' she asked.

'Yes, I'd like that.'

I watched her as she went to her dressing table and located a photograph in a metal frame. I smiled at her little frock with a Ninja turtle print, her white socks, and the way she felt and explored the surface of the table with her fingers with practical efficiency. I also saw the scar on her forehead and the discolouration of her left eye that lacked the dark colour intensity of the other. I felt a great rush of love for this child, my daughter, to think that I had helped create her filled me with a sense of awe and made me desperate to be a part of her life. I hoped that I could help her in any way possible.

'Here, this is Bozo,' she handed me the metal framed picture.

'Ah, yes. He's lovely,' I exclaimed and looked at the image of a large brown dog seated next to Clare on the lounge chair downstairs.

'He's naughty. He's not really allowed on the sofa.'

'I see,' I replied. 'He's big, isn't he?'

'He's missing.' Clare responded, her voice taking on a more serious tone.

'He's been gone nearly two weeks. Grandpa put a thing in the paper, but we haven't

heard anything.'

'You will,' I said reassuringly, 'and if not, well maybe he's just having a

kind of holiday with some different people.'

Clare's mouth contorted and she twisted her lips to one side as she thought about what I'd said.

'But he was happy here. He's my dog and I miss him. He was naughty sometimes but so am I, will you help me look for him?' She faced me. Her expression begged me to say yes.

'Well, I'll try but I don't ...' I thought about what I was saying, 'I'll do my best and if I see him, I'll let you know.' I looked again at the picture and then at Clare.

Her small, rounded hand searched for mine and she sat silent for a moment and gave a sigh.

In the room there were many childish things on her dressing table, the patterned wallpaper; a group of dolls in various stages of undress in one corner; books with large print and colourful illustrations waiting to be read. I thought to myself what a protected world she lived in compared to the harsh realities of life, a world where animals had a fluffy toy quality about them, and adults were to be trusted. How nice it would be if the world were like that.

I also wondered how she would feel when she got older and realised her father had killed two people. How she would think of me then. I glanced at myself in the mirror, sitting on the bed with my daughter's hand in mine, my somewhat angular features and frame contrasting with the small delicacy of the young child.

'Let's go downstairs and see Mummy,' I realised the joy I'd missed and the pleasure of seeing my daughter grow from a baby.

She was, though I knew I was biased, the nicest kid I had ever seen. She had similar qualities to her mother in her mannerisms and expressions. I wanted to just grab her and hug her to me and ask her forgiveness and try to explain everything. I consoled myself with the thought that one day when she was mature enough to understand, I would tell her. In the meantime, I would try and do something for her to make her happy. I looked at the photograph of Clare with her arm around Bozo.

'Have you any other photographs?' I asked.

The little girl tilted her head to one side.

'Of me and Bozo?' she replied.

'Yes, or one of you and Bozo separately?'

Clare jumped up from the bed; took out a packet of photos from the top of her small chest of drawers and withdrew a bundle of snap shots.

'Here, these are some more photos taken on the same day. You can tell cos Mummy says I'm wearing the same dress.'

'I see,' I responded, and took the pictures.

'You can have any one of those you like,' Clare added.

'Thanks, that's kind of you.' I thumbed through the photos and chose two, one of Clare and another of Bozo on his own, in the yard. It was obviously taken from quite close as the dog's head appeared larger than reality.

'Can I have these two?' I asked.

'Which ones have you choosed?'

'The one of you sitting at the table in the garden with Bozo looking at the camera.'

'Is it a good one?' Clare asked.

'It is a good one of both of you,' I replied.

'Mummy says one day I can see them for myself.'

'I'm sure you will,' I replied, and thought how I would give my own sight willingly if it would restore hers. If only there were as my wife now believed, some supreme being with whom I could strike a bargain, and if the Devil himself walked in and offered me a deal at that moment I felt that I would have grabbed it.

'Thanks for the photos, come on, and let's go see your Mum.'

'Where have you been?' the little girl enquired, her voice contained a tone that almost scolded.

I was again momentarily caught off guard.

'Er, where did your mother say I went?'

Clare thought for a second and was about to answer when Sally's voice called from downstairs.

'Your drinks are ready.'

'We'd better go downstairs and have something to drink now, eh?' I said, grateful for Sally's well-timed intervention.

The little girl again took my hand. 'Are you thirsty?' she asked.

'Yes, a little. Are you?' I responded.

'So so,' she said. 'But people often drink when they're not thirsty.' She replied.

'I know lots of people who drink when they're thirsty.' I stated,

But Susan Kato's Dad, he drinks beer when he's not thirsty,' Clare continued.

'Sometimes it's good to drink for the taste.' I countered.

'But beer tastes horrible,' she wrinkled her face.

'How do you know?' I remarked.

'Because I tasted Uncle David's once. It was horrible.'

I mentally noted my daughter's use of Uncle David and thought that I must come to terms with it. After all it was, as I had protested so many times, what I wanted.

We made our way downstairs and discussed the ins and outs of drink as Sally placed the tray on the coffee table, sat down in a nearby chair and crossed her stockinged legs as she did so, the sound of which caused me to cast a quick glance in her direction. I had been in prison for five years and the proximity of my ex-wife and the sight of her shapely legs brought the fact vividly to bear.

Sally noticed where my eyes went and readjusted her skirt to cover her knees. I felt momentarily embarrassed. It was as if, in that second, I had been rejected; I averted my gaze.

'Please sit down and, er, here, here's your drink,' Sally said, leaned across and placed my mineral water on a small cork mat.

'And here's yours, darling,' she continued, placing a glass of fruit juice with a straw in Clare's hand, waiting until the small fingers had grasped it tightly. Clare thanked her, put the straw between her lips and gurgled audibly as she drank.

'Clare,' Sally scolded lightly. The little girl giggled and apologised. I smiled as she continued to drink with less noise.

'So, five years is a long time,' Sally stated.

'Yeah, and I haven't really done much in those five years. Er, what did you say to ...?' I nodded in Clare's direction.

'Oh, um' that you were away. I didn't actually say where.'

'I see,' I said and looked at my daughter as she continued to suck the liquid through the straw, her cheeks hollowed as she did so. Clare paused for a moment.

'Where did you go?' she asked.

I looked across at Sally. 'I, er,' I was about to say that I was a bad man and was locked up, but then thought this would lead to too many questions, the answers to which would not sound particularly good to a small girl.

'I, er, was working in a library, far from here.'

Again, I looked at Sally for confirmation that I had said the right thing. Sally remained expressionless.

'Was it good?' Clare asked.

'No, not particularly. It was boring.'

The little girl looked puzzled. 'Then why did you do it for such a long time then?'

'Er, I had to. It was my job,' I replied. After all it was true. I had worked in the library, and it was my job.

'Don't make such a noise when you drink, Clare, it's bad manners.' Sally interjected as the little girl searched with the base of the straw for a favourable angle from which to draw up the last few drops in the glass.'

'Sorry,' she said.

'Your father told me about David and your interest in the church.'

'Yes, I thought he might,' Sally replied with a smile.' 'I don't think he really approves.'

'Oh, I wouldn't say that I think he wants you to be happy, that's all.'

I couldn't help thinking of the night I had come back from Tokyo and made love to her, and the many wonderful times spent together. I noted her mouth, still the same, and her beautiful white teeth when she smiled; a few recently etched lines in the corner of her eyes could not mar her overall beauty.

"God, she's lovely," I thought.

My imagination began to get the better of me and I visualised myself as I made love to her.

The physical response to my thoughts made me readjust my position on the small sofa and pursue another line of thought. My daughter's voice helped me out.

'Daddy's going to help me find Bozo.'

'Oh, that's good, but I don't think he will have any more success than Grandad so don't expect too much.'

'I won't promise anything, but I'll make a few inquiries I may be able to find out a couple of things.'

'That's kind of you,' Sally said.'

'I'll try. How long has it been?' I asked.

'Nearly two weeks; then after a short pause, 'What are your plans now?' she enquired.

'I don't really have any now, it depends.'

'Are you going away again?' Clare interrupted'

'I don't know,' I replied.'

'Why? Why do you have to go again?'

'Daddy hasn't decided yet but maybe he has to go because of his job.' Sally added.

'Why do people have to work?' the little girl continued.'

I tousled her hair.

'Make sure you marry a rich man and then you won't have to work.'

We sat in the small room for another hour; Clare held my hand as she listened to her mother recount events of the last few years, of Rochester and my relations with whom she'd kept in touch. I said I must visit them now that I was out. My Aunt had written to me a few times, but my uncle had fallen ill, and it was difficult for him to travel.

I could not speak of my own experiences mainly because my daughter was there but also because those years were something I wished to forget.

As I sat and talked to Sally with Clare in the crook of my arm, it seemed far removed from the harsh and austere conditions of Greenacres.

Sally had given me a meal and Clare had given me a guided tour of their small backyard. We ate outside at an old sandstone table with a canopy overhead. The weather had improved, and a winter's sun had brightened the day considerably allowing us to bask in its warmth. Sally had removed her clothes from the line for us to appreciate the many potted plants situated around the small space.

I hadn't wanted to leave but knew I must. She had given me no indication as to the way she felt and no encouragement. She'd every right to kick me out and not even speak to me but had behaved in a warm if reserved manner. Clare had fallen asleep, and I extricated myself from the chair, she didn't wake. I looked down at her as she slept.

'Does she always sleep like this in the afternoon?'

'No, not usually,' Sally replied, 'but she was so excited last night she didn't get much sleep.'

I knew how she felt. 'Well, thanks for letting me see her.'

'She's your daughter. You can see her when you like,' Sally answered.

'It's just that...,' I felt a little awkward, 'it's... well... I don't want to interfere with your life.'

'Don't worry, I won't let you interfere. We can discuss that later.' She spoke with a quiet assurance that emphasised her point.

'Well, I'll call you before I come, to find out if it's OK. Perhaps I can take her out somewhere, the zoo or maybe, no, not a good idea? ' I said.

'Why not the zoo?' Sally asked. 'She can hear, and you can describe the animals. She'd just like a day out with you, I'm sure.'

'Yeah, why not? That'd be good.'

We stood and looked down at our daughter; I eventually broke the silence.

'I'd best go then. Thanks again. It was great to see you.'

I looked into her eyes.

'Have you really forgiven me? I can't believe that you have been so... good after what I did, but Sal I did it for your sake and now I realise I was stupid, selfish and crazy to deny myself your love and support and I'm sorry for all the upset and hurt...'

'It's in the past now,' Sally interrupted.

'Yes, you're right. But I just wanted to tell you. I thought it would be best for you.'

She turned to me and spoke.

'There is no denying I was deeply hurt. I visited the prison many times and you refused to see me, I wrote to you, and you didn't answer one of my letters,

I was so angry, frustrated, and desperate; I hated you for it, hated you for being so cruel and thoughtless and finally resigned myself to, as you said what you wanted, getting on with my life with my beautiful daughter. I was ready to stand by you, support you, but no your stupid stubbornness.'

Her eyes flashed and her voice began to grow louder as she relived the past, and then lowered as she took control of her emotions.

'I found another means of support in the church. I survived and now I'm happy.

As I said it is in the past, bad feelings only hurt the one who harbours them.

Now is now and what is done is done. She gave a quick smile.

'I sound a bit like a Chinese philosopher, don't I?' Must be my ancestry coming through.'

I wanted to hold her but resisted the temptation. Instead, I tapped her lightly on the hand and turned to go.

'I'll call you,' I said as I made toward the door, 'and arrange a time to take Clare out.'

'OK, whenever,' Sally replied. 'Are you going to start up another dojo here?'

'Your Dad said I could have the old room back, maybe … I don't know. As I said it depends.'

We reached the front door and spoke above the noise of the traffic.

'Take care,' she said.

'I will, and you.'

I looked back just once as I walked away and made my way toward Darling Harbour.

That evening, as I sat in my Marrickville apartment and watched a rather poor remake of the 'Big Sleep', my mind wandered back to when I first met Sal and our consequent relationship over the years, our marriage, and the happy times we had together before my arrest. I thought of the first man I had killed and then the second. I thought of Granston and Green and knew I could have quite happily killed them both with my bare hands. I had no conscience about it and thought maybe I would have probably enjoyed it. The lethal dose that I had pumped into Granston caused me no concern; it was, to me, Karma and I was merely instrumental in its fulfilment.

The television screen momentarily took my mind elsewhere, but it always returned to Sally. Again, I thought of the touch of her skin, her sexuality and wondered if she was still the same passionate woman I had loved. The idea of someone else with her made me feel depressed; I had to live with it.

I turned the television off, stretched across the small coffee table and picked up a pen, took a sheet of paper from a pad and penned a few lines to Deuce. The letter was mainly small talk and a request for him to call me within the next few days. I knew that the letter would be read and no doubt the call monitored but I wanted to make some effort on behalf of my daughter, Unaware of the consequences of my action.

Chapter Twelve

Twelve - Dogs off the leash

O ver the next two days I signed on at the offices of Social Security and became another statistic.

I had always loved Centennial Park and would often go for a run around the circumference when I lived in Pyrmont. It hadn't changed, I walked round the perimeter and mused I was no longer a young man and had accomplished little in my life. Two girls rode horses around the inner circular riding track. I heard their laughter and excitement as their steeds broke into a canter, it reminded me of Clare. Maybe she would one day enjoy a ride in the park. A couple of swamp hens disputed a strip of water, rose, flapped their wings, and rushed at each other, necks outstretched, the one with the least resolve broke off at the last moment and skipped over the water in a flurry of feathers and high-pitched calls.

The winter's sun shone, and the filtered warmth brought the promise of spring to the bird population. Male pigeons strutted, cooed, and bobbed their heads as they pursued a disinterested female. Ducks and geese gave vocal vent to their amorous intentions and sized up prospective mates. Ibis and crows probed litter bins and scattered paper and boxes in their search for titbits.

Joggers, elderly walkers, dogs, and a high school football team added to the collage of life in the park as I sat myself down on a bench and quietly observed.

When I got back to my flat, I received a telephone call from Deuce. He had got my letter, been granted parole and would be out in three weeks. I couldn't ask outright if he knew anything about dog fighting or those involved and disguised my question, if anyone could find out it would be him.

'Can you do me a favour,' I asked. 'I'm gonna write a book on dog fighting and thought maybe you could find out any information for me, like the kind of people who are involved and that sort of stuff.'

'Are you serious?' Deuce responded with a note of disbelief.

'Yeah, very. Ask around,' I replied.' I gave him my address.

'I'll see what I can find out.' Deuce realised I had some ulterior motive although he hadn't the faintest idea what it might be.

A prisoner called McCready; a young Aboriginal gave him some information. McCready had previously been involved in the scene in Queensland and then later in Sydney before he was gaoled for car theft and robbery. He had driven through a shop window and helped himself to the contents.

·········

John Simpson had retired with time on his hands to pursue various hobbies, one of them listening into police communication around the city as well as his visits to Longbeach.

He sat in the living room of his house, sipped a cup of tea, and browsed through a newspaper; his appearance gave the impression his occupation could be, or have been, a bank manager or insurance clerk; he reached over to a table on his left, picked up his wallet, took out a crumpled photograph from within and inspected it.

The picture was of a girl of twenty-two, a young man, approximately the same age stood next to her. They both smiled, the photo conveyed a sense of a happy occasion. After scrutiny of the well-thumbed snapshot, he returned to the newspaper article, took a pair of scissors from a nearby drawer and began to cut it out.

I received Deuce's letter sometime later, written in large childlike, almost unreadable letters. The message was short but contained an optimistic note.

"Dear Tony, how are you? Talked with Macready. Go to the Three Lights pub in Redfern about your dog book. See a bloke called Goulburn. He knows about dogs. Say I sent you. See you in a fortnight. Deuce."

I smiled at the note and imagined Deuce hunched up in the yard or sat on his bunk in our once shared cell as he wrote. I folded the piece of paper and tucked it in the back pocket of my jeans.

I 'd been up for some time, trained for an hour or so at the local gym, bench pressed, worked my abdominal muscles to maintain my strength and mulled over Ron's offer about the dojo. I came to a decision; I would take him up on it and visit him later that afternoon.

Time had passed and I hadn't seen my daughter since that first occasion. I rang Sally and arranged to take Clare to the zoo. I also decided to duck over to the "Three Lights" sometime that evening, check in with my parole officer first, then maybe the next morning fix myself up with a car.

The public transport system was, to say the least, not the fastest way to get from A to B, the trains notoriously unreliable. I'd called Ron and asked him to keep his eye out for me in the way of cars for sale and if anything turned up to let me know. With my own transport it would be easier to organise a job and a place to live.

Around eight in the evening I found myself outside the pub the "Three Lights." in Redfern, an area close to Central Station and populated by many Aboriginal and mixed-race inhabitants.

It was dark and drizzled. There had been an unseasonable amount of rain over the last month and Spring weather was taking its time to get here.

I walked into the pub; several pairs of eyes watched me as I made my way to the bar.

I was the only white face among many black and although there was no open hostility, I could sense I was not the most welcome of patrons. The barman, a man of mixed race, eyed me as I approached.

'Yeah?' he enquired.

I pulled the piece of paper from my back pocket.

'I'm looking for a bloke called Goulburn.'

A man sat at the bar slowly turned his head and looked for the author of the voice that had enquired as to the whereabouts of Goulburn.

The barman shook his head.

'Don't know, never heard of him.'

The man at the bar spoke. 'What do you want this, er, Goulburn for?'

'A bloke called Deuce said maybe I could find him here,' I responded.

The barman looked at the man sitting at the bar, the man nodded. The barman turned to me.

'He's Goulburn' he said.

I turned toward him.

Several other patrons had become more interested in the conversation and I felt the hairs on the back of my neck tingle.

'You a cop?' Goulburn asked.

I laughed; I looked the man straight in the eye. 'Are you the Lone Ranger?'

Goulburn's facial expression changed from curiosity to anger and back to controlled interest within a split second.

I continued. 'Deuce and I, er, shared a flat together.'

He regarded me, rose from the stool upon which he'd perched and moved closer. I didn't move and quickly assessed the situation; I worked out which man to strike first if I had to secure the quickest exit.

'What are you drinking?' he asked.

I was uncertain how to react to this offer. "Was it genuine or to be followed up with a sarcastic remark?"

I felt I was in a scene from some Western film standing at the bar about to draw my gun. 'Mineral water please,' I remarked and thought that maybe I should have said milk. Nobody reacted to my request for a non-alcoholic drink.

Goulburn addressed the barman. 'Mineral water and a beer, Biff.' Biff nodded and went for the drinks.

'Let's sit down.' He gestured to a table.

I acknowledged and sat, still cautious. The other patrons sensed that the moment of tension had passed and satisfied that I wasn't a cop, carried on with whatever business they had been doing prior to my entrance.

'So why do you want me?' the man asked.'

'Deuce wrote me.' I handed the letter to him.

'Said maybe you could help.'

Goulburn read it.

'What kind of help? McCready, Fuckin' idiot,' he murmured.

I waited until the man had finished.

'What book?' Goulburn enquired.

'Oh, that's nothing.'

I explained my daughter was keen on her dog and it got nicked. Maybe for fighting, maybe not, just a long shot, but I'd like to get it back if it's being used in dog fights.'

Goulburn listened. 'Geez, that is a long shot,' he said after a moment's pause. 'What kind of dog?'

'Er, Staffordshire or something, here.' I took out my wallet and showed Goulburn a photo of Bozo.

Biff called over that our drinks were at the bar. I stood up from the table.

'I'll get these.'

Goulburn continued to scrutinise the snap as I crossed to the bar. I paid the barman and carried the two drinks back to the table.

'That's a big staffy,' Goulburn commented.

'Yeah, I don't know much about dogs. I think it came from the States.'

'Yeah, it looks like a pit bull. Could be an Amstaff or cross.'

'Amstaff?' I enquired.

'Yeah. American Staffordshire. Bigger than your Aussie staff which are Pommy dogs originally, well, so were the Amstaffs but they like 'em bigger in the States, could've been nicked for fighting. They're the same heritage as the Pitty in fact.'

'Pitty?' I asked.

'Pitbull' virtually the same dog only Am staffs are being bred to a breed standard these days, guaranteed to fuck' em up.

'American Staffordshire sounds familiar, where can I find out?' I asked.

Goulburn took a sip of his beer.

'I'll ask around. I'm not into it much these days, there's a few out west now. Did it still have its nuts?'

'Yes, there was another photo, and they were quite prominent.'

'How long has it been missing?'

'I dunno. Three weeks or so,' I replied.

'Hmm. could be at the bottom of the harbour by now unless it's proving a good 'un or unless it's still training. Or who knows. Could be anywhere; could be someone's pet. How old was it?'

'I dunno,' I replied. 'About two or three.'

Goulburn nodded but said nothing.

'Does it make a difference?' I asked.

'Sometimes,' Goulburn answered. 'Give me your number and I'll call youse if anything happens or if yer wanna go see for yerself. It may have just pissed off somewhere or been shipped up north. It's a real long shot mate.'

'Yeah, I realise that. Anyway, thanks for your help.'

'No worries.'

I drank the remnants of the mineral water and went from the pub.

That evening Sally had become worried about her father. She had invited him round for dinner at seven thirty, by eight fifteen there was still no sign of him.

She had called his office but there was no answer and left a message on his machine. Her logic told her that her father was fine and though unlikely, had probably forgotten about dinner or become caught up with a friend. He was getting on a bit and could be rather absent minded, but she couldn't relax and had an inexplicable sixth sense that something wasn't right.

She rang David and explained the situation. David tried to allay her fears and put forward the same logic that Sally herself had used.

'I'm just concerned, David, that's all. I have this feeling.'

'Okay, look. I'll come over to you and either look after Clare or I'll go over to your father's.'

It was ten thirty when Sally drove over to her father's place. She telephoned before she left but still only got his answering machine. She knocked loudly, rang the bell of his front door, and waited a few minutes before she took out her spare key and entered his house.

She walked down the hallway and into the lounge room. A radio issued soft late-night music; her father always left it on with the lights on a timer when he went out to dissuade any would be thief. The stillness of the night emphasised the sound in the unoccupied room. She continued into the kitchen and then upstairs but there was no sign of her father. It was eleven p.m.

She stood in the hallway and tried to think what to do. Earlier in the evening she had called his closest friends but none of them had seen him.

The thought struck her that maybe she was being a little dramatic. After all her father was a grown man and perhaps there were some aspects of himself that he preferred to be kept secret from her. She pondered for a moment and then dismissed the idea. She felt her apprehension return, went to the telephone, and pressed some digits. After a while, a voice at the other end of the line answered.

'David, look, he's not here and he obviously hasn't been home. What do you think I should do?'

'Maybe you should try the office and then call me from there and then we'll decide.' David replied.

'I think he's probably staying at someone's place, a friend or someone.' He continued.

'No, I don't think so. He particularly wanted to come over and see Clare. Look, I'll go, the sooner I go the sooner I get back. Sorry to drag you out so late.'

'Don't worry about it. Call me as soon as you can,' David answered.

She left Ron's house after making sure that she'd locked up when a thought struck her.

"His car of course. Why didn't I think of it before?" She turned the corner and looked up and down the street.

There was no sign of his car in the street; he always parked in the same spot.

"Maybe he has had an accident.' She decided to check his office before she called any of the hospitals.

George Street was deserted; the only vehicles she saw were a police patrol car and a council truck that drove close to the kerb to spray water to clean the gutters; a large rotary brush swept up any litter with a loud swish.

She parked her car outside the school. Took her keys from her bag and approached the door. It was an old building secured by a heavy metal barred gate that she unlocked and closed behind her; went to the lift and pushed the dark grey security key into the slot provided; they weren't in use until six o'clock in the morning when the cleaners arrived. She used the stairs, reached the third floor, and made her way to her father's office. It was dark in the building except for a dull emergency light.

She pressed the switch; the neon light outside the office buzzed and flickered into life. Her eyes grew accustomed to the brightness.

It was dark in her father's office and the doors were closed. She was about to turn back down the stairs when she remembered that she should call David.

She took her key and inserted it in the lock of the glass door. The pressure of her arm caused it to swing open. It wasn't locked. She entered the office, switched on the light, and stopped in her tracks; her heart leapt.

She could see her father's arm from behind his desk.

'Oh, my God!' she exclaimed, and rushed to the prostrate man.

Ron's face was severely bruised and coagulated blood adhered to his clothing. Sally cradled his head and took his pulse. It was a weak irregular beat.

'Oh my God,' she repeated. 'Dad, Dad!' She fumbled for the telephone and picked up the receiver. The line was dead. It had been wrenched from the socket.

'Oh, no!' She stood up,

'I won't be long, Dad. I'll get help.' She didn't know whether her father could hear or not, but he was still alive, although barely.

She raced down the stairs into the street and caught sight of a distant light as a cab came toward her.

Standing in the middle of the road she waved her arms frantically in the air. The car pulled in. She grabbed the handle of the door and opened it.

'Please use your radio. Get an ambulance. It's an emergency.'

'What's up, miss?' the cab driver enquired.

'It's my father. He's in that building in a serious condition Please, please hurry.'

The urgency in her voice and the indication that she was on the verge of hysteria prompted the cab driver into action.

'Don 63 to base, Don 63 to base'

There was a moment's pause.

'Go ahead Don 63.' a voice answered from the radio,

'Could you get an ambulance to 231 George Street ASAP. Emergency, an elderly gentleman heart attack or something Over.'

'Don 63. Heart attack? Over.'

'Yeah, that's all I know a woman just flagged me down; her father or something.'

'Roger Don 63.'

The cab driver looked at Sally. 'Be here soon, miss, where's your father?'

'He's upstairs. I'll go back, and thanks,' Sally replied, turned, and headed back to the building.

'Do you want me to come up?'

Sally was already out of ear shot; her mind focussed on her father's condition. The cab driver left his vehicle and followed Sally into the building. He climbed the stairs and saw the light on the third floor and followed the corridor round. He went through the glass doors and found Sally as she tearfully stroked her father's hair away from his eyes. Sally was surprised by the sudden appearance of the cab driver'

'It's okay, miss. Thought you might need a hand, I used to do a bit of first aid.' The driver caught sight of Ron's face and went to him.

'Oh dear,' he said. He noticed the elderly man's condition and knew it wasn't a heart attack.

'Try not to move him. Is there a blanket or something? He must be pretty cold; it's not the warmest of nights.'

'Er, I don't know.' Sally took off her jacket and draped it around Ron's body. 'There's a fire in the other room I'll bring it in,' she added.

'I think you should also inform the Police miss; yer dad looks as though he's been attacked by someone. Maybe there was a robbery. Is there anything missing?'

'I don't know. I don't think so.' Sally looked around the room. Apart from a few papers on the floor and the furniture being slightly disarrayed the place appeared to be normal. It hadn't been rifled.

'There could be, I don't know, I'll check later, although there's never any money left here only petty cash.' She returned to her father and tried to make him as comfortable as possible.

The cab driver went back to his taxi and radioed for the police just as the ambulance siren wailed in the distance. He stood outside in the cold night as the flashing lights approached. It drew up behind him and two paramedics got out of the cabin.

'Upstairs, third floor.' The Cabby instructed.

They nodded, took some equipment from the rear of the vehicle, and went into the building.

Sally waited until her father was in the ambulance and then followed in her car to the hospital. She accompanied the paramedics. He was wheeled in on a trolley by a nurse who waited outside casualty for their arrival. Sally gave a brief sigh of relief as her father was pushed through the green doors and knew that at least he was in capable hands.

She learned from the paramedics that he was in a bad way and had internal injuries, concussion, and facial lacerations. The next day or so would be the most critical.

"My God, it's nearly one O'clock. I must ring David. He must be worried sick."

There was a phone nearby and Sally felt the anxiety and worry of the last few hours begin to take their toll.

Tears welled up in her eyes and the urge to cry overcame her. She broke down and sobbed.

A nurse came over and gently coaxed her into a chair. There were two older people and a teenager sat in the same area.

'Come now, miss, he'll be right. Just take a seat, eh?' the nurse comforted.

The older woman looked across at Sally.

'Can I get yer a cuppa or something?

Sally took control of herself.

'No, I'm fine, thank you. That's nice of you all the same.'

The nurse sat a few more moments with Sally until she had regained her composure.

'It's okay. I'm alright now. Thank you, you're very kind.'

The nurse stood up, gave her hand a reassuring squeeze, and went about her duties. Sally crossed to the phone once again and this time got through.

'David, I'm sorry to be so long. Something terrible has happened.'

········•·····

Early the next morning I jogged past a gym in Glebe, stopped and walked back. I needed a job to tide me over, I intended to start a dojo, but it could be some time before I had enough students to earn a living.

Jimmy Winston, the man I'd met many years ago in Melbourne, ran the place, saw me enter but didn't recognise me. He was with a young fighter and shouted instructions as the youth bobbed and weaved and delivered a flurry of punches at a bag suspended from the ceiling. There were four others like it hanging in the gym. In the centre stood a large roped off ring and portraits of famous pugilists on the walls either side.

Jimmy looked across at me. 'Yeah mate. What can I do youse for?'

I came closer. 'Oh, just thought I'd drop in to see if the place is still going.'

Jimmy peered into my face.

'Wait a minute where do I know you from? He squinted and took a closer look.

'I stretched out my hand,

'Tony Mason. We met in Melbourne a few years ago. How are you, Jimmy?'

'Fuck me yeah I remember. Good, yeah, good. Tony Mason yeah, I heard that you …. So yer back in circulation then?'

'Looks like it,' I replied.

'Yeah, you were pretty good if my memory serves me. Are you planning to stay in Sydney?' Jimmy asked.

'For a while. See what happens. I don't have any real plans.'

'You should 'ave been a pro fighter instead of all that Kung Fu stuff. There's no money in it unless of course yer another Bruce Lee or Chuck Norris and then it's all from movies.

'Yer still training?' Jimmy went on.

'Yeah, that's what I came down for. I'm after a job and came to see if you needed anyone.'

'Yer pushing it a bit now, aren't yer?' Jimmy asked and looked me up and down. 'Yer still look in good shape, although you're probably slowed down a lot but.'

'Maybe, although I don't think so,' I retorted.

Jimmy looked across at the young fighter who'd stopped his bag work and listened to our conversation.

"Oi, keep going,' Jimmy shouted.

The young boxer turned his attention back to the bag.

'So, you think I'm past it'?

'Well, I think you definitely passed your prime but.'

I don't know why but I felt my ego bruised by his comment and smiled at the use of "but" to finish a sentence.

'I'll go a couple of rounds with this guy.' I nodded in the direction of his protégé.

'Come on mate, I don't think that's a good idea.' Jimmy responded.

He had twenty years on me, but I wanted to show Jimmy that I was not exactly over the hill. The young fighter looked at me.

Jimmy smiled. OK. Yeah, why not?'

'Just two rounds, he needs a sparring partner' Jimmy stated. 'See how yer go.'

The young man's expression indicated that he was not happy with the idea but, okay, it was me, the older man, my choice.

'There's head gear and gloves in the changing room locker number ten. It's open. Help yourself but.' Jimmy indicated.

'Right.'

As I sauntered across the gym and into the changing rooms. I heard his fighter say 'Are you serious? You want me to spar him? He' gotta be twenty years older than me for sure.

I ignored the "flattery.'

Jimmy looked at his protégé.

'Let's put it like this, hit him if yer can. I don't know what he's like now and maybe I'm assuming too much, but if he's as good as he was the last time, I saw him, you won't be able to hit him.'

I climbed into the ring with the young boxer.

'Where's your head gear?' Jimmy asked.

'Don't need it. It cuts down my vision,' I replied.

Jimmy pulled a face.

'Not so sure about that mate.' He thought about it and reluctantly conceded. 'Okay, be it on yer own head, it's down to you, mate.'

'No worries,' I said.

'Just two rounds, okay?'

As I stood and faced the young fighter I thought. Why am I doing this, is it for my ego"? I had done virtually the same thing years ago but then I'd had an objective to test my resolve and learn a different skill. Now I needed to know if I still had it. Plus, I thought I could show Jimmy that I had something to offer his fighters. I needed a job.

Jimmy shouted and clanged the bell.

The young fighter came out full of confidence with the impression he thought himself superior as he sized me up. I fought a more defensive round. I couldn't use my feet as weapons and had to control my reactions to stop myself from an attack with my front leg. He shot out a left jab which I avoided, and then followed up with a series of combinations but only found the leather of my gloves. I fell in with the fighter's rhythm and needed only to evade his attack. The comparative ease with which I neutralised his punches caused him to tuck his chin in and start to pile on the pressure. I sensed the younger man's irritation and remained on the defensive.

Jimmy watched from the ropes as we circled one another, his protégé took the initiative and attacked; I continued to remain comfortably out of range and avoided each punch as though it were telegraphed seconds before he threw it. With age the speed of physical reaction diminishes, but after years of practice timing improves and can give the appearance of fast reactions; fortunately, it's one of the few things that can improve with age.

I kept my eyes on the young boxer and flicked out a straight left that caught him square on the nose. The sound of the glove as it smacked into the face of Jimmy's hope for the future caused him to throw in a bit of advice.

'Let him come to you,' he yelled.

The young man's pride was hurt more than anything else; that this "old" man should so easily get through his defence. He tucked his elbows in and protected his head, took his trainer's advice, and let me come to him. I stepped forward, feinted with a left to his head which brought his guard up and then followed it through with a right to the breadbasket.

He was a few pounds heavier than me and had had six pro fights and won them all; he was no pushover. I blocked his attack and stepped away from my now riled opponent.

Jimmy shook his head knowingly but said nothing.

'Just take it easy, kid,' I said as I clinched with the young fighter.

'Get fucked,' the younger man replied and pushed me away.

Jimmy checked his watch and rang the bell. We broke and returned to our respective corners. Jimmy came up to me.

'You okay? You wanna go on?' he enquired.

'I'm okay. Just your fighter getting his jocks in a twist,' I said.

'Yeah, he's a bit hot-headed. Yer know the problem with youth, hormones racing and all that stuff.'

Jimmy approached his fighter.

I listened to his reprimand. 'Take it easy. It's just a spar, nothing serious. Don't lose yer cool. Youse alright to go on?'

'Yeah, cocky old bastard keeps grinning at me. One more round and I'll have him. I just wanna get one good one through to knock that smug look off his face.'

Jimmy said nothing but looked at his stopwatch.

'Okay.' He rang the bell.

We stepped out into the arena and commenced battle.

The young man tore into the offensive once again and threw jabs, uppercuts, and right crosses with precision but still without any contact. He ducked down and threw an uppercut which I evaded and leaned back. There was one hundred per cent intent behind it and I caught the man's elbow on the way up and pushed at the same time, pinning his arm to his chest, it took him off balance, I threw a punch to the young fighter's ribs, this time with a lot more force. The punch winded him and sent him to his knees. Jimmy looked anxious.

He managed to get up. He was still in pain.

Once he was on his feet, I shot a combination of punches, each one found their target, and to finish, a controlled uppercut which I didn't land but made it obvious to the younger man that if I had he would have been flat on his back.'

He was impressed and concluded the rest of the round with a few punches but with less serious intent.

The bell sounded and I patted the youth's head with my glove. 'Thanks for that,' I said.

'No worries, 'Yer good, yer bloody good. Where did yer learn to fight like that? Maybe give me a few pointers would youse?'

I smiled. 'Jimmy's your man. He'll put you right.'

Jimmy approached me.

'Well, yer still seem to be okay. Maybe a bit slower,' he said. 'Yer a bloody fool. Yer could 'ave possibly been a rich man by now. Gone over to the States when youse was younger but. It breaks my heart to see such a waste. I guess I can use you. Come in early next week and we'll talk hours.'

I nodded. 'Thanks.' I left the Gym with a sense that I had taken a step in the right direction to get back on my feet.

When I arrived home, I could tell something was wrong. The door to my apartment was open but I couldn't see inside from the doorway. I tensed up and listened. Rick had flown to Greece days before, so I knew it wasn't him and nobody else had a key.

"It must be a break in. Probably kids," I slowly pushed the door open wider; the furniture was overturned, the television and radio smashed, and the walls covered with graffiti.

I felt a great flush of anger sweep through me. How could anyone be such an arsehole, so wantonly destructive? I disliked people who destroyed things. It totally opposed the creative instincts and was so easy to do; it used no higher principles of thought only the motivation of a person possessed by a base emotion.

I felt saddened that Rick's possessions had been so viciously vandalised. Nothing appeared to have been stolen, only destroyed. There was a large patch of water in the kitchen and my food had been piled on the floor and urinated upon. A word written on the wall in the kitchen made it abundantly clear why I had been broken into. The words "Free mason?" was written in ketchup, the letters still clearly discernible as they began to drip.

Granston!

"How the hell did he find me?" I looked around at the damage to the rest of the apartment, the bedrooms had been equally treated, with shit smeared on the walls and over the sheets, the smell was vile, and I clenched my fist in rage and frustration.

'Bastards' I muttered to myself, 'the bastards.'

It was an act of invasion that brought back the memory of the past five years.

I should have killed him. A mental picture of Granston's evil face came into my mind and I felt my body tense with rage; the image of Granston continued until I had beaten his head into a mass of pulp. I savoured the image and then realised what I was doing.

That brought me down to his level and made me something of a hypocrite. I'd spent virtually all my life devoted to martial arts. It had given me strength in moments of stress and a body that was coordinated and functioned well, supremely fit, and healthy, but my mental philosophy had always been a struggle. Like most men I sought peace of mind and the myth that the martial arts are imbued with a mystic quality is more in the eyes of others than in those of the practitioner.

I'd become highly skilled, but most people can do the same if they practice long and hard enough, my biggest struggle was with myself and my search for inner tranquillity. The years in prison had made me bitter. I no longer had faith in the judicial system as a means of justice and now ran with the pack in matters of self–preservation. I knew I would confront Granston sooner or later but if so, would risk my parole and be back behind bars. I sensed something would probably turn me into an even more bitter man. What should I do? I looked around the room; the smell of crap in the air, the hatred in the atmosphere, invaded my reverie. I picked up the phone; it had been ripped from the socket but still functioned. I knew that until Granston was either returned to prison or dead. I would have to spend my life looking over my shoulder.

I sat down on one of the kitchen chairs and worked out my next move. First, I would clean up and assess the damage, and then I would go and buy a new television and radio. I decided to hire a cleaning company for the carpet and graffiti and worked out that in all I would have to spend all my bank balance. I was glad that I had the prospect of an income with Jimmy although my car would have to wait.

It was while I sat amongst the debris and contemplated that the phone rang. It was Sally. Her voice sounded anxious and upset.

'It's Dad, he's been hurt,'

'Hurt?' I repeated. 'How? What happened?'

'He was attacked last night at the office and left for dead. He's got a broken jaw and internal injuries.'

'Where are you now?' I asked.

'I'm at St. James' Hospital.'

'I'll come over right away,' .

'No, it's okay. There's nothing you can do. He's in a coma and they don't know what's going to happen. It could go either way.'

'I'm really sorry to hear that Sal, 'I'm coming over.'

I replaced the receiver, stood up and shook my head. Granston, it had to be, how else could he have known my address? I thought back to my contact with Deuce. I'd given Ron's address to him. I hadn't given him mine because I knew it was only temporary and I could have moved before Deuce was given parole although I had given him my phone number.

This time Granston had gone too far. Ron was a kind, considerate man and didn't deserve to be beaten up; at his age the trauma, if he survived, would cause him to have repercussions for the rest of his life.

I got changed and left the house to catch a bus to the city. The weather was warmer, and the sun felt good on my face. From a tree close to the bus stop the song of a mynah bird pierced the air and an elderly lady with an aged poodle passed by. Her dog tottered along on in front of her on unsteady legs, dressed in a pink woolly coat as insulation from the cold.

It would have been comical if my mind had not been preoccupied with other things. I took a quick look to see if I could discern anything that betrayed the presence of Granston. There was none that I could tell. The bus arrived after what seemed to me to be an eternity and I thought that I must get a timetable if I can't afford a car, or I'd be forced to spend endless time at bus stops.

I boarded the bus, fixed my Walkman, and sat and listened to the music of the thirties, Noel Coward "Mad dogs and Englishman."

The frivolous lyrics carried me away from the mundane and into the realms of fantasy where reality was Utopia.

Sally was still at the hospital when I arrived. She spoke to two men, obviously police. I stopped and then thought. "What the hell, why shouldn't I," and approached the trio.

'How is he?' I interrupted.

'He's still the same,' Sally answered.

The two Police officers looked questioningly at me.

'He's my father-in-law,' what happened?' I asked.

'We'll speak to you again in a moment, Mrs Mason,' Detective Sergeant Camileri, one of the police officers, commented as they moved away from us.

'Have they any idea who did it and why?' I asked, although already in my own mind I was sure of the answers. I didn't know what to do. "Should I tell the police all I knew or settle it in my own way?"

We stood in the hospital ward, and I tried to be of as much comfort as possible.

'You've been up all night?' I asked.

'Yes. I couldn't sleep. I had a few hours here but that's all.'

'Where's Clare? Does she know?' I asked.

'No. She's at home. David's with her. I'll go back this afternoon and return later. They said they'd call if anything happens; there's not much I can do.'

The two Policemen re-joined us.

'Could we have a word with you, Sir?'

I thought how young the cop looked.

'Sure, what?'

'Where were you last night at approximately seven o'clock?'

'Surely you don't believe that...'

The younger policeman interrupted Sally before she had time to complete her sentence.

'We don't believe anything, Mrs Mason. We just have to follow every line of enquiry however ridiculous it may sound.'

The older man stepped forward.

'I'm Detective Sergeant Jackson and this is Detective Constable Camileri. Would you mind answering the question, sir.'

I cast a quick glance at Sally.

'I was in a pub in Redfern. "The Three Lights."'

'Well, there's a coincidence. That's an Abo pub, isn't it?' Camileri interjected.

'You mean do Aboriginal people drink there? Yes, many do.' I answered.

'What were you doing there last night? Why there? I know for fact whiteys aren't particularly popular guests.'

'Maybe it's just coppers they don't like,' I replied. 'I was having a drink any law against that?'

'Alright Constable.' The senior officer interrupted. 'Thank you. Mr Mason we'll check your story.'

'Please do.' I smiled at the thought of them in the "Three Lights." They'd get a very cordial reception and not the liquid kind.

'We'll be in touch, Mrs Mason.'

'Yes, yes of course,' Sally answered.

'Oh, just one more thing does the name Deuce mean anything to you?' My interest was awakened as I heard the name of my ex-cell mate.

'No, it doesn't. Why?' Sally asked.

'The name was written on your father's notepad on his desk, along with the words, "The Three Lights." '

The Sergeant turned and looked at me. 'The pub you visited last night, did you arrange to meet anyone there, sir, or do you know why he should write the name of the pub down?'

'No, I didn't arrange a meeting and no I don't know why he would have written it.' I answered.

'My father was always writing things down on pieces of paper. He could have written it days ago. I don't know, I'm sorry I can't help you.' Sally added.

'That's okay. We'll be in touch. Goodbye Mr. Mason.'

I nodded a farewell and watched them depart.

Sally turned to me. 'You must have changed in prison. You never used to drink before.'

'I don't drink. I ...'

I was cut short by the appearance of a photographer, a camera, and a newspaper reporter.

'Could we have a word, Mrs. Mason?'

Sally turned to me. 'I'm sorry.'

········

Granston and Green had returned to their Newtown address. A third member, a friend of Green's, had teamed up with them; his nick name was "Barrel" given to him when he was a youth because of his physique. He had changed considerably since then, but the name had stuck.

He was a "Dragon," a member of an outlaw motorcycle gang, about forty-eight with an orange beard, hair that gave him a wild look and huge tattooed forearms. With his stud covered leather jacket, "Dragon's" patch and discoloured teeth, he looked the sort of character you wouldn't like to come up against.

He was from a "Chapter" in Perth and had known Green for some time; they'd committed a few robberies together. He'd also spent several years "inside" and lived by the rule of muscle. His prime source of income was from illicitly made speed and other designer drugs. He rode a twelve hundred cc customised Harley Davidson which he constantly cleaned when his hefty frame was not astride it. Green had contacted him; they wanted to plan a robbery and needed a third man. Barrel was only too keen to oblige.

'Well, well, what do yer fuckin' know,' Green said as he watched television. 'Masons got a fuckin' tart.'

'Really,' exclaimed Granston, and stared at the screen.

There was a picture of Sally and a story of how her father had been savagely beaten.

'Why didn't we wait for the cunt at his place and do 'im?' Green asked.

'He may not 'ave come back. And besides, now he knows he can sweat; now, he won't sleep too good.'

'But say he pisses off?' Green responded.

'No, he's got a missus and a father-in-law. I wanna play with the bastard. I wanna make him suffer. She ain't a bad looking bitch, is she? 'Ere give us the telephone book,' Granston commanded.

Barrel threw the book across to Granston. He opened it.

'Let's see.' His eyes narrowed and his finger went up and down the columns of names: Mansion Manter I.... Mason, Oh, here we are, which suburb is it?'

'The bloke just mentioned she was from Ultimo,' Barrel stated.

'Mrs Sally Mason, Ultimo. Ah, that narrows it down.' Granston commented.

'I like the name Sally,' Barrel interjected. I once fucked a Sally. Guess what 'er other name was?'

Green looked across at the huge ginger bearded man squashed into a chair as he swilled a can of beer.

'I dunno. What?' Green asked.

'O'Mally. Yeah, straight. Er name was Sally O'Mally.'

'Where did you fuck 'er? In an alley?' Green asked.

The big, bearded man rocked back in the chair and gave a laugh that sounded like a distressed walrus.

'Yeah, in an alley. I fucked Sally O'Mally in an alley.'

Green joined in the guffaws.

Granston's face changed from concentration into an evil smile; he ignored the puerile comments of his colleagues; he stretched across and picked up the phone.

'Knock it for a sec,' he said, 'I wanna make a call.'

Green and Barrel lowered the volume of their amusement as Granston punched out the digits then pressed the receiver to his ear. A voice answered. It was Clare.

'Hello,' she enquired.

Granston adopted a tangibly oily tone.

'Who is that?' he asked.

'Who am I speaking to?'

'Clare Mason. Who are you?'

Granston could tell his conversation was with a small child and continued. 'I'm a friend of your daddy. What's Mum's name?'

'Mrs Mason. What's your name?' the childish voice enquired.

'Oh, er, Tommy,' Granston replied. 'Tell daddy I'll call later.'

'I'm seeing him Saturday. We're going to the zoo,' Clare stated.

'Oh, that's nice,' Granston continued. 'You enjoy yourself at the zoo with your dad, okay? And I'll call back later. Alright 'bye then.'

'Alright, goodbye.' Clare replaced the receiver and Granston grinned at his two companions.

'Let's go and call on Mrs Mason. Let's do naughty things to her.' Granston's snigger changed to an inaudible grunt of pleasure at the prospect.

·········

After I'd met the two cops at the hospital they returned to their car.

'I know that bloke from somewhere,' Jackson said, his features illustrated his effort to recall   where from. 'Mason? Mason?' he repeated. 'I just can't put my finger on it.'

Camileri climbed into the car. 'Well, we'll do a check on him. See what we come up with.'

'Yeah, but I just know that I've seen him somewhere …'

'Feeling hungry?' Jackson enquired of his companion.

'Yeah, a bit peckish.'

'Right. To Macdonald's and get that light flashing.'

Camileri grinned and started the car. 'No worries.'

I had stayed at the hospital with Sally for a while before she left. I remembered the state of my apartment and decided I should go back and do something about the shit on the walls and bed. I didn't mention to her that I knew who it was who beat up her father, or the real reason why I went to the "Three Lights," but made up my mind to get Granston before he did any more damage. I gathered that Deuce had been released, but why had he called on Ron, and what had he said?

Granston must have beaten my address from Ron, and I felt myself burn with hatred at the thought of such cowardly and vicious behaviour meted out to a defenceless elderly man, I also wondered why he had chosen to smash up my apartment rather than attack me personally.

On the bus back from the city my mind dwelt on recent events, the vulnerability of Sally and my daughter; I decided, I would, after I had got my apartment organised, go to the "Three Lights." and find out why Ron had written Deuce's name on his note pad, then go back to the hospital.

Chapter Thirteen

Thirteen – The Three Lights

B ack at the flat I went into the kitchen and took a bucket from under the sink.

I wanted to get some cleaning done before the professionals came to make the place more liveable. Both bedrooms had their walls smeared with faeces and I thought about the best way to tackle the problem as I filled the pale. Sheets and other washable items went in the washing machine as I began the task to rid the place of the terrible stench.

It took me hours. I placed the damaged furniture and television close to the front door. With the intention of replacing them as soon as possible. Fortunately, the bed had not been touched, apart from the sheets and covers. Before I left for the Pub, I called the hospital, there was no change in Ron's condition.

I grabbed a bite to eat on route to the "Three Lights" to save me the trouble of buying in more food. Granston had thrown all I had onto the kitchen floor before whoever it was pissed on it.

It was dark when I arrived. 'As I approached, music and the sound of billiard balls bouncing off each other came from within.

The place was more crowded this time. I peered across the room through the haze of smoke and recognised Biff on his way to the bar. Several of the billiard players eyed me as I passed.

'I'm looking for Goulburn,' I said in a firm but quiet tone.

'Ain't here, mate, should be around but no sign.'

I scanned the smoky bar room for any sign of Goulburn and did a double take on a man slumped across one of the tables, I made my way over to him and lifted his head. It was Deuce.

'Hey, Deuce, it's me.'

Deuce slumped forward totally unaware of anything. I pulled him up from the table and heaved him to his feet.

'Fuckin'…what's going …' Deuce's voice trailed off as his head swung from his neck like a Toy placed on the rear window of a car.

With Deuce's protestation came interest from several bar patrons as I attempted to drag him out, they began to form a circle around me. I sensed there could be trouble. Deuce tottered on rubbery legs as I turned and faced the men.

'What the fuck youse doin', man?' one of the younger men enquired.

I had always had a stubborn streak and reacted against aggression with defiance, a characteristic that had landed me in trouble. I hadn't changed. Instead of an explanation I said nothing but stared straight into the man's face.

'What youse doing, man?' the young man shouted again.

'I'm standing here holding this bloke with my finger up his arse,' I replied quietly.

He took a few seconds to register my answer.

'Eh, fuckin' cheeky dick sucker,' the young man responded and took a step forward.

'Hold on,' a loud voice interrupted.

The men turned in the direction of the command. It was Goulburn.

'Just cool it, take it easy...I see you found yer mate,' Goulburn added and stepped into the circle.

'Yeah,' I replied, 'looks a bit under the weather.'

Deuce lifted his face and squinted into mine. His head nodded and swayed his eyes glazed and bloodshot. He mouthed recognition of my shaven head immediately in front of him.

The effort to speak and his condition caused him to heave, and his body jerked in convulsive movements that regurgitated the contents of his stomach as I supported him. The circle of men moved back almost as one as the warm liquid vomit splashed to the floor.

'Fuckin' 'ell,' Goulburn said, and stepped out of the line of puke.

I said nothing. I had taken the brunt of Deuce's stomach contents down my front; my trousers and T-shirt were soaked. There was a few moments' silence and then a roar of laughter from the men, who dispersed back to the pool tables.

'Geez, man.' Biff had come from behind the bar and pulled chairs and tables out of the vomit zone. 'Get him outside,' he said, betraying his lack of sympathy for my condition.

'That's what I was trying to do.' I said feeling decidedly uncomfortable.

'I'll give youse a hand,' Goulburn offered, took Deuce's other arm, and guided him toward the door.

'Fuckin'ell, it stinks.

Where yer goin'?' Goulburn asked.

'Maybe back to my place. Let him sleep it off and then talk in the morning.'

'Where's your place?' Goulburn asked.

'Marrickville, Phew! What's he been drinking?' I muttered.

'Youse better come with me. I'll give youse a ride.'

'Yeah? Great thanks.' I remarked.

'Yeah, youse never get a cab, man. Besides, cabs don't come down to this pub.'

'I can believe that,' I said.

Goulburn didn't answer but took his arm and wiped a string of saliva that dribbled down from Deuce's mouth.

'My truck's this way. You'd better sit in the back with 'im, or you'll stink the cab out,'

'No worries,' I replied and looked around to locate Goulburn's car.

'It's the Ute over there.' Goulburn pointed with a nod of his head.

We half carried, half dragged the drunken Deuce to the utility, heaved him over the tail board and I jumped in with him, the dampness of my trousers and shirt made me cold in the night air.

'Whereabouts in Marrickville?' Goulburn asked.

'Off Illawarra Road,' I replied. 'I'll give you a tap on the cabin when we're close.'

'Illawarra. Which end?' he enquired.

'Before you cross over the main road.'

'Okay, no worries.' He climbed in and we set off.

The journey back to Marrickville was even colder, the evening temperature had dropped to about eleven degrees, and I was grateful to arrive. I banged on the cabin.

Goulburn stopped and looked from the window.

'It's the next on the right,' I said.

The Ute pulled up outside the flats and I jumped down.

'Hang on here for a sec. I'll just go and open up.'

I shot a quick glance around me, checked to see if there were any signs of interested parties and cautiously went up the stairs. I pushed my door open; there was no sign of entry.

Prior to my departure I had threaded a thin piece of cotton across the entrance. It was still intact. I went back down the stairs to help Goulburn.

We laid Deuce on the bed in the spare room and closed the door.

Goulburn glanced around the flat.

'What happened?' he enquired and took stock of the slashed furniture and smashed television set.

'I, er. had visitors.'

'Granston?' Goulburn asked.

I looked up. 'How did you know?'

'I saw Deuce this arvo. He told me. He went to your father in laws office. He'd lost your contact address said that some prick inside nicked it, but he remembered it, He said he owed you a drink.'

'Granston got to my father–in–law, and he's in hospital.' I answered.

'Shit.' Goulburn replied, 'bad, is he?

'Intensive care.'

'Fuck he must have done 'im soon after Deuce left.'

'Yeah, thanks for the lift. Did you want a drink?'

'No, I'm right. I'll get back. I heard youse are pretty hard, right man?' Goulburn gave a broad grin and revealed a set of white teeth.

I gave a half smile in response. 'Don't believe all you hear.'

'Oh, about the dog, there's a match coming up soon. I'll give yer details later, man. If yer come with me, you'll have no worries.'

'Thanks, that'll be good,' I replied.

"Don't get too excited the chances of one being yer kids' dog, pretty remote.

See yer." Goulburn turned, went out and pushed the door closed behind him.

My vomit covered clothes had become dryer but stunk; I threw them in the bin, had a shower and got to bed at around midnight although I had to get up once to go into the bedroom where Deuce slept to turn him over, his snores pierced the still night air with a sound like a rasp drawn across a steel plate. I pulled the only dry blanket over me and slept.

I rose next morning at six o'clock and went for a run.

The weather was windy, and the sunrise partly obscured by grey black clouds. I ran the length of Illawarra Road to the golf course at the bridge over Cooks River and stopped under a tree to stretch and go through a few moves. I had taken a chance and left Deuce with a note on the door asking him to wait; I wanted to talk to him and hoped he'd be there when I returned after all the bother of finding him.

I arrived back an hour later; the note had not moved; Deuce was still asleep. I took a shower, realised I had no food in the house and decided to go to the milk bar at the top of the road to buy some grub. I returned a half hour later; Deuce was still asleep.

The smell of toast failed to raise him; I'd spent two months in the confines of a small cell with Deuce and knew him well.

It was eight thirty when I telephoned Sally.

'How is your father?' I asked.

'I called the hospital last night and there was no change.'

'I'm going to the hospital this morning actually, in about ten minutes,' Sally stated.

'Oh, right. What about Clare?' I enquired'

'I thought you were going to take her to the zoo this afternoon,' Sally said.

'Well, I thought under the circumstances you would have changed your mind.'

'No, it would do her good and there's nothing you can do. She's looking forward to it.'

'Okay, I'll see you when I get there.'

'No, I'm leaving soon. David will be here,' Sally remarked.'

I concealed my surprise. 'Right, okay, I'll pick her up about eleven o'clock.'

'That's fine,' Sally responded. 'Can you get her back by six?'

I acknowledged and replaced the receiver; I had no desire to see David and wondered if he had spent the night with Sally. A twinge of curiosity played on my mind. I buttered a piece of toast, finished my breakfast, and went into the bedroom to wake Deuce.

'Hey, wakey, wakey, roll call......'

Deuce prized his eyes open. 'Wha ...?' he muttered.

I caught a whiff of his breath – a combination of stale vomit and beer.

'Phew,' I remarked.

Deuce sat up. 'Roll call. Shit – uh ––' He looked at me and stared blankly ahead.

'What's up?'

'Time to get up,' I stated.

Deuce's bloodshot eyes surveyed the room.

'Where am I?' he said.

'My place, Marrickville.'

Deuce stared at me as his mental faculties began to organise themselves into a semblance of normality.

'Hi, man, how's it goin'?' He muttered.

'Okay,' I replied. 'You want something to drink? Tea or something?'

'No, man, no. it's okay. I'm right.'

'I'll make you a cup of tea, but I've only got honey.'

'Yeah OK, that's fine,' Deuce said and ran his hand through his hair. 'I'll be out in a sec. Where's the shit 'ouse?'

'Through there.' I nodded in the direction of the toilet. 'But you have to use the bucket outside.'

'What?' he queried.

'Just pulling yer leg. Do us both a favour shut the bloody door. I've seen enough of you
sitting on the throne, and have a shower whilst yer in there, there's a blue towel on the rack; use that one.'

Deuce grunted something, raised himself from the bed and staggered into the bathroom.

·····•·•····

It was ten thirty on that same morning that Granston and Green drove a stolen car they'd appropriated earlier, to Sally's house. The plates of the white Nineteen eighty-six Falcon had been changed and the pair so brazen in their disregard for the law had at one time parked the vehicle within thirty metres of a police station.

The previous owner had been proud of his car and kept it immaculate for the period that he'd enjoyed it, thus the glove compartment was well equipped for the road user. Granston thumbed through the latest edition of the Gregory's. Green was at the wheel.

'Down Harris Street and it's one of the roads off.' Granston stated.

'I'll have to go around,' Green replied. 'It's one way down Harris now, the bastards changed it.'

'Everything's fuckin' changed in this 'ole,' Granston scowled.

Barrel had gone off to 'score some shit' as he put it and said he'd catch up later, the two men confident they could handle the situation.

Granston took a swig of a half empty whisky bottle and grinned. 'I'm looking forward to this. I could do with a bit of cunt.' He chuckled.

The car drew up outside Sally's house but there was nowhere to park; they continued down the road and parked in a "no waiting zone."

It mattered little to either of them; the question of fines on a stolen car with untraceable plates was beyond contemplation and deserved a snigger. The two men walked back to Sally's house and pushed open the squeaky iron gate. Granston knocked on the door.

From within came the sound of movement before the door was opened.

'Hello,' Clare said.

'Hello,' Granston answered. 'You must be Clare?'

Clare smiled.

'Yes, that's right. Who are you?'

Granston regarded the little girl closely, then looked back to Green who stood immediately behind him.

'Er, I'm a friend of your Daddy and Mummy.'

'They're not here,' Clare said. 'Mummy went out a few minutes ago to see a friend in hospital. Just Uncle David's here.'

Granston moved his hand in front of Clare's face. There was no reaction. He turned to Green and nodded. Swiftly he pulled the little girl forward and clamped his hand over her mouth. Green backed through the gate and the two men walked quickly to the car. Clare was bundled inside and driven away.

David had been in the garden doing a repair job on Sally's fence when he entered the house. he could see from the kitchen that the front door was open and wondered why Clare had opened it.

'Clare why is the front door open?' he called.

There was no reply. He came through the house to the front. He looked both ways down the road.

'That's strange,' he mumbled. 'Clare are you upstairs?' The only sound he heard was the uninterrupted hum of traffic from Miller Street.

'She could have said goodbye at least,' he said to himself, assuming I had picked her up to take her on her outing.

Chapter Fourteen

Fourteen - Cops

Back at my flat I made some tea, a couple more rounds of toast and sat down at the kitchen table. After a lot of noise and gurgles Deuce reappeared fifteen minutes later.

'You look a bit better,' I said. 'I thought you had finished with booze,'

'Yeah, but I came under some bad happenings man.'

'What happened?' I enquired.

'Me missus give me a hard time.'

'I didn't know you were married.'

'No, she never come to see me. Well maybe a few times, anyways.'

'My father-in-law got beaten up.' I said and looked for any change in Deuce's expression.'

'Beaten up, eh that's no-good mate, what happened?'

'I was thinking maybe you could tell me,'

'What?' He looked puzzled.

'The police have got hold of your name. Ron wrote it down on a pad, my ex-wife found him at his office, savagely beaten.'

Deuce pondered my last remark.

'Yeah, I went to see 'im,' he said he didn't know yer at first and then I explained about yer address and stuff, and he said he'd tell yers. I told him I'd be at the "Three Lights." You got the message then?'

'No. I got the message from the law. They didn't understand it, but I guess they may figure it out once they see my record.'

'How did Granston know Ron's address? 'I asked.

Deuce sucked in his breath.

'Fuck man, shit. I lost the address you give me. Russel, I bet he must have somehow got hold of it. Fuck I'm sorry bro I'm real sorry. I swear I had nothing to do with yer father-in-law. I just paid a social call.'

'I didn't think that. Goulburn told me you went to see him.'

'What happened to the furniture?' Deuce remarked, as he took a slurp of his tea.

'As you can see by my flat, I had visitors.'

'Granston?' Deuce remarked.

'Yeah.'

'Fuckin' shit bag,' Deuce growled.

'Evil, the man's evil. We have a name for men like him.'

Deuce was cut short by the sound of the phone. I got up and answered it. There was a silence and then a voice spoke. I felt the muscle in my hand contract involuntarily. I knew instantly who it was.

'Ello Mazzer ol mate. How's it goin'?' the voice hissed.

I didn't reply.

'How's the flat? Yer like shit, do you? I've got someone 'ere I'd like yer to talk to.'

There was silence, and then the voice of a small, terrified girl.

'Daddy, please Daddy.,' the voice began to waver and became a loud cry. 'daddy!

'Hello, daddy, it's me again.' Granston sneered.

I felt as though I had been stabbed through the heart with a steel blade, physically sick.

'You touch her, and I'll kill you.' I shouted.

'Now, now, that's not nice, is it? She's only a little girl but I think she needs to grow up a little, experience the adult pleasures of life, if yer get my drift.'

I felt powerless.

'What do you want? I'll do anything you want. Just don't harm her,' I pleaded.

'Yer doin' what I want, yer suffering and I'm gonna make yer suffer more. I'm gonna cut my finger and I'm gonna make her little snatch so sore it's gonna bleed and then our blood will mix. Sees yer Puss, just think about it.'

The phone clicked off. I felt as if my head was going to explode. I stood in the room; my eyes filled with tears of desperation.

'Oh, God, no. Please no. Don't let him do it. Please, God, no.'

Deuce had caught part of the conversation.

'What's up?' He could see I was in a state of shock.

'Granston's got my daughter,' I managed to blurt out.

'Fuckin' 'ell, no good man.'

From deep within me I seemed to regain my composure. It was as if I had found some inner tranquillity.

'I'm gonna find her,' I stated in a calm almost casual way.

At that moment there was a knock on the battered door.

I nodded to Deuce to go into the bedroom, and then looked through the glass identity hole. It was Jackson and Camileri.

··········

The two Police officers had returned to the station after they left me. Camileri ran a check and discovered my past but hadn't come up with any connection to Deuce until they had contacted Longbeach; the Governor mentioned Deuce's name as my cell mate, and I'd recently been in touch with him.

Jackson also recalled my case as he was in Court that day to give evidence for the prosecution at another trial and happened to be in the vicinity, so sat in for a few moments.

'Yeah, the cat case. It was in the papers, killed some bloke for running down a cat,' Jackson mused.

'A bit of an overreaction if you ask me,' Camileri said.

'Yeah, but the bloke he clobbered was a real arsehole if I remember, a real villain. It wasn't a straightforward case,'

Jackson added.

'He got done cos he was into Kung Fu or something, expert or whatever. 'I don't remember the exact facts, but he got sent down for eight years. Geez, how time flies when yer havin' fun.'

They'd traced me through my Parole officer and figured that I must have been with Deuce or looked for him at the "Three Lights."

Jackson was the first to speak when I opened the door.

'Mr. Mason, mind if we ask you some questions?'

I looked at the two men and realised I had no choice. 'What?' I stated.

'Do you mind if we come in?'

'Well, er,' I didn't want them to come in but knew that if I refused, they would probably come up with some charge to take me in.

'Yeah, sure.'

The two men entered the apartment. They noted the television set and the slashed furniture but made no comment.

'What is it you want to ask me?' I enquired.

'Are you familiar with a man called Deuce?'

I nodded. 'Yeah, you know I am.'

'Have you seen him recently?'

'Yeah, I've seen him.'

'When and where?' Camileri asked.

'Last night as you no doubt know at the Three Lights pub.'

The two cops exchanged glances at each other.

'Why didn't you mention you knew him at the hospital?'

'I guess it slipped my mind.'

'Any idea why he contacted your father-in-law or why he should want to harm him?'

My mind was preoccupied with Granston and my daughter; I just wanted to get rid of them.

'He wanted to get in touch with me,' I replied.

'Oh? Why was that? Any particular reason?'

'We were cell mates. I guess he missed me, we, er, made a date when we got out. Look, I've got things to do.'

'So, you were really close then?' Camileri stated.

I acknowledged his innuendo with a quick look of contempt.

'Are you alone?' Jackson asked, as he took in the table with the two cups.

I said nothing.

'Do you mind if we look around?'

I was not impressed but knew there was little I could do. 'Sure, go for it.'

Jackson made to go towards the bedroom when Deuce stepped out. Camileri caught sight of the ebony skinned man and his hand automatically went for his gun.

'On the floor.' He yelled.

'Look man....' Deuce stuttered.

'On the floor and shut up.' Camileri repeated.

Deuce bent down on one knee and eased himself down onto the carpet.

I stood and watched and thought Camileri had seen too many American cop films.

'It's okay, Camileri, relax,' Jackson said.

Deuce remained still.

'Look, man, youse chasing the wrong possum.' He mumbled still face down.

I wondered why Deuce had come out. He could have easily made it through the window and down the tree. Camileri lowered his gun and Deuce, relieved by the gesture, breathed easier.

Jackson turned to Camileri.

'Let him up.'

Deuce got back on his feet after much effort and a few vocal protestations.

'Go on.' Jackson said.

Deuce looked at me and then back at the two men; he spoke.

'It's a bloke called Granston he's got Tony's kid I went to his dad in laws place to get Tony to meet me at the 'Lights, Granston's the one who beat up on that Ron fella.'

I said nothing, I had no faith in the law although knew that Deuce meant well.

'Granston,' Jackson repeated.

'What's he got to do with you?'

'He was in Longbeach, Tony crossed him, upset him shit loads. He's out,' Deuce replied.

'Yeah, we know. He's pulled a few local robberies lately. What's this about your kid?' Jackson turned to me.

'He's got my kid. I don't know how. Granston called me a few minutes ago. Look, I need to find out if my wife's okay and what's happened to my daughter.'

'Your wife doesn't know? Where does she think her daughter is?'

'I dunno. I was supposed to take her to the zoo; she probably thinks she's with me.'

Jackson sensed the urgency in my voice. The cops listened as I recounted the events that led to this moment. I failed to mention the actual details of the encounter in the shower, I considered it unimportant and said only that we had an altercation prior to my parole.

'Please can I try and contact my wife. I mean my ex-wife?' I repeated.

'What about all this?' Camileri said and indicated the broken electrical equipment and slashed furniture.

I thought about my daughter and Sally. I still had control of myself and tried to formulate a course of action. In a way I was not unhappy about the fact that the police were involved. They had a wider network to call on and even if I had no faith in them, it was another avenue of hope.

'Granston,' I said.

Jackson pulled out his radio phone and shook his head.

'Why the bloody hell didn't yer give us all this in the first place? Maybe we could have collared him before he got to your daughter.'

'Sure. I went inside for five fucking years. You think I believe in justice? You said he'd done a few jobs. You haven't collared him yet.'

Jackson put out an alert describing Clare.

'Maybe if you'd told us, we'd have had somewhere to look,' Camileri interrupted.

'This is going nowhere,' Jackson said. 'We'll go to your wife's house and send someone over to the hospital and take it from there. If your wife is at the hospital then she doesn't know about her daughter, or was her daughter going to the hospital with her?'

'No. I was meant to pick her up from the house at eleven. There was a bloke looking after her until I arrived.'

'Oh? Who was that?' Camileri asked.

'A bloke called David. I never met him, a friend of my, er, ex–wife,' I hesitated.

It seemed a strange situation; one that I would never have dreamed of when I married Sally.

'I see. Well, we'll get over to your ex –wife's place.' Jackson added, 'and talk to this David.'

'I'm going over there too, you can stay here if you want,' I said to Deuce. 'I don't know what time I'll be back.'

Deuce sensed that I needed some support. He still had a hangover from the night before and didn't particularly feel energetic.

'No worries,' he said.

'There's not much grub in the cupboard but help yourself.'

Deuce nodded. 'Yeah, right.'

'I'm sorry, there's no TV.'

'I never watch it,' Deuce replied.

'Yeah, oh well then I'll see you later.'

The three of us left the apartment and Deuce flopped down on the sofa.

'How are you gonna get there? Jackson asked.

'Bus.' I answered.

Jackson shook his head as he moved toward their car and beckoned to me. 'Jump in.'

·····•••·····

When we arrived at Pyrmont. The house was vacant, and the front door closed.

Jackson rang the doorbell there was no answer. 'Hmn doesn't look like anyone's home.'

'I'll have a look around the back.'

From there I could see the house was empty and showed no signs of forced entry or otherwise.

"What happened to that David bloke?" I thought. "Wasn't he supposed to be here?"

'Anyone around back?' Jackson asked.

'No,' I replied.

'What's this David bloke's other name?' Camileri asked'

'I don't know,' I replied.

'Come on Camel let's go.' Jackson stated.

"Camel" raised his eyebrows and shook his head.

'I shouldn't call him Camel really he gets the hump.'

'Where are you going?' I asked not really in the mood for humour.

Jackson looked at me, 'To see your wife.'

'Can I come with you'?

I felt responsible for all that had happened and knew that Sally would be hurt, I hadn't told her the truth about her father's attack and now her daughter had been kidnapped and was about to suffer a fate too horrific to contemplate. I felt my stomach turn at the thought. I knew I had to tell Sally face to face.

Jackson glanced at Camileri. 'Ok.'

On our way to the hospital Sally was informed of recent events and had given the police David's family name.

On being located he was surprised and shocked to learn what had occurred and was on his way to the hospital. He had assumed that I had called earlier and taken Clare, not wished to see him, and left.

Whilst he understood my reluctance to meet him face to face, he thought it rather ill-mannered of me to go off with Clare and not tell him. He'd heard about my reputation and in turn been somewhat nervous about an encounter but demonstrated guts to agree to wait with Clare in the first place.

Sally looked tired and distressed at the hospital. I caught sight of her as she talked to a female police officer outside my father-in-law's room.

I felt guilty and ashamed that I'd been responsible once again and brought about such unhappiness to a person I cared so much for. I walked with the two cops toward Sally unaware of our presence until Jackson spoke.

'Mrs Mason.'

Sally looked up. Her eyes filled with tears and her features betrayed her anxiety.

'Where is she? Where's my daughter? What's happened to her?' She fought to regain her composure.

'What do you mean when you say you think she's been taken?

By whom and why? Please tell me what's going on.' Sally implored hysterically.

I wanted to comfort her, to hold her, tell her everything would be okay but knew I wouldn't convince her.

'It's my fault, Sal, your father, Clare, all that's happened. It's down to me.'

'What do you mean?' Sally looked at me.

'Your Dad was beaten up by a thug who wanted to find me.

Clare has been taken to get at me.'

'Get at you? I don't understand?' Sally said, her eyes searched mine for the answers.

'Your husband had a run in with a prisoner who has since escaped and is out to get him,' Jackson stated.

'We have reason to believe it was him who took your daughter, but we'll get her back. Don't worry.'

Sally took little comfort from Jackson's effort to ease her anxiety.

'I'll do anything, Sal, to get Clare back. Anything they want. Believe me.'

I moved closer to her, offering her support. But she shunned my advance and buried her face in her hands.

·····•·····

A man of approximately fifty years, dressed in a pair of light slacks and green pullover, came through the doors. He stopped, caught sight of Sally, and went straight to her, touched her lightly on the shoulder, and said something I didn't catch. Sally broke down and sobbed, she put her head on the man's chest as he comforted her.

The two cops stood for a moment and felt awkward before Camileri interjected.

'Are you David Lasio?'

The man turned briefly in the direction of the detective's voice.

'Yes.'

I felt uneasy and nodded to Jackson to indicate my departure. I hesitated for a moment and then thought better of saying anything to my wife or ex–wife should I say.

'Okay if I go?' I asked.

'Yeah. but leave this to us.'

I said nothing, left the hospital, caught a taxi back to my flat and tried to figure out what the hell to do.

Deuce was asleep on the sofa. I shook him.

'What the ... oh, geez, shit. What happened? Anything?' Deuce enquired; his mind still fogged by a recent nap as he tried to give the impression he was fully in control of his faculties.

Chapter Fifteen

Fifteen - Kings Cross

I walked over to the window and looked out.

'No, and I haven't any idea what to do. Did anyone call?'

'No, 'Deuce remarked.

I fought to keep from my mind images of my daughter in Granston's company. I knew that thoughts of this nature only hurt me and were totally negative for both her and I. It was torture more painful than anything else and Granston knew, he would prolong it for as long as he could.

Deuce's expression changed.

'Wait a minute, what about Granston's brother? He used to visit him sometimes.'

'Who?'

'What was his name?'

Deuce assumed a thoughtful expression. 'What was the bastard's name? Evil lookin' cunt, like his brother. Oh, shit, I dunno. But I don't s'pose it matters, but he runs a place for slags in the Cross, Vic street.'

Kings Cross, a suburb with a chequered history alive with numerous clubs and bars, scantily dressed street walkers, adult bookshops and Spruikers outside night spots, strip clubs inviting passers–by to "come in and be entertained."

'Whereabouts?' I inquired, a glimmer of hope.

'I dunno the exact address but I know roughly where. Granston would often blow off about how he was gonna ask his brother to send him a tart over.

'Where yer goin'? Deuce enquired.

'To the Cross to find Granston's brother.'

'Ang on.' Deuce added, 'mind if I have an apple. I just fancy one.'

I didn't bother to answer.

Deuce selected an apple, rubbed it against his trousers and took a bite.

'Let's go.'

Before we left the flat, I threaded a piece of cotton across the door and went down the stairs.

We were halfway up Illawarra Road when a utility drew alongside, and Goulburn's face peered from the window.

'Where's yer going?' He asked.

Deuce acknowledged his companion and strode over to the side of the car.

'Down the Cross.'

'Jump in. I'll take youse .' We didn't wait to be asked a second time and climbed in alongside Goulburn.

'Yer smell a bit sweeter today,' Goulburn remarked.

'Yeah,' I replied.

'What's up?' Goulburn asked, and sensed from my demeanour that something was not right.

Deuce explained to him as we drove.

'Fuckin' bastards,' Goulburn added after he had listened to his companion.

'How are yer gonna find 'im?'

'Ask around,' Deuce stated. 'Some of the girls should know 'im.'

'Yeah,' Goulburn agreed.

I sat quietly all the while Deuce had related the past events to his colleague and stared out at the traffic, my mind absorbed by thoughts of Clare's rescue and how I could achieve it. I couldn't allow myself to dwell upon my daughter's vulnerability but thought only of her survival.

'Whereabouts in the Cross?' Goulburn asked.

Deuce looked at the streets as they passed by.

'Wait down here, Vic Street. Drop us 'ere.'

'No worries. I'll hang around for a while.'

I looked at Goulburn and wondered why this man should want to help.

'It's okay if you're busy. I'll be right,' I said.

'No worries, I'll wait a bit. I run my own business; I can please myself. Go for it,' Goulburn replied.

Deuce got out and took a quick look around.

'It's somewhere round 'ere,' he said, 'in Vic Road but I'm buggered if I know the number.'

Goulburn parked the Ute and waited as Deuce, and I walked down the street; we looked in each doorway for a red light. A girl, obviously a prostitute, stood gazing in the opposite direction outside one of the houses.

'Ask her,' Deuce said and nodded toward the girl.

I waited until we got closer and then spoke.

'Excuse me, miss, do you happen to know a bloke called Granston?'

The girl walked off and ignored me.

'Friendly sort,' Deuce remarked as he watched the girl totter off, her buttocks wobbling in time with her unsteady steps.

'Look at that arse', like two fuckin' pigs fightin' under a blanket.'

I took little notice and walked up the path of a house that displayed a red light. I rang the doorbell whilst Deuce waited in the street. A tall Asian girl with dark hair answered the door.

'Come in,' she said and touched me lightly on the arm; she beckoned me to follow her up red carpeted stairs that led to a closed door at the top. She pushed it open, said something to the occupants, a pair of young men, one dressed as a Roman gladiator, the other as a surfie, who scampered out and disappeared along the corridor.

'Wait here,' the girl instructed, she turned to go downstairs.

'Wait a minute,' I said. 'I'm looking for someone. A mate of mine.'

The girl stopped and came up one more step of the stairs. Even though she was on the same step as me she was still a fraction taller.

'Oh? Who's that?' she enquired.

'A bloke called Granston.' I looked for some reaction in the girl's face. There was none.

'Don't know 'im,' she replied.

'He, er, runs a business in this area so I'm told.'

'You a cop?' the girl asked.

'Do I look like a cop?' I replied.

'You can't tell these days. The most unlikely people turn out to be cops.'

'I'm not a cop,' I assured her. 'Do you know Granston?'

'What's he look like?' she asked.

I had never seen Granston's brother but knew that Deuce said he looked like Granston. I described him as best I could.

The girl listened.

'Could be anybody, try four houses down. But don't say you called here.'

I thanked her and left. Had she told me the truth or just wanted to get rid of me?

Deuce had just rolled a cigarette when I came out. He stood next to the truck; Goulburn was seated behind the wheel.

'Any luck?' Deuce enquired.

'I dunno. Maybe something. You said Granston's brother looks like him? Same hair or what?'

Deuce thought. 'Not so greasy, but, yeah, you can tell they're brothers. Why?'

'Just this girl wanted to know what he looked like, and I didn't know. She says to try four houses down.'

'Right.' Deuce replied.

Goulburn approved the plan and indicated he would wait. I walked down the street to the house the girl had suggested.

Deuce followed close behind. When we got there the door was open; nobody about. We stood in the hallway at the bottom of the stairs; from above we could hear screams.

'What the fuck's that all about?' Deuce asked as he tossed his cigarette out of the front door.

'Wait here,' I instructed.

Deuce complied although he felt uneasy if this was Granston's brother's place and Granston showed up.

I climbed the stairs and listened outside the room.

'You filthy little shit,' a voice boomed out followed by the sound of a slap and the screams of a woman. I pushed open the door and saw a man, naked to the waste hitting a girl on the bed as she tried to defend herself. He had already made her nose bleed; she wore a mini skirt and blood spattered her face and hair.

The man wheeled round at my entrance.

'Who the fuck are you? Get out.'

I stayed where I was.

'I said get out!'

The man got up from the bed and rushed at me. The room was small and didn't allow much space to manoeuvre; the bed took up the largest area. There was a chair and a mirror, the only other furniture in the room. I stepped back through the door as the man advanced, then to my left. The man abruptly stopped and slammed the door shut. A key turned in the lock.

I heard him mutter an obscenity and go back to the girl.

He was about to hit her again when I lost it and front kicked the door open, it shattered in two, one half held by a screw to the now twisted hinge.

The loud bang gave the man more of a shock than the spectacle.

I stood in the doorway, my eyes clearly indicative of my mood.

'Leave her alone,' I commanded in a quick but authoritative tone.

The man recovered from the explosive interruption, stood up and angrily charged at me. I side stepped, grabbed him, and used his momentum to send him through the door and against a wall. I followed him out; he turned to face me as I delivered a stamp kick to his knee, then a side kick to his stomach which sent him head over heels down the stairs. Deuce stepped to one side as the man clattered to a halt at the bottom; he screamed in pain.

'My leg, my leg!' he yelled.

The dislocated limb gave a macabre appearance; it was at an awkward angle to the joint.

I went back inside to the girl.

'Are you okay?' I asked.

The girl looked up. 'Yeah, I'm okay.'

Cries of pain echoed from downstairs, then the sound of a conversation followed by footsteps on the stairs. I tensed ready for fight or flight'

A lank haired man with similar facial features to Granston appeared in the doorway.

'What the fuck's 'appening?' The man slowly advanced toward me.

'It's okay, Jase,' the girl called out, 'it's okay, he helped me.'

The man stopped.

'It was the arsehole downstairs,' she went on.

'What the black bastard?'

'No, he wasn't black.'

Granston looked at me.

'What do you want?'

'I'm looking for your brother,' I said, my eyes fixed on the man in front of me.

'Don't talk to me about that cunt, the arsehole. Is yer a mate of 'is? Cos if yer are yer can piss off double quick.'

I looked at Jason and was surprised by his reaction. I wasn't sure whether he lied or not, but either way knew I'd get nothing out of him. I felt the urge to beat him into pulp for being Granston's brother.

'Why? What do yer want my brother for?' Jason asked.

From downstairs I could hear Deuce help the injured man out of the house. It became quieter.

'He's got my daughter. She's five years old. She's blind and he's got her.'

Jason shrugged.

'Yeah, sounds like the prick. He's no good. If ya catch up with 'im give 'im one from me.'

'You've no idea where he is?' I asked.

'Nope, sorry, mate, can't help yer.'

The girl had dressed and made to leave the room. Granston turned to her as she walked past.

'I'll talk to you later,' he said.

'Sorry, mate, as I said, can't help yer. Now if you'll excuse me. Who fucked this door up? My fuckin' door. Who did it?'

'The bastard bloke,' the girl hastily said.

I felt disappointed and yet I was not wholly convinced that Jason had told me the truth. I left the room and went downstairs.

Deuce was on his way back in. Goulburn carried a baseball bat.

'It's okay but thanks,' I said as I made for the front door. A siren could be heard in the distance.

The man I kicked down the stairs was attended to by an elderly woman who had come out from one of the houses in answer to his cries of pain and called the ambulance.

Deuce had propped the man up against the wall and left him there, sure that he would get attention but not too sympathetic to his plight. I heard the siren and walked away from the house. The man caught sight of me and screamed abuse. I ignored him.

'What now?' Deuce asked.

'He's lying. I'm sure of it,' I said. 'He gave the impression he hates his brother.'

'Bullshit. He wouldn't visit him if he hated him,' Deuce added.

'Let's get away from this area. The cops might show up,' Goulburn interrupted.

I agreed.

Jason Granston waited for the sound of the ambulance to fade then went to the phone.

He punched out a few digits and waited. A voice responded.

'Just had visitors, a shaven headed bloke and a coon.'

'Get me a shooter,' the voice on the other end of the line hissed. 'I'll come over. Meet you at the usual place.' Granston said.

'It might be difficult gettin' a piece', Jason responded.

'Get one. I don't care how much. I'll see yer soon. One hour.'

'He says you 'ave his kid?' Jason asked.

The phone clicked off.

········•·•····

We drove down the road and stopped at the traffic intersection. I was deep in thought when a girl stepped up to the open window of the car. She was the one at the house on whose behalf I had intervened.

'He's lying, he saw his brother yesterday. He came to the house.'

'Where's Granston?' I asked. The lights changed and I leapt from the truck.

Goulburn moved off from the intersection. The girl looked nervously around.

'If he sees me talking to you, I'm dead.'

'What do you know about Granston? Please tell me.'

I put my hands on the girl's shoulders and looked into her eyes.

'He's got my kid and I don't know what he's going to do to her. I may be too late already.'

The girl bit her lower lip and glanced over her shoulder.

'Try Newtown. Gowrie Street, number eighteen. That's all I'm gonna say.'

The girl broke free from me and hurried off.

I caught sight of Goulburn and Deuce; they'd driven back up the street. I ran to the Ute.

'Can you take me to Newtown. I think I may have something.'

Goulburn acknowledged with a grin. 'Let's go.'

Twenty minutes later the Ute turned into Gowrie Street, and I counted off the numbers of the houses. It was a small terrace with a broken gate and if it were like most of the houses in that street there would be an alley that ran along the back with access to the garden.

This is eighteen.' I said. 'I'm going around the back and over the fence to see if there's any sign of life. Let's hope that girl hasn't given as a duff line,'

I walked past several houses, then turned left, then left again and ended up in a narrow lane directly behind the house. I peered through the crack in the fence and saw a frosted window which I took to be a bathroom.

Deuce and Goulburn had remained in the truck.

'Wait 'ere, I'll be back,' Goulburn said to Deuce and threw a quick glance over his shoulder before he followed me down the alley.

I was by the fence when he came up beside me. 'Anything? 'He asked.

'I'm going over the fence to try the house.'

Goulburn considered it dodgy. For a start if it was the right house there was no way to know how many people were inside; if it wasn't, I ran the risk of someone calling the cops and might end up on a charge of break and entering.

Goulburn had an idea.

'Hang on. Why don't I knock on the front door and make some excuse, I'm looking for a mate or something? I can tell maybe how many blokes or if it's the right place. They won't suspect me. I don't know any of 'em. What does this bloke look like?'

I gave him a quick description of Granston. 'Okay.' I agreed, 'I'll hop over the fence and get closer to the house.'

Goulburn went around to the front.

As he disappeared around the corner, I scaled the fence and dropped down on the other side. There was a small outside toilet where I took cover and waited. I then went from the shed to the back door and hoped "neighbourhood watch" were not active in this part of town. I could hear music.

Goulburn had rung the bell and been greeted after his third attempt with an obscenity which requested him to 'Fuck off.'

He replied to the voice from inside.

'I'm looking for a mate,' he called.

'Go to the zoo,' a voice answered.

Goulburn stayed outside the front door for a few minutes and then moved off. He came back around to the alley.

I heard a voice and caught a glimpse of the author through the back–door window. I didn't recognise him; I reckoned he was alone otherwise there would have been an exchange of conversation and sounds that indicated the presence of others.

I couldn't be sure and wondered if I was camped outside the wrong house. There was no way of knowing; I had to go in.

Goulburn had returned to the rear of the house via the alley and peered through the fence. He could see me crouched outside the back door.

Deuce had kept out of sight as much as possible with the knowledge that if Granston was inside the house and looked out he could have been recognised. He now joined Goulburn at the fence.

'Where is he?' Deuce enquired.

Goulburn nodded towards the house.

Deuce looked through the crack.

'What's he gonna do?' he asked.

Goulburn shook his head. 'I dunno. Maybe go in I guess.'

In the meantime, I'd checked the back of the building. There was a window, probably a bedroom, directly above a small conservatory. The opposite garden fence would provide a suitable point to climb and from there provide access to the room. I didn't know from where in the house the voice had come from. If they had my daughter, then they'd seen Goulburn quite clearly at the front and chose to recognise that the man was not a cop or any threat.

I reckoned that if they could see the front then they'd also keep an eye on the back. I had to cross in front of some French windows to get to the fence. Having already come over the back and up to the rear door unnoticed I reasoned I could probably make it to the other side of the yard, I made a dash, leapt onto the fence, and shinned up the conservatory.

Next door a dog, previously disinterested, began to bark furiously without warning as I contacted the fence and jumped up. He snapped and snarled; I balanced momentarily above him.

Deuce stepped quickly to the neighbour's fence to distract the animal. The dog raced down the path and began to bark at him.

He spoke a few words to the dog to encourage it to remain at the end of the yard.

I climbed as quietly and quickly as possible to the window; I looked in. A bed and a small chair, on the bed my daughter tied with her hands behind her back, naked except for a gag bound around her mouth. My heart sank. I was filled with rage and anxiety. Was I too late? Had Granston carried out his threat?

Clare lay perfectly still. The window was ajar, and I prised it further open until I was able to let myself in. I heard a television from downstairs and a cough, but no voices. I went from the window to the side of the bed and laid my hand on Clare's shoulder. She was shivering with cold; I shook her gently and whispered in her ear.

'It's Daddy. Everything is alright. I'm taking you home.'

I removed my shirt, draped it around her and quickly untied the bonds.

I purposely left the gag on her mouth as I was sure she would make some sound which could alert whoever was downstairs. I felt unkind because but knew it was in her best interest.

I carefully lifted her from the bed and made toward the window. Her eyes were open, but she remained perfectly still, I leaned through the window, sat her down on the roof and told her not to move. I joined her, picked her up and descended.

Goulburn had seen her placed on the roof and the start of my decent. He called to Deuce.

'He's got her,' he said.

Deuce came to his side. 'Yeah?'

'I'm goin' in,' Goulburn stated.

'Poor little cow,' Deuce commented as his companion heaved himself over the fence.

Barrel was the only occupant of the house, Granston and Green had gone to the Cross to follow up an address that Jason had given them in the hope of obtaining a gun. Clare had been left in his care while they were away.

I could only assume Granston felt secure in the knowledge that the police made no connection with this place in Newtown and himself.

Barrel had been concerned when Goulburn had knocked on the door but when he saw it was an Aboriginal, he relaxed, more irritated at the interruption of his meal. He was sat in the front room and had a limited vision of the back door and yard; thus, I was able to scale the fence unnoticed.

The dog continued to bark with increased frenzy as I climbed down from the roof. The racket caused Barrel to rise from his chair and go toward the back door. He caught sight of Deuce as Goulburn opened the gate to let him in.

'Fuck you,' he muttered and picked up a baseball bat from the corner of the room, he rushed outside.

The backdoor crashed open, and they were confronted by the sight of the large man with red beard and wild red hair, a baseball bat in his right hand and a look of disdain on his face.

'What do yer want youse little bastards? Come to nick something 'ave youse?'

Deuce felt his bowels contract and Goulburn's knees weakened a little.

'Come on, then,'

'I'm lookin' for a mate. I told yer. I thought he lived here,' Goulburn stammered somewhat unconvincingly.

'Yeah? Well, no fuckin' Abbos live here.'

I heard the back-door crash open and saw Barrel face my two companions and remained where I was to figure out the best course of action.

I squeezed Clare and whispered in her ear. The little girl was motionless, her blind eyes stared blankly ahead, and the constriction of the tape wrinkled her face.

'Soon be okay, darling,' I soothed, 'soon be home.'

Goulburn shouted to Deuce, 'Run for it!' The two men turned and raced back down the yard threw open the gate and hurtled through, chased by Barrel who swung the baseball bat wildly to catch them.

They raced up the alley, Barrel in pursuit.

I took my chance, quickly threw Clare over my shoulder in a fireman's lift and dropped down onto the fence, my one free hand as my support, the dog, who had barked throughout the whole escapade, increased its intensity as my foot touched the fence and I dropped to the ground on the opposite side. I carefully eased Clare down, pulled the tape from her mouth, and at the same time tried not to hurt her. The little girl said nothing, and I thought the worst. She must be in shock, poor little kid.

My hatred of Granston rose to new heights but I controlled my anger to escape and get my daughter to safety. I faced a dilemma; I could either go through the house or through the gate. I had no idea if there was anyone in the building or for that matter where Barrel was. I decided to go for the gate and lead her by the hand, but because she was barefoot had to carry her. I was about to go through when the shape of Barrel blocked my path. The sight of me in front of him with Clare caught him totally off guard.

He let out a yell and stood rooted to the spot.

'Where do yer think yer goin'?' he boomed and swung the bat.

My main concern was for my daughter, and I hastily pushed her away as the bat prescribed an arc towards my head. Clare crashed into the side fence and sank down. I heard her cry as I ducked; the bat sailed over my head with a distinct rush of air. I shot a quick glance in her the direction. My mind raced, I had to draw Barrel away from her. He went toward her. I pursued him and stopped when he turned to face me. The man stood undecided, whether to grab the girl or deal with me. He knew who I was, having heard about me from Green and Granston but had total confidence in his own prowess and even more so with the feel of the baseball bat in his hand.

He decided to deal with me. I stepped back to face him.

'I'm gonna break yer head,' Barrel scowled.

I walked back to lead him away from my daughter; she stirred momentarily, then remained still and sobbed. The dog continued to bark, and I saw two figures behind Barrel come through the gate. Barrel continued his advance.

I shouted, 'grab Clare,' and tensed ready to take the initiative.

Deuce stepped forward and bundled the small girl in his arms as Barrel swung round and caught sight of him.

'Yer fuckin' shit,' he snorted and lumbered toward Deuce who was trying to go through the gate.

I ran forward and punched Barrel in the kidneys. The movement of the man in the same direction as my punch lessened the effect but still caused him considerable discomfort. He gave a groan of pain and turned to face me.

His eyes filled with hatred, he gritted his teeth, a vein stood out in the centre of his forehead and accentuated his formidable appearance. He said nothing, grunted, then lumbered towards me. He had taken two steps when he let out a cry, stumbled forward and dropped the baseball bat. Goulburn had hurled a large stone with considerable force at the man's head and struck him at the base of the skull.

Barrel's eyes lost their anger and began to glaze momentarily.

I ran forward and smashed my instep into Barrel's groin then followed it up with a straight punch to the throat. He gurgled, slumped back, and collapsed to the ground like some drunken elephant.

Deuce had taken Clare from the garden and tried to reassure her as best he could. She still cried but her blindness made her like some hooded bird of prey and curtailed her movements; she made no attempt to escape. Bewildered, terrified, thirsty, and carried in the arms of a person she could only smell.

Deuce, aware his breath might not be so good endeavoured not to breathe over her. She was heavy for him, but he ran as fast as he could down the alley. The utility was a hundred yards or so away.

Confident Goulburn and I could deal with Barrel he strove to get Clare to safety regardless; he reached the Ute, opened the door, climbed in, and placed the little girl on the seat next to him. She continued to sob; a bruise began to show on the side of her face where I had pushed her into the fence.

'Come on kid. Yer okay now. Don't worry.'

'I want my Mum. I want my Mummy,' Clare sobbed and rubbed her eyes.

'It's okay,' Deuce soothed. 'Soon you'll be with yer mum.'

He took the small girl's hand, rubbed it gently, and pulled my shirt around her frail body as he spoke.

'Yer dad will be here soon, sweetheart. Then we'll go home.' Deuce had two daughters of his own; hadn't exactly been a model father and spent most of his free time in pubs or "worked away" while his kids grew up. He retained a strong belief in his culture but fell short in the practice. He looked at the small girl draped in the oversized shirt, her eyes filled with tears; his thoughts went to his own daughters and the grandchildren he'd never seen.

"I must do that; I must go up north."

His thoughts were interrupted, a Ford Falcon cruised slowly up the street. Deuce had ever been mindful of Granston and what would happen if he showed up, he viewed every car with suspicion. The lank dark hair of the man in the rear–view mirror of the Ute was easily recognisable; Deuce put his arm around Clare.

'Get down kid.' He pushed the little girl forward.

'It's okay, kid, don't worry. It's some people we don't want to see. It's okay.'

He tried to reassure her as she once more found herself in a position of discomfort in the presence of a strange man. She had no idea of events outside of the Ute or of where she was and endured yet another experience far removed from her once protected world of teddy bears and kindergarten playgrounds. She gave way to her emotions and began to scream hysterically. Deuce clamped his hand firmly over her mouth and forced her down.

'It's okay kid, believe me, I'm not going to hurt yer. I'm yer dad's mate. It's okay, just be quiet. Be quiet for a second, okay?'

Granston and Green cruised alongside the utility and then for no apparent reason took off up the street and out of sight. Further down the road a car started its engine.

Deuce watched Granston's car take the corner and peered cautiously over the dashboard of the utility until they were out of sight. He didn't trust Granston. Why had the car suddenly taken off?

He released his grip over Clare's mouth, and she gave vent to her hysterics.

'It's okay. No-one's gonna hurt yer.'

His words seemed to have no effect on the little girl's emotional condition, and she continued to scream. Deuce was at a loss what to do. It didn't look good to anyone who passed for him to be alone with this small white girl and her in hysterics. He tried to quieten her. The noise would draw attention to them if it hadn't already.

He stretched across her and wound up the window as a face appeared in the frame.

Deuce was taken by surprise and gave a sigh of relief when he saw it was me. The door opened on the other side and Goulburn jumped in. I reached in and took Clare's hand.

'It's me, Clare,' I said. 'It's me.' Deuce moved over; I put her on my knee.

'Let's get out of here,'

Goulburn turned the keys and the Ute raced off down the road.

'Swing a right, don't go left.'

'Why's that?' Goulburn asked, and flicked the indicator switch to the right.

'Granston and Green,' Deuce replied.

I sat next to Deuce and hugged Clare as I tried to calm her. She had her face pressed to my shoulder and her cries had abated from hysteria to intermittent sobs.

'Where?' I asked.

'They came down the road and then took off for no reason that I could see.' Deuce replied.

Chapter Sixteen

Sixteen - Cold blooded murder

Granston had a gut feeling that something was wrong and, like Deuce, had a built-in survival instinct.

He took no chances and chose to drive by, stopped next to a phone booth; entered and picked up the phone. The phone rang unanswered for a minute before Granston slammed down the receiver. He returned to the car.

'What's up?' Green enquired.

'I dunno. That fat arsehole's not answering or he's off his face. I got the feelin' somethin's up. Let's take a drive.' Granston climbed back into the car.

·············

I managed to calm my daughter although she still cried for her mother.

'How is she?' Deuce asked.

'I dunno,' I replied.

'Did Granston...'

Deuce didn't know how to phrase the question, but I understood what he implied and saved him the trouble.

'We'll find out after a doctor's seen her, I guess.'

'Where do yer wanna go?' Goulburn asked.

'It'll have to be the cops,' I said.

Deuce looked at me. 'Is that wise?' he asked.

'I've no choice. This kid needs her mother and protection and to see a doctor. Maybe Granston will try again.'

'Which one?' Goulburn asked in relation to the whereabouts of police stations.

'George Street, I guess. That's where that Jackson cop's based.'

Goulburn nodded and headed toward the city centre. As we drove past Sydney University and into Broadway, I held my daughter to me. Her hair blew into my face from the open window; I kissed the top of her head and spoke softly.

I wanted to ask her what had happened, if the repulsive Granston had touched her in any way, but I held back. This wasn't the time or place, and specially trained counsellors had the technique and experience to cause less trauma than my emotionally motivated questions.

The Ute pulled up in George Street. 'You'd better not come with me,

thanks for your help. I owe you.' I addressed Goulburn, 'Can I give you some cash for petrol?'

'No worries, mate,' Goulburn responded and patted my shoulder.

'Take care of her and watch out for Granston.'

'Yeah.'

I turned and carried my daughter across the busy road and into the entrance of the police station, giving a quick glance over my shoulder in time to catch a farewell wave from Deuce.

The officer on the reception was a woman of about thirty; she regarded me with curiosity as I approached.

'Yes, sir, how can I help you?' The police officer calmly enquired.

'I want to see Sergeant Jackson, please.'

'In respect to what, sir?' the woman asked.

'In respect that this is my daughter she was kidnapped, possibly molested and infected with HIV, and I've just got her back.'

The woman looked at me, I stood naked to the waist with intensity in my eyes and held a small girl draped in a shirt, obviously distressed.

'You'd better come through, sir,' the officer lifted the counter to allow me access.

I was shown to a room with green vinyl covered benches and a table in the middle.

'Take a seat and there'll be someone down in a minute.'

'Please tell Sergeant Jackson that my wife needs to know what's happened.'

Ten minutes later Jackson arrived. He had been out on a call and had come back straight away when he got the message. Sally was also on her way over. Another police officer, a woman, had come down from upstairs and spoken to Clare who was provided with a fruit juice drink and some lollies. A doctor had also carried out a preliminary examination to ascertain her standard of general health and she' been given a blanket to keep her warm.

'How did you know where your daughter was?' Jackson asked.

I told him the address but failed to give him the whole story as to how I had come by it. Jackson knew that there were holes in my statement but did not press the point. A team was immediately sent to Newtown with a search warrant but found no trace of Barrel or Granston, only Clare's dress which confirmed my story.

I heard Sally's voice outside the door; she appeared a second later, breathless and flushed. She ran to Clare, picked her up and smothered her in her embrace as she showered kisses of relief onto her head and face. Clare hugged her mother in return and began to cry.

I said nothing but regarded the picture of maternal love relieved that at least they were reunited. I still felt sick in my stomach when I thought about what might have happened and whether Clare had been interfered with or not. She seemed alright on the surface and had relaxed considerably with the woman Police officer, even asking about her dog on a couple of occasions whether the Police had found him.

What was going on in her head and how much the experience had affected her I had no idea. I approached Sally.

'I'm sorry Sal, about all this.'

Sally looked at me, I was naked to the waist, my head bowed and my eyes tired and strained. I felt as though I had aged since I last saw her, and the spring was gone from my step. She regarded me with a touch of pity, or was it disdain?

'Tony just please go away.'

I'm sorry Sa......

'Just go away!' My father is in hospital and my daughter.... God knows what could have happened.... Just go please.

I felt helpless. I wanted to be a source of comfort to my wife, but my presence accentuated her discomfort; I was responsible for all that had happened. I left the room and answered a few more questions from Jackson.

'I told you, leave Granston to us. We'll get him. We've got people watching his brother's place and his Newtown address. If he goes to either one, we'll have 'im.

Pick up your shirt from the desk then get out of here.'

When the counsellor questioned Clare, the small girl gave nothing away. She would not speak about what had happened at the house and just moved her head up and down and side to side.

A further, more thorough examination was given in hospital and showed evidence of bruising around her lower regions, but she could go home.

A cop had been assigned to stay at the house until Granston had been captured and Clare would undergo further tests and questions when she felt less traumatised.

I left the Police station and made my way back to my apartment, punctuated by glances behind me.

I thought about my daughter and the fact that she'd asked about her dog. I wondered about her mother's attitude and new-found religious beliefs, the events of the last few days, of Ron in hospital, his kindness in the past and his love for his granddaughter, the implications of Clare being infected with HIV and the shock of her kidnap. I felt no enthusiasm for the future and for the first time in my life had no desire to live. Even when I was in prison, I still had hope.

But now life seemed altogether meaningless, without purpose, and only bringing pain to those who deserved it least. Talk about Karma; fuck me, I must have done something bad in a previous life.

I reached my flat and checked the cotton. It was still intact, entered, flopped onto the sofa and stared into space.

In the bedroom I searched through my bag and pulled out an address book; thumbed through the pages, found the one I wanted, picked up the phone and punched out some numbers. A voice answered and repeated them.

'Hello, mate,' I said.

'Tony,' the voice responded.

'Are you out? Where are you?'

It was the familiar voice of Rochester. 'I'm in Sydney,' I replied.

'Just thought I'd let you know I'm around again.'

'When are you coming up to Queensland?' Rochester enquired.

'I've no plans just yet.'

'I'm, er... You wouldn't believe it; strangely enough I'm coming down to Sydney the day after tomorrow.'

'Great,' I replied. 'Well, look, I'll give you, my number. You can stay here if you want. It's okay. I've had a few problems but I'm getting sorted out.'

'No that's' OK. I'm fixed up with a hotel, the company's expense, tax deductible and all that stuff but give me your number and we'll get together. How are things? Also, funnily enough an old friend of yours, well I say old, I really mean an extremely attractive friend, is in Sydney for a month.' Rochester went on.

'Oh yes, who?' I had already guessed who it was from Rochester's description.

'Satchiko,' he continued.

'Oh, that's nice. I had a feeling that he wanted to play cupid. Please give her my love.'

'I'll do that. She's out with Akiko now. Gone to some Japanese book shop, look, I'll talk to you when I see you. Catch up on all that's happened. Be great.'

'Yeah, it'll be good.' I agreed.

'Please call me. Bye.' I replaced the receiver. Rochester, my dear friend, I needed someone to talk to and he had a down to earth, if not comical, approach to life that I had always found lifted my spirits.

The phone rang and caught me off guard. I took a deep breath and picked up the receiver. I listened and waited for the caller to speak. A voice at the other end said,

'It's Goulburn, about your dog. I'll pick you up tomorrow night at seven thirty. That's if you're still interested.'

I told him I was.

'How's yer kid?' Goulburn enquired.

'I don't know yet. There are signs of, you know, but whether she's infected or not is another thing.'

Goulburn didn't comment. There was nothing he could say.

'I'll see yer tomorrow,' he replied. I confirmed the time and replaced the receiver.

Simpson had been washing up when he heard his two-way radio crackle into life.

'Kings Cross two, 18 Gowrie Street Newtown, neighbours report incident, man injured, known associate Paul Granston, over.'

'Roger that Kings Cross two, over.'

Simpson hastily dried his hands and grabbed his car keys.

Granston had tried to get through to his home several times but with no response; eventually he had called his brother who told him that the cops had been around, asked questions and that the place was watched. The lank haired man scowled and went back to the car where Green sat behind the wheel. He pulled from his pocket a small piece of paper along with some tightly wrapped silver foil. He folded the paper, opened the foil, and poured the contents onto the paper.

Pressed one finger against his right nostril and sucked the powder up his left.

His eyes watered and his facial muscles relaxed he sat in the car next to Green and became highly animated.

'Drive back around the block near my place,' he hissed.

'Why don't we just blow this shit 'ole? Go up Queensland. We're pushing our luck here, Gran.'

'Do as I fucking say.' He screamed.

'I've got one more thing to do before I piss off. Don't go down Gowrie Street. Just stop at the car park. We need a different car.'

The two men pulled up at a shopping precinct car park and left the Falcon.

Granston nodded in the direction of a late model BMW.

'That'll do us.'

He forced down the driver's side window and set off the alarm, slipped into the driver's seat, pulled the bonnet catch, quickly got out, raised it, and silenced the alarm with a pocketknife. He had had experience of car alarms in the past. Technology had changed considerably over the last ten years, but he had kept up with it whilst in prison from "experts" and treated it as a necessary talent for when he got out.

Granston had nerves of steel and all the while the alarm blared, he remained calm and confident, most likely due to the cocaine. Green on the other hand had succumbed to nervous twitches, he felt uncomfortable and cast several glances over his shoulder. Granston forced the steering lock, broke it, and hotwired the ignition in the space of a few seconds.

'Here, you drive,' Granston said.

The car burst into life, accelerated out of the car park and on to the road.

'Stop at the top of Gowrie,' Granston mumbled. He peered down the street as he spoke.

Green slowed to a halt, a car behind blared its horn.

'Get fucked!' Green screamed out of the window as the driver of the car mouthed abuse as he overtook them.

Granston ignored it and squinted intently down the road at an unmarked police car.

'Too many fuckin' aerials on that car. Cops. I can almost smell the bastards,' he muttered. 'Let's get out of here.'

Green willingly complied and the car accelerated up the street.

Simpson had raced to Gowrie Street. He thought it highly unlikely that Granston would return but wanted to check the place out and if necessary, come back and wait. He knew that Granston was no fool although he could be reckless and there was a slim, a very slim chance he would return for some reason or other. Simpson wearing a broad brimmed hat and scarf had parked when he heard the horn of the driver behind Green.

He cast a glance at the BMW as it drove past and sat for a minute or two before it dawned on him that it looked like Granston in the car. He couldn't believe it.

He had to find out whether it was him and went in pursuit. The BMW turned the corner further up the road.

Where to?' Green asked. 'Queensland?'

'Not yet. Just a quick visit to the free mason.'

Granston pulled a revolver from his pocket and spun the chamber to check the number of bullets.

'A very quick visit.'

The journey took fifteen minutes; it was dark when the two men arrived. The Holden kept a respectable distance behind Green and had remained unnoticed in the dusky light.

Green had turned the corner into the street.

'Shit!' Granston exclaimed. He had caught sight of a car parked outside my flat and a man sat in the driver's seat.

'Cops! Fuckin' Cops! They're all over the poxy place!'

Simpson came around the corner and caught sight of the halted BMW; he was taken by surprise and drove quickly past. He still wasn't sure it was Granston but couldn't risk getting too close to find out so pulled into a parking space behind the cop car, unaware it was police.

He turned off his ignition and observed Granston and Green in his rear mirror.

Camileri had staked out the house on the hunch that Granston would show and noticed the Holden pull up. He watched Simpson in the rear-view mirror; and wondered why he appeared to be nervous for some reason. Camileri got out of his car and walked back to the Holden.

The old man saw him coming and hastily threw his coat onto the back seat to cover the two-way radio.

Camileri knocked on the car window and flashed his badge; Simpson wound it down.

'Evening, sir. Are you alright?'

'Er, yes, perfectly officer,' the old man retorted.

'May I see your licence please sir.'

'What for?' the old man questioned and then added, 'er, yes of course.' He fumbled in his jacket pocket.

Camileri waited whilst the old man went delicately through the garment on the back seat.

'Live around here do you, sir?'

'Er, no. As a matter of fact, no.'

'Visiting friends are you, sir?' Camileri continued.

The old man was caught off guard and had no idea what to say. He desperately tried to think of an excuse as to why he had stopped.

'No. I, er, I didn't feel particularly well. I stopped for a moment just to rest, and I thought I recognised someone I knew.'

Camileri looked through the old man's licence and handed it back. 'That's okay, Mr Simpson,' Camileri said.

'Is there anything wrong officer?' he enquired.

'No, nothing at all, sir,' the Policeman answered.

'Well, I'm feeling a little better. I'll be on my way.'

Granston and Green had observed the proceedings.

They were too far away to discern Simpson's features and could tell only that it was a man in a hat.

'What now Gran?

'Shut up and let me think.' Granston caressed the pistol and stared blankly through the windscreen. '

We don't know for sure he's in there' Granston said. 'This is getting fuckin' annoying. I need to get that little shit, but I want to do it my way.' He continued.

'That pig sitting in that cop car has to be dealt with.'

Camileri strolled back to his car as Simpson, drove off.

Granston wondered who was in the car but was unsure whether it had any connection with me.

'Fuck him, pull up alongside the cop.' Granston ordered. Green started the car; the engine coughed into life. The sound caused Camileri to glance casually in their direction.

'Do it!' Granston yelled. 'Pull up alongside him.'

Green yanked on the wheel of the car and the tyres screeched as it swept past on the opposite side of the road then did a U- turn. Camileri saw the car pull up alongside him, but Granston had ducked down out of sight, Green lowered the window,

Camileri leaned across and lowered his. He stared curiously at Green; instinct told him that something was wrong. His realisation came too late. Granston, gun in hand, sprang up like some evil Jack-in-the-box and grinned at Camileri. Green turned his face and clapped his hands over his ears as Granston pulled the trigger. Camilleri's expression changed to a look of horror and his hand went involuntarily to his face to protect himself.

The bullet slammed through his palm, through his head and out into the wall of a house in the direct line of fire.

Granston whooped at the top of his voice.

Yes!! take that yer stinky grunter, fuck you fuck you.' Green started to pull away.

'Wait' Granston hollered 'Stay here keep the car running. I'm gonna pay a visit.' Granston was almost maniacal.

'Fuck Gran we can't stay here. It's crazy.'

'Fuckin' shut up and wait!' he screamed.

The shot motivated me to race to the window and I caught sight of Green behind the wheel of the BMW, also the unmarked cop car with Camileri slumped forward over the steering wheel. I glimpsed Granston leave the car and realised he must be on his way up: he had a gun. I ran to the bedroom opened the window and quickly hid in the wardrobe. Seconds later I heard his footsteps on the stairs and then his boot kicked the door open. He scanned the flat before he came into the bedroom and made for the window.

He searched the ground below through the branches of the tree for any trace of me. The sound of a police siren prompted him to leave. A stream of profanity followed before he turned and raced out.

Green had become anxious; several people peered from nearby houses as Granston raced down the stairs and into the car. Green pushed his foot hard down on the accelerator, burnt rubber and roared up the street.

The fact that a cop had been murdered seemed to have no effect on their emotional state.

'That little prick did a runner out the window.' Granston snarled.

'What are we gonna do, Gran?' Green asked.

'We'll check into a hotel up the Cross, blow him away tomorrow and then go to Queensland,' Granston replied.

'Why don't we just go now?' Green asked although he already knew the answer.

·········

Simpson had reached home, driven into his narrow driveway and switched the engine off, tired and shaken. It had been a fruitless day; his chest had begun to give him discomfort and he needed to take a tablet.

He went into the bathroom, took a bottle of pills from the cupboard, unscrewed the cap, placed one on his tongue, and cupped some water in his hand to help the pill down. His reflection looked back at him, his lined face, and tired eyes a product of his recent lack of sleep.

The news of Camileri's death crackled from his two-way radio with the mention of Paul Granston as a suspect.

'You bastard,' he muttered. 'you bastard.'

Earlier I had climbed out from the cupboard, relieved to hear their car depart. Within minutes the place was alive with cops, and I knew that soon I would hear heavy boots on the stairs. I didn't have to wait long.

The front door on one hinge flew open, Sergeant Jackson burst in.

He stood and glared at me.

'What's going on?' I asked.

'Don't come the innocent. You know what, one of my police officers has just been murdered in cold blood outside your flat.'

'I'm really sorry to hear that.'

I didn't have a great deal of affection for Camileri, but I didn't wish him dead.

Jackson seemed to soften and sat down on a nearby chair, obviously upset.

'It was Granston,' I said.

Jackson looked at me.

'It's obvious his main objective is to kill you.'

I got the impression that Jackson would not have been overly bothered if Granston had shot me instead of his partner. He picked up my keys from the table as he spoke and played with a wooden carved monkey that hung from the ring.

'Have you any idea where this man is?

I shook my head, 'No. I'm sorry.'

He stood up. 'Your daughter wasn't raped if that's any consolation.'

I felt relief but was still concerned about Granston's threat to infect her with his blood.

Jackson continued.

'I know it's been pretty rough for you over the last few days and life hasn't been exactly handing out cookies, but leave Granston to us. If you hear anything tell us about it. I know that probably goes against the grain but it's the only way.'

'Have you got kids?' I asked.

'Yeah. I've got a son and a daughter.' Jackson shook his head.

'I know what you're going to say. Sure, I'd feel the same, but it's not the way.'

I turned and faced him.'

'You say that after one of your men has just been killed? I'm sorry I don't have much faith in the law or justice. When I was younger my father brought me up to believe that if you did something wrong you got punished and that cops were the good guys and crooks the bad ones. It's not that black and white. It's all bullshit.

Yeah, sure I'm bitter. I went inside for five years for defending myself. If they'd have beaten me up and left me in the gutter or killed me, what then? They'd have got off with it, a sad childhood or some fuckin' lame bullshit connived by some overpaid barrister. Remember I used to be in the business.'

Jackson shook his head and sighed.

'I just thought I could appeal to your rationality. You'll end up inside again if you take the law into your own hands. I'll come down on you like a ton of bricks. This isn't some bloody stupid American movie where the hero metes out justice and leaves a trail of dead baddies and gets away with it. This is real life. Real life.' He repeated.

'So, face it. I know that it's like banging yer head against a wall sometimes, but there has to be rules or at least an effort to maintain them.' Jackson threw my keys onto the table and made for the door.

'I'm putting a man to watch your ex-wife and daughter and one here for one night. That's all I can do. Maybe be best to look for another place for a while.

'I can take care of myself.' I replied.

'Yeah, I heard,' Jackson said sarcastically. 'Maybe you should take a bit more care of other people.'

I felt that was a bit below the belt.

Jackson noticed the sudden flash in my eyes.

'Ah, got through, did I? Good, if it concerns you, you can help more by being out of prison.'

There was a high-pitched ringing sound and Jackson reached into his pocket and pulled out his radio phone.

'Yeah, OK I'll be down in a minute.'

Jackson slowly retracted the small aerial of the phone and grasped the compact instrument tightly.

He gave another deep sigh and shook his head as his mind took in the full implications of the loss of his friend Camileri.

He closed the damaged door quietly and I heard his footsteps descend the stairs.

·········

I hardly slept that night as visions of Clare, of Granston, ran continually through my mind. At four o'clock I got up and practised meditation until the anxiety subsided to a level where I could exercise some reasonable control.

From within I sought to calm myself under adverse conditions, with the knowledge that to torture myself with negative thoughts was detrimental; I had fought my mind for most of the night before I finally decided to change the situation.

I sat for an hour and focussed my attention on a most beautiful place. I had done this many times whilst I was in prison and had become more at ease, and although the problems had not gone away, I felt more confident in my ability to handle them. When I switched on the light it was five thirty and still dark. The huge tree outside the bedroom window looked like some black statue risen from the earth, its serpent like branches twisted in all directions brushed against the glass. I decided to go for a run and later look at some furniture to replace the damage done by Granston.

The Police officer posted outside my house sat up when he saw me come out and stepped from the car.

Before he could say anything, I told him I was going for a run and would be about thirty minutes. I ran down the road; he decided it'd be better to watch my apartment than chase after me, double checked to see if there was anyone else in the vicinity, satisfied himself that he was the only one stupid enough to be awake at this time of day, apart from me, and got back into the car.

His radio microphone crackled as he reported my movements to cover himself in case I was gunned down whilst on my run.

Chapter Seventeen

Seventeen - A trip to the country

G ranston and Green had booked into a hotel at the Cross and hired a couple of girls for the night. Granston had no regard for his sexual partner, treated her as merely an object for his degraded lust and subjected her to various abhorrent acts before his twisted mind stimulated his ejaculation.

She was also at risk from the HIV virus, he cared little for his own condition and didn't want to know whether he was positive or not but knew the amount of infected blood pumped into his veins made it a near certainty he was.

An empty bottle of whiskey lay on the floor of his room; it was three in the afternoon when he heard the knock on the door.

The hotel was a cheap dive on the main street, he booked for two nights and had no intention to part with any money when he vacated.

Room service had knocked earlier and entered but left when she saw Granston still asleep.

Two hours later she came back into the room.

'Excuse me, sir.'

Granston prised open his eyes and focussed on the woman.

'What do yer want?' he growled.

'To change the sheets, sir,' she replied.

Granston shook his head. 'Oh, shit, what time is it?'

'Three o'clock, sir,' the woman replied.

Granston was still partly dressed, his lank greasy hair and unshaven face filled the girl with apprehension. She could sense the man was evil.

He had been out of prison for some time and obtained clothes from his brother but had worn the same socks ever since. There was a pungent odour of feet in the air which added to the unpleasantness of the girl's situation.

'Three o'clock.' Granston swung his legs over the side of the bed, stood up and tottered on unsteady feet into the bathroom; she heard him throw water over his face and then squat on the porcelain, He flushed the toilet and came out.

Without a word he put his shoes on, pulled his shirt over his tattooed body, and left.

He walked down the corridor for a few paces and banged on the door of room 201. There was no answer.

'Green!' Granston called. 'You up?'

Still no answer. Granston entered. The room was bare, and the bed made but no sign of Green or any of his clothes. Granston stopped in his tracks. 'Fuck!' he shouted and raced back to his room. The girl was about to change the sheets when Granston raced in.

'Just go outside for a minute,' he said to the girl.

'I'm nearly finished, sir.'

Granston glared at her. A cold flush of fear made her catch her breath and she hastily left. Granston lifted the mattress and felt for the pistol, located it, shoved the cold steel down the front of his trousers and pulled his shirt down to cover the handle. He left the room.

The girl waited in the corridor as Granston swept past and went downstairs to reception.

The bald man behind the desk chewed on a sandwich as he read a newspaper.

'Did my mate go out this morning?' Granston enquired.

The receptionist looked at Granston with equal apprehension.

'Er. Yes, he left about eight this morning, he said you'd pick up the tab.'

'The fuckin' shit.' Granston hissed.

The man said nothing; he surmised that any comment might add fuel to Granston's obvious displeasure at the news of his companion's departure.

Granston walked away from the reception, his head still foggy from the night before as he tried to think of his next move. His one objective remained unfulfilled and needed to be achieved. The car they'd left the night before was gone; Granston gave vent to a string of expletives and went in search of a telephone box. After a brisk walk down, the main street he located one.

He pressed several numbers and waited.

'Yeah?' a voice answered. It was Jason. 'I need some money,' Granston grunted.

'Yer fuckin' hot. Just lay low. Just cool it and I'll get back to yer,' Jason replied.

'I need some money, Jase. I'm fuckin' off real soon but I need some bread.'

Jason recognised his brother's tone of voice. He knew he was in a reckless mood and totally out of control, but he was still his brother.

'Okay, I'll meet you at the usual place.'

The usual place was a coffee shop not far from the hotel where Granston had stayed. 'Half six.'

'Half six?' Granston replied. 'Why so long?'

'I've got something to do. I can't make it earlier. Take it or leave it.'

Granston contorted his face.

'Okay, okay, half six,' he repeated and hung up.

He had fifty dollars and decided to go and eat then get himself a car to travel.

·········

In the meantime, I had been busy, visited two big stores and wandered around the furniture and electrical departments before I decided what to buy.

I put down a deposit, arranged a delivery date and hoped there'd be no repetition of Granston's visit. I called Sally and wanted to speak to Clare, but she didn't want to speak to me. I was hurt she felt that way but could understand. Sally on the other hand, to my surprise, despite everything, although lacking any warmth in her voice, told me to be patient as Clare was still upset.

I said it was OK but feared she would associate me with her unpleasant experiences; Sally assured me that she was reticent now with everyone except her. I asked how Ron was and brightened up when I heard he'd regained consciousness and on the mend.

'I'll drop in and see him as soon as I can.'

'Leave it for a day or two. He's still very weak. I'm going over myself later but only for about ten minutes. I'm taking Clare,' Sally said.

'Please give him my best,' and then I remembered. 'Oh, Rochester's coming down to Sydney.'

'Great, when?' Sally asked.

'In a couple of days, he's going to call me.'

'Please give him a hug for me.'

'I will,' I replied. 'I'll call you tomorrow and see how Clare is... Is that cop there?'

'Yes, he's here and Dad's being watched at the hospital. Terrible thing about that police officer.'

'Yeah,' I replied. 'I'll be in touch,'

I returned from the department store and stopped on the way home to have a bite to eat at a Japanese noodle bar; it reminded me of my time spent in Tokyo. I spoke to the waitress briefly in Japanese and realised how much of the language I'd forgotten; also saddened by the knowledge I had a criminal record and couldn't return to Japan and work, unless of course I got a fake passport. "It's a possibility." I mused. I had enough contacts to get a phoney one but what was the point? I'd have to start all over again.

The waitress's looks reminded me of Satchiko, and I wondered if she would contact me.

It had been over six years; it would be nice to see her; surely, she must have married. Maybe she had come to Australia with her husband.

I felt alone and down as I left the restaurant still absorbed in my thoughts; I checked my watch and remembered my meeting with Goulburn at seven thirty.

By seven o'clock I was back at my apartment, got changed and told myself I must get back to some serious exercise, weight work outs, and fix up a start date at Jimmy's boxing gym.

Granston, meanwhile, had met his brother Jason and been given two thousand dollars.

'You shouldn't 'ave shot that pig. That was stupid.' His brother admonished.

'I'm goin' up north,' Granston explained.

'Good move.'

'But I'm gonna fuck that bald-headed little shit up before I go.'

'Leave it out. Forget about 'im, yer pushin' yer luck just being around here. Forget it,' Jason argued.

'Forget it?' Granston scowled. 'He stuck me with an HIV syringe. He busted my jaw and my arm and yer say just forget it.'

'Look, fuckin' leave it for a bit. Maybe six months, he'll relax his guard and then bingo, no worries. Now every bloody grunter is out lookin' for yers.'

Granston could see the logic in his brother's argument but was driven by fanatical hatred. Besides, in six months he may not be capable of much at all.

'They've been watching me. I had to play it close to the wall to meet yer here.' Jason muttered.

'It's too risky. Take my advice and go now.'

Granston stood up from the table. 'What's the time?' he said.

'Quarter to seven,' Jason answered.

'I'm off. I'll see yer.' Granston walked away.

Jason remained at the table and watched his brother go before he himself rose, paid the cashier, and left.

Granston had walked up and down Victoria Street before he chose a two-seater Honda sports. It was comfortable, fast, and ideal for the drive to Queensland. Within two minutes he was behind the wheel heading down William Street, his left hand rested on the revolver tucked down the front of his trousers.

He pulled it from his belt and laid it on the seat beside him. It was seven twenty.

·········

I'd had a shower and fixed a temporary bolt on the door when Deuce arrived. I was surprised to see him.

'I didn't reckon on you coming with us,' I remarked.

'Goulburn can't make it, but he's given me all the crap to get in and he's leant me the Ute.'

'That's good of him; do you know where it is?' I asked.

'It's outside where I parked it,' Deuce grinned at his own joke. 'Yeah, about an hour and a half out west, I got a rough idea where it is.'

' What time does it start?'

'About half eight. How's the kid and yer mate?' Deuce asked.

'She's a bit better but she didn't want to talk to me,' I answered.

'Probably thinks it's all yer fault what happened to her.'

'Thanks, that makes me feel much better,'

Deuce raised his eyebrows and shrugged.

'She'll handle it. Yer just have to hang in there.'

I looked at my ex-cell mate, said nothing, pushed the front door open and gestured he go first. He complied and went down the steps as I fixed the cotton.

Simpson's car needed a service He glanced at the Holden then went to the rear of his yard and pulled the cover off a red 1968 MGB. A present he had bought for his daughter and kept in perfect condition although he hardly ever used it, and then only at weekends.

He lifted the bonnet, reconnected the battery and turned the engine over, it was reluctant to fire up and sucked up what little power left in it. He disconnected the leads and carried the battery from his garage down to a service station a few metres from his house.

The sun shone from a brilliant blue sky although the presence of clouds warned possible change later in the day. A man in overalls worked on a car, the old man approached.

'Tom,'

The mechanic looked up. 'John, what brings you here, mate?' He looked at the Battery,'' 'Hang on, put it down here.' Tom removed a large spanner from the top of a work bench.

'Flat, is it?

Yes, 'It's from my MG, I was thinking I'd like to take it for a spin.'

Tom strolled over to the battery.

'It's been some time since you've used it, eh?' he enquired.

Simpson nodded 'Yes, though summer's coming and all that.'

Tom took the battery and tested it on an electronic device in the corner of his workshop. .

He came back and shook his head.

'What I would suggest John is that you get a new one. I could charge this one up but it's pretty old matey, like us, and it's not worth it.'

Simpson had known the mechanic for years and accepted his advice.

He returned home carrying a new battery.

Upon his arrival he went to a cabinet at the back of his garage, unlocked it and took out an object he hadn't used for years.

It was past seven thirty when Granston tentatively turned into Illawarra Road. He checked to see if there were any cops' cars parked in the immediate vicinity and caught sight of us coming in the opposite direction. He slammed on the brakes and did a three–point turn.

He wanted to be sure he could get close enough to kill me. His plan, to confront me when I left the car; to see my face as he pulled the trigger; take my life in the most unpleasant way, but necessity dictated that he must do it quickly.

He followed our utility but kept a comfortable distance behind, His original idea was to come alongside and fire a hail of bullets, but that had been dismissed as it could stand a chance of failure. Instead, he told himself to wait longer before he tasted the sweet fruit of vengeance.

The venue of the dog fight was at a place called Dural; forty–five minutes' drive from the city, depending on traffic. We stopped to buy some petrol whilst Deuce checked the Gregory's to locate the exact area.

The dog fight was held in a brick barn building that belonged to a local farmer who had an interest in the "sport."

Granston continued to follow us but had no idea where we were headed.

When we pulled in for fuel he'd stopped and was about to take his chance and drive into the petrol station, when a bloody great tanker pulled in from the opposite side and blocked his entrance. There were several other cars on the pumps which made a surprise confrontation and a quick getaway less likely. The tanker manoeuvred closer to deliver its load and lurched to a halt with a hiss of air brakes.

The driver climbed down from the cab and sauntered into the office. Granston decided to wait for a better opportunity. He parked a few yards down the road and waited.

Neither of us connected Granston with the convertible. We drove out of the garage and continued the journey; Granston waited to give us time to get ahead and then followed.

I had located the position of the farm on the map when a sign 'Shelly's Lodge appeared in the headlights. Deuce squinted into the blackness.

'There it is.' He indicated he was about to turn left.

I was thinking what I would do and how I would identify Bozo. To get her dog back would be something worthwhile for me. I'd told Deuce about the situation on the drive and he, whilst he wished to encourage me, secretly thought the whole episode was a long shot without any hope of a result but agreed to come along for support.

'You'll offer to buy the dog if yer sees it then?' Deuce asked.

'Well, I'll ask a few questions first,' I stated, 'and then see.'

Deuce looked at me. He could see the determined expression on my face that indicated there could be a few problems ahead.

A man was posted at the gate to the entrance of the farm and another at the entrance to the actual building. Both had two-way radios and spectators had to give a password before they could proceed. The man at the entrance to the farm driveway had a torch, waved us down and flashed it into Deuce's face, he wound down the window.

Deuce looked into the beam of light and put his hand up to shield his eyes.

'I'm a mate of Goulburn,' he said. 'Oh yeah, cherries,' he added.

The light momentarily shone on me and then clicked off. A voice spoke from out of the darkness.

'OK, mate, go up the drive and to yer left. There's a place to dump yer car by the barn.'

We continued up the drive.

Granston had slowed down and witnessed the procedure from two hundred yards down the road from the farm entrance. He could not discern any shapes, only the rear lights of the car and the flash of a torch. He reasoned that wherever our destination we had to pass some form of interrogation and he would be subject to the same if he wished to follow.

He waited until we'd gone up the drive and then drove on.

A torch was shone in his face in the same manner that we had been subjected. Granston wound down the window.

'I'm with them two,' Granston stated.

The person behind the torch looked closely at the man illuminated in the beam.

The shadows cast on his face by the light seemed to enhance the evilness of Granston and the cold cruel eyes that stared up from the car, as those of a shark about to tear a lump of flesh out of somebody.

'What's the word?' the man asked.

'Eh?' Granston enquired.

'The word, what's the password?'

Granston coughed. 'Er, do yer know I've fuckin' forgot. Er, Deuce told me.'

'Whose Deuce?'

'The bloke in that car. Shit, what is it?'

Granston assumed a puzzled expression as though he searched for something in his mind. He opened the car door and climbed out; the man stepped back.

'Just a minute I've got it here I wrote it down. Ah, here it is.' He pulled the pistol from the front of his trousers and pointed it at the man's head.

The man with the torch froze with terror as the gun was levelled at him.

'Turn around arse hole,' Granston ordered. The man did as he was bid; Granston slammed the pistol butt against his head with all his force. The man gave a gasp and fell to the ground. Granston stared down at the fallen gatekeeper and had to contain himself from emptying his gun into him. He then dragged the man's body and rolled it into a ditch. He got back to his car as a pair of headlights swung off the road and flashed into the driveway; he picked up the torch and stood in the way of the car as it approached, the driver wound down the window.

'Password,' Granston demanded.

'Cherries,' the driver replied and then asked in a casual manner, 'Where's Jake?'

'Went for a shit,' Granston replied. This seemed to satisfy the enquirer who wound up his window and continued. Granston watched the rear lights of the vehicle until it turned left into the car park. He climbed back into his car, drove up the path, reversed it, and parked close to the entrance in preparation for a quick getaway.

Deuce and I left the Ute and strolled over to the venue from where the sound of dogs could be heard. The car park was almost full, I was surprised at the amount of people who wanted to see such a spectacle and reminded of when I was in Japan and read about the Japanese fighting dogs, Tozas, who were treated like sumo wrestlers, the fights being legal and held once a year near the base of Mount Fuji. The dogs appeared before the contest draped in various ornate clothes and tapestries that indicated their heritage and prowess. The fights themselves, almost ritualistic, were not generally fought to the death, the animals renowned for their stoic silence throughout the battle.

I had little knowledge of the so-called sport but whether in Japan, Mexico, or Australia, I thought the idea of using animals to fight each other for entertainment was cruel and contemptuous.

A huge man stood in the doorway of the barn and barred our way.

'Cherries,' Deuce stated.

The man stepped aside. He was well built and wore a T-shirt which accentuated his muscular body. He had a confidence that bordered on arrogance and gave Deuce and I a cursory glance as we passed.

The building was partly filled with farm equipment and signs of recent agricultural activity which implied it was still used for its original purpose.

At one end, close to the entrance, a hundred and fifty or so people, mainly men, milled around a square arena designated as the space for the canine combatants. It consisted of a fenced off area of approximately a metre high and four metres square.

A line was drawn across the centre; two dogs were in the arena with four or five people in the "Pit." The dogs were leashed; the handlers talked among themselves.

I could sense the mood of anticipation in the crowd. It was the second fight of the evening; the previous match had been won after an hour and both dogs had suffered extensive damage. The square was blood soaked and a man cleaned up with a cloth. I wondered if we were too late but discovered the dogs had both been black in colour and small in stature.

I surveyed the room. Men stood in groups; some gesticulated as they recounted the previous bout. Money changed hands, a small bar at one end of the building, crude but adequate, dispensed alcohol. I took the photograph out of my pocket and studied it.

"Was this a fool's errand, had I subjected myself to something I held in disdain for nothing?"

A man with a brown dog entered the space; he was fair haired, about thirty-two, of medium build, wore a red sweater, and black trousers. His face was freckled, and he had the typical appearance of either a farmer or a builder's labourer.

Deuce had mingled with the crowd and made his way back to where I stood.

'Wanna beer?'

I shook my head.

'That dog over there, look at this what do you reckon?' I handed the photo to Deuce. He looked at the snap and then at the dog.

'Looks pretty much like 'im to me,' the Aborigine replied. 'But ...' He mused over the photograph again.

'I wouldn't like to put my life on it but, yeah, I'd say that's the same dog. Look on his nose. There's a black mark.'

I looked in the direction of the dog once more and then over Deuce's shoulder at the snap; took it back from him and stuffed it my pocket.

Water was sloshed over the dogs already in the "arena" and the animals towelled down after close inspection of the buckets that contained the liquid, a precaution against poison on their coats. The dogs were both in the region of thirty kilograms, each solidly muscled.

One was white; the other fawn with a trace of white on his face, the fawn dog's ears had been cropped which gave his head a square chunky appearance. He was a pit bull terrier descended from a line of dogs first introduced into Australia from America several years earlier and proven game in the pit. He was three years old and in peak condition.

The other dog was a bull terrier /pit bull cross, an equally impressive gladiator against pigs and other members of his own species. He was white and called Frisco, after a famous dog of the same breeding, "Frisco Sport" that fought in America and won many battles in the dog fight days of the early twentieth century.

The fawn dog, Tarquin, was encouraged by his owner to tear his opponent apart, the man squatted down and talked to the animal with the intensity of a second in a boxing ring. The dog, no doubt heard a string of sounds, but the intonation and volume indicated to the canine gladiator he was in favour and, like most of his breed, eager to please.

The two dogs were 'faced,' the handlers stepped out. All eyes turned to the pit.

As we watched I tried to think of the best way to retrieve Clare's dog.

Chapter Eighteen

Eighteen - A real dog's breakfast

G ranston left his car and followed the road to the barn; he'd kept to the side of the path and saw the bouncer at the entrance as he approached; cars were parked to the left of the building.

He had no idea he was at a dogfight; he'd heard dogs bark but assumed they were farm dogs reacting to the noise of so many people.

When he was within fifty yards, he took cover behind a tree to wait and watch before he made any move to discover what was going on. He reasoned whatever it was it was illegal, due to the security and use of a password. The lights of a car illuminated the driveway; he stepped back behind the tree. The driver parked the car walked over to the barn and delivered the required password; the doorman stepped aside.

The two dogs flew at each other across the pit and met in the middle. They ripped and slashed, gripped each other and shook with all their might once they got a hold.

They were both experienced fighting dogs, their lacerated heads, and torn ears the result of many such encounters. A lot of money had been bet on the outcome and their handlers shouted encouragement to their contestants from the side of the "pit." The crowd also egged the animals on. I was surprised at the ferocity and single mindedness of the dogs. Totally consumed in the task of defeating their adversary.

The fawn dog, Tarquin, sought a throat hold but Frisco was too wise for such a manoeuvre and lowered his head, clamped on Tarquin's shoulder, and wrestled him back into the corner. Every muscle of Frisco's body was visible through his fur; he shook his head to try to tear his opponents flesh away from the bone.

Tarquin fought back to hold his ground against the sheer power of the white dog's energy and sought a counter hold. Again, Frisco was aware of the fawn dog's strategy and turned his body away from the teeth of his opponent. Frisco was one of those rare dogs who was not only fast and strong but had a powerful bite, and a comparatively long neck which gave him good reach.

Pit bulls have great power in their jaws, that in combination with agility and strength are winning qualities.

I turned away as the dogs fought their way around the pit for another quarter of an hour, neither showing any sign of fatigue. Frisco still retained his grip, blood streamed down the flank of Tarquin mixed with Frisco's saliva. The white dog's hind legs tensed and heaved with all his strength; Tarquin slid back across the pit. Frisco was quick to take advantage and changed his grip from shoulder to throat and clamped onto his opponent's windpipe.

The fawn dog was in trouble, the whites of his eyes clearly showed. I felt pity for both dogs.

Frisco sensed victory and settled down to wait for his foe to collapse. The snarls and growls ceased, the only sound was Tarquin's distress as he gasped for breath, his lungs in need of the oxygen that Frisco's grip denied.

The crowd fell silent; Frisco's owner grinned at the spectacle of his dog killing another. I was about to do something foolish and jump into the arena when Tarquin's owner held up his hand in defeat. Frisco's owner acknowledged the submission and made his way into the pit. The "referee" indicated the bull terrier cross as the winner. The crowd murmured its approval, the dogs were separated with a break stick inserted into the side of the jaws.

Tarquin was still alive although would not have survived much longer. He was wet with the combined saliva of the two dogs, steam rose from his battered body, and he panted furiously to take in air.

He had a gash in his shoulder, and his jaw torn from the initial onslaught.

He was in a state of shock and dehydration. His future debatable; dogs that lose were not held in high esteem and if big money were at stake angry owners would take out their frustration on their dogs in the cruellest of fashion, another "admirable" characteristic of dog fights.

I thought the whole thing degenerate and cruel but at the same time admired the spirit and ability of the animals. The owners would insist their dogs loved to fight but failed to mention the trauma, shock and terrible wounds inflicted in the process, and the aftereffects as their dog lay collapsed on the ground in a desperate attempt to suck in oxygen, dehydrated and covered in deep lacerations. In a strange way I empathised with their determination and character. Perhaps they served to inspire me to fulfil the purpose of my being there.

Deuce had also watched and felt equal disgust.

'Let's get outa this fuckin' place, I don't like watching dogs tear each other up,' he muttered.

'OK Yeah,' I made my way over to where the fair headed man stood talking to two other "dog lovers."

Deuce watched me as I pushed my way through the throng of people gathered around the small arena.

'Shit, I shouldn't have said that.' Deuce mumbled to himself, knowing I was highly motivated and the man with the dog wasn't likely to just hand it over. He felt a contraction in his bowel and took a swig of beer before he tentatively followed me.

The fair headed man looked up as I spoke.

'Nice dog,' I remarked.

'Yeah,' the man replied and returned to the conversation with his companions.

'Where did you get him?' I continued.

The man looked at me, the two other men waited for the response of their companion.

'Eh?' he grunted.

'I was wondering where you'd get a dog like him.'

The man obviously thought I was an idiot but sensed there was something about me which prompted an answer.

'Ask around, grab a paper. Talk to the bloke over there.' He gestured toward a small weasel like character who spoke to a woman as he intermittently swilled a can of beer.

'Do you breed them?' I asked.

'No, mate, I don't.'

'How old is he?' I enquired.

'Not so old,' the man replied.

I looked down at the dog.

'Do you want to sell him?

The man grinned.

'Maybe in an hour or so, mate.' He turned to his companions who nodded in amusement. 'Maybe I'll give him to yer.' He yanked on the dog's leash and made his way through the crowd to the pit.

I followed and pulled the photograph from my pocket.

'Hang on, mate!' The man turned. I shoved the photograph under his nose.

'Is that the same dog?' I asked.

He cast a quick glance at the photograph.

'I dunno, is it?'

'Take a close look,' I instructed and held the photograph closer.

The man looked at the snapshot.

'No, mate, that's not Red,'

'I think it is,' I continued.

The fair headed man changed the hand that held the leash and faced me.

'Now look, mate. I don't know what you're on about so just leave it alone.

Okay? I'll talk to you later.'

The man turned to walk away.

I placed my hand on his shoulder and pulled him around.

'I'm saying that dog doesn't belong to you.'

The man became visibly agitated.

'Look, arsehole, I'm tellin' yer this dog is mine and I've got fuckin' papers. Now piss off.'

One of the men who'd acted as referee in previous bouts beckoned the fair headed man into the arena.

'Let me see the papers,' I stated.

'Are you fuckin' nuts?' the man replied. 'I don't carry no fuckin' papers around with me. Just piss off!'

The two men who'd previously spoken to him came up to me.

'What's up, Jim?' one of the men asked. Jim pointed towards me.

'This cunt is givin' me aggro.'

'Alright, mate, out.' said one of the men as he grabbed my arm.

No sooner had the hand touched me I dropped down and slammed my elbow into the man's ribs. He groaned, fell to the floor, and clutched his stomach. The second man lashed out at me and became the recipient of a block and a punch to his mouth that dislodged several teeth and sent him to the floor his face bloodied.

Jim turned and tried to run. I stepped forward and with a kick caught the man's leg, swept it from under him, he crashed to the floor. Several people in the crowd parted to allow him access.

The action of the fist fight had prompted the dog to look in the direction of the melee and lick the face of his previous owner as he hit the ground. I snatched the lead from him and led the dog away.

The organiser had witnessed the affray and sought the assistance of the bouncer posted on the door; he came in like some angry bear rudely awakened from winter's hibernation.

Deuce hovered around in the background, the adrenalin coursed freely through his veins as he witnessed my altercation with Jim and his colleagues and hoped against all odds that the rest of the spectators wouldn't realise what happened and side with the dog's owner.

Deuce made for the exit and kept a watchful eye out for Jim, who'd picked himself up from the floor yelled abuse as he made his way through the crowd toward us.

The bouncer barred my way.

'Where're yer goin'?' he asked.

'I'm taking this dog for a walk,' I replied.

The dog had at one time been in the hands of his "owner" then dragged away in another direction. At no time did the animal show any semblance of loyalty to Jim, who previously had control of him and seemed quite happy to go where he was directed.

The bouncer glared at me.

'Give me the dog,' he said and stretched out his hand.

I shook my head.

'I have no quarrel with you. This dog belongs to my kid and I'm taking it back to her.'

Jim reached the scene and sided with the bouncer. He made a grab for the leash, and I delivered a fast uraken, (back handed strike), to his jaw, he tottered back before he fell into the arms of one of the spectators.

The bouncer stretched out his arm to grab me; I deflected it and stepped to the side. The pressure of the crowd had begun to restrict my movements and I handed Deuce the dog's leash.

'Take him to the Ute,' I said hastily.

'Stay where yer are!' the bouncer ordered.

Deuce looked at the huge man and then at me. He didn't want to upset me, but the size and obvious strength of my adversary compelled him to wait until there was a more positive result from the disagreement.

Granston had remained by the tree and watched who went into the building. He witnessed the exit of Tarquin, wrapped in a blanket.

'Dog fightin',' he muttered.

He had no idea what my motives were and assumed it was purely entertainment value that had brought me so far out of town; he didn't connect Clare with my actions. He ran his hand through his lank greasy hair and fondled the handle of the pistol tucked in his trousers.

He contemplated his next move. Initially he'd decided to rush in, blast me and then retreat but changed his plan; he wanted to make me suffer, to savour the pleasure of seeing me writhe in agony and already decided upon which parts of my anatomy were to be his targets. The best way to achieve his objective was when the bouncer left the entrance door and went inside.

He stepped from the cover of the tree and walked towards the building.

Back in the barn I faced the bouncer.

'Look, I don't want trouble. I just want the dog.'

'If yer don't want trouble just give the dog back,' the bouncer argued.

'I'm sorry,' it belongs to my kid, and I can't let it get ripped up for the amusement of this lot.'

The bouncer lunged forward in another attempt to grab me; I surmised that he was strong, and I didn't want to go to the ground where I would be vulnerable from attack by any helpers. I brought my fist down with all my force on the man's enormous forearm and simultaneously snapped a back-hand punch to the bridge of his nose. Blood streamed from his nostrils onto his T-shirt. He was momentarily stunned but by no means out of the fight. He wiped his arm across his face, and I took the exposed stomach as an invitation to throw a side kick into his guts which sent him into a group of people directly behind him.

The man took several onlookers down with him as he fell, their bodies helped to cushion his fall. For a moment, confusion; people yelled and shouted as they tried to regain their feet.

Deuce made for the door and skirted around the affray as he led the dog away.

The bouncer, true to his title but as a recipient rather than the perpetrator, bounced up again. With the assistance of several arms, he staggered to his feet, winded by the kick.

His face was covered in blood; he moved forward; his eyes fixed on me.

'I said I didn't want trouble with you. Now let's call it a day, eh?' I coaxed.

The man had not only suffered physical assault, but his pride had been badly dented. He was about twenty-three years old, superbly fit and a black belt holder in two martial arts. He just couldn't believe that he was not capable of dealing with this puny upstart. He threw a kick. He was fast but I was faster. My timing was accurate and as the man raised his leg to execute a mawashi geri or round house kick, he found himself flat on his back, this time with a broken leg. I'd shot a stamp kick to the bouncer's support leg at the same time as he'd thrown the roundhouse, caught him on the knee and sent him straight down. It wasn't a spectacular technique but efficient. To use flashy techniques would be inefficient and impractical. Karate has always been about either avoiding a fight or if unavoidable, dealing with it in any manner that works. This time he didn't get up. The onlookers stood back as I walked toward the door.

The fair headed man had regained his senses, he nursed a bruise to the left side of his face; he screamed abuse as I left. Fortunately for me no one was, unlike their dogs, game enough to try and stop me.

Deuce had waited by the door, took a step through, and came to an abrupt halt face to face with Granston who stood, pistol levelled at his head.

Deuce froze.

My attention had been occupied with what was behind me rather than in front and I collided with Deuce. Granston caught sight of me, aimed the pistol and pulled the trigger. The blast from the gun caused several dogs, Bozo included, to bark furiously. I recognised the evil shape of Granston a fraction of a second before he raised the gun and took off like a rabbit. I barged my way through the mob to some doors directly opposite. Granston saw he'd missed and pushed his way through the crowd now in a state of panic after the gun shot. I had come up against the doors, too strong to kick down and securely padlocked.

I faced Granston, who made his way towards me to be sure of his target. Most of the punters had made a hasty exit when the way was clear behind him, and the sound of car engines reached my ears. Granston was cautious and shot occasional quick glances over his shoulder. Deuce took a step forward; Granston swung around and released another bullet.

I saw Deuce's heart sink and he probably felt violently sick, the bullet whistled past his head and thudded into the wall behind him. He turned and ran for cover.

A man dressed in a raincoat and a wide brimmed hat looking like someone from a Tarantino film entered as the crowd rushed to the door. He'd kept close to the wall as he edged his way along, it was Simpson.

Granston had almost come within range of me when I saw Simpson from the corner of my eye. Granston was too intent on his mission to notice him. He wanted to cripple me before the final shot. He'd wasted two bullets.

I dived to his left to run past him. He swung round.

'Yer dead shit man.' Granston's finger tightened on the trigger.

I rolled over and was back on my feet in a matter of seconds.

No time to think, there was a loud explosion and I watched in disbelief as Granston's head seemed to burst, particles of flesh and blood splattered in all directions, his hair straightened and resembled a red Indian puppet before he collapsed, his face distorted beyond recognition.

Simpson had pulled a sawn–off shotgun from beneath his coat and blasted Granston with both barrels, pellets had hit the walls opposite and created puffs of dust as they 'd struck the brickwork.

The few people who had remained in the doorway of the building scattered shouting and screaming as the shotgun blast reverberated in the enclosed area. I stayed put, Deuce had cautiously returned and released the dog when Granston first entered; he waited until he was sure the man was no longer a threat. Simpson stood stock still, the weapon in his hand held loosely down by his side. He took no notice as Deuce passed him; his eyes stared at the remains of the man he'd killed.

I'd recovered from the shock of Granston's attack and walked toward Simpson. I looked down at the body of my nemesis. The old man remained unmoved. The shotgun clattered to the floor.

'Are yer okay?' Deuce asked me.

'Yeah, no problems.'

He turned toward Simpson.

'Why did you do that?' he asked.

Simpson hung his head. 'I tried, I really tried.'

'Tried what? Deuce asked.

'To forgive.'

Deuce shot a glance at me.

"Fuck mate we gotta get out here quick. This is serious shit.'

Simpson had come to terms Granston was evil, a man beyond any redemption and needed to be eradicated. He was an ordinary decent sort, had worked as a clerk for the railways most of his life and lived with his wife for forty years before she died of cancer three years previously. Her death was tragic enough, but he carried an even heavier emotional burden, that of his daughter's demise.

He had used a double-barrelled shotgun kept in a cabinet in his garage. A family heir loom. It was over fifty years old, and the cartridges were detonated by two external hammers pulled back manually and released by the triggers as opposed to more contemporary weapons that had internal mechanism to discharge shot. He'd constructed near the cabinet at the back of the garage a small workshop, where he'd cut eighteen inches off the barrels, a crime to perform on such a precision crafted gun but easier to conceal.

His MG was parked outside my flat as he considered me to be the most likely one that Granston would go after. Unbeknown to Deuce and I he'd watched us leave then saw Granston follow. He took up pursuit, lost him around a bend not far from the destination but managed to see the Honda drive up the road and into the farms entrance.

When he heard the revolver go off, he'd thrown caution to the wind, rushed into the building and met several panic-stricken spectators on their way out. Seeing Granston with a gun pointed at me he discharged both barrels directly at his head.

I was still curious 'Why did you kill him?' I asked.

The old man slowly turned his face towards us.

'I did it for Jeanie,' he said quietly.

'Who's Jeanie?' Deuce enquired.'

The old man didn't answer but looked skyward...

'It's over Jeanie. I did it, you can rest now,' he murmured.

I didn't know exactly what the old man had meant but guessed that Jeanie was someone close to Simpson whom Granston had probably come into contact in the past.

A couple of curious faces peered through the doorway of the barn and the bouncer who'd been on the floor with his face pressed into the dirt was being helped by two men. Car engines revved in the car park and vehicles hurtled down the drive.

Deuce spoke to Simpson.

'Look, mate, you'd better get out of here someone's bound to call the cops if they haven't done so already.'

A dog entered the building made its way over to Granston and sniffed his mutilated head.

Simpson looked confused.

'I've got nothing to live for. He destroyed the one thing I held most precious.'

'Don't throw the rest of your life away because of him he's not worth it. Go, just go. We didn't see anything; you saved my life.'

Simpson looked at me and then at Granston, picked up the shotgun and shuffled out. I watched him depart and called the dog. 'Come here, boy – here.' The dog gave a wag of his tail and trotted up to me; I took hold of the leash that trailed behind him.

Deuce was anxious to leave, 'We'd better split, man.'

'Yeah,' I answered. 'You got a pencil or something to write with?'

Deuce shrugged, 'No mate, why?'

'He's HIV and there's a lot of blood around.'

Deuce cast a hasty look around the interior. There was no sign of anything to write on.

I walked across to a corner of the now deserted building, picked up a small piece of wood propped up against the wall, and returned to the body of Granston who lay in a pool of coagulated blood.

I prescribed an 'H' then an 'I' then a 'V' in the crimson liquid, wiped my prints from the wood and threw it down beside the corpse; took my last look at Granston. I felt no remorse or pity for him.

I had changed, perhaps not for the better.

'Let's go.' I tugged on the dog's leash; we left the building.

There were still a couple of people in the car park, a vehicle stopped next to me. The bouncer looked out from the passenger's side and glowered from the interior of the car. By the expression on his face, I could see he was still in pain.

'You're a fuckin' troublemaker, mate. You'll end up in real shit, mate. I'm gonna…'

'You're what?' I interrupted and took a step toward the car. The driver put his foot hard down on the accelerator and rocketed off with a screech of tyres.

'Arsehole!' Deuce yelled out as the vehicle bounced down the track.

The dog sat between us in the front as Deuce drove.

'Shit, man, that was heavy,' he remarked. 'Heavy.'

I felt relief that I'd got my daughter's dog back and Granston was no longer a threat to me or my family.

A sense of relief? Yes, but knew I couldn't relax until I was sure my daughter was not infected. If she were, I would face that problem when and if it arose.

As we drove down the country road towards the city my lack of remorse at the sight of my nemesis sprawled on the floor with hardly any head made me investigate myself and question my character.

·········

I had long since abandoned my early beliefs and had adopted a more philosophical approach to life and, if anything, leaned towards the concept of reincarnation and the development of the spirit.

"My spiritual progress in this area must have taken a step backward today." I thought.

Bozo had collapsed and slept with his large head on my lap. I ruffled his ears.

'Nice lookin' dog,' Deuce commented. 'What yer gonna do now?' he asked.

'I dunno. Get rid of this mutt and then maybe head up to Queensland, Brisbane somewhere that's if my parole allows.'

'The grunters will suspect you were involved, somehow.'

'But I've done nothing wrong. I didn't kill Granston,'

'No, but you were at an illegal gathering which goes against yer parole regulations.'

'So, were you, how are they going to prove it? And I don't think they'd bother just to pin that on me.'

'Don't trust 'em, mate. Don't yer believe it they're all a bunch of cunts.'

'Not to put too fine a point on it.'

Deuce pulled up outside my apartment. It was eleven fifteen. I thought of Sal but then decided not to disturb her as she may not be alone, and I didn't want to embarrass her if she wasn't. I guess it depended how "Christian" she had become and whether her relationship with David was platonic, as they were not married.

'Don't forget there are still Green and Granston's brother around and that fat arse dickhead mate of theirs.' Deuce reminded me.

I shrugged. 'I don't think they'll hang around, Granston's brother may be a problem. Anyway, I've got a dog to protect me now.'

Deuce glanced at Bozo. He'd lick em to death.

'I don't think he'd be much good unless yer were attacked by another dog.'

I put out my hand. 'Thanks for your help mate and tell Goulburn I'm grateful.'

'No worries,' Deuce replied. 'I'd do it all again. I hope yer kid and yer father-in-law are okay.'

'Thanks.' I said, 'Keep in touch..'

'See yer.' He drove off.

I watched the car disappear around a corner before I went upstairs to my apartment, the dog led the way, panting and pulling, eager to go on a trip of discovery. The cotton was still intact, and I pushed open the door. I felt tired and the adrenalin rushes I had experienced throughout the course of the evening had left me shagged out. I released the dog; it immediately ran from room to room, sniffing and exploring every inch of the apartment.

I sank into one of the chairs as he came over and sat a few feet in front of me, he barked. I leaned forward.

'Quiet, you horrible dog,' I stroked his brick like head.

'I bet you're bloody hungry, aren't you?' I heaved myself out of the chair and went into the kitchen. There was nothing to eat.

I noticed on the table a card which read 'Healthy pizza.' 'What time does this place close?' I said half to myself and half to Bozo, who looked up at me with a cocked ear.

'One o'clock. Well do you fancy a pizza, a healthy one? Hang on I remember reading onions and chocolate weren't good for dogs.'

I looked at the menu. 'How about some pasta?'

Bozo wagged his tail, 'without onions. Okay, let's do it.' I picked up the phone.

An hour later the dog was asleep on the floor with an extended belly, and I was asleep in the chair. I woke up momentarily, dragged myself into the bedroom and collapsed on the bed fully dressed. A few minutes later I felt a large lump of warm fur flop down beside me. I didn't have the energy to kick him off; I rolled over and went to sleep. The dog gave an audible sigh and settled down in Rik's monstrous bed.

It was seven o'clock when I was awakened by the wet tongue of Bozo as he licked my face and greeted by the sight of the dark muzzle of my canine bed mate. The shock caused me to pull back sharply before I realised where I was and what had happened.

'Jesus you're a friendly bugger, aren't you? Where's Clare?' I said. 'Where's Clare?'

The dog pricked up its ears and cocked his head to one side then woofed.

'Shh, shush,' I said, and put my hand on the dog's nose, 'you'll wake everyone up. Come on, let's go for a walk, otherwise there'll be a big curly one on the carpet.'

I swung my legs over the side of the bed, got up, splashed some water over my face and changed into my track suit and running shoes, fixed the dog's lead and set off toward the park.

I suspected that Bozo had not enjoyed a morning walk lately and had probably been kept on a chain. He wasn't badly scarred, as the other dogs had been, which made me think that maybe he hadn't fought, which could be the case and kind of confirmed to me that he was indeed Bozo. We got back an hour later. I bought a tin of dog food from the milk bar up the road before I headed home. I fed him, had a shower, and listened to the radio as I cooked my breakfast.

'The Police are investigating the death of a man in Dural last night, believed to have been attending a dog fight.'

The newscaster went on to say that the police received an anonymous call around about ten o'clock on Saturday night.

I poured myself a cup of tea. The news continued about some international celebrity being pelted with eggs whilst he visited Sydney Town Hall and then the resignation of a prominent politician in Japan on corruption charges.

This caused me no particular interest and I would have ignored it had not the announcer gone on to say the police wish to question a man called Jason Granston in connection with a drugs raid in Kings Cross.

'Well, that'll keep him busy for a while,' I commented.

Bozo had parked himself on the sofa and contentedly licked his foot. He interrupted his ablutions at the sound of my voice and then carried on, satisfied all was well.

'We live in a great world, mate. Come on, let's get you back to where you belong.'

I was about to depart when there was a knock on the door. Bozo looked alert and went to the door.

'It's okay, it's okay, I told the dog. 'Who is it?' I asked.

'It's Detective Jackson.'

I silently cursed but opened the door. 'Come in before you're tempted to kick it down.'

'Thanks.' Jackson stepped into the apartment and stopped when he saw the dog. Bozo wagged his tail and approached the Policeman.

'Got yerself a dog ?' he stroked the animal's head.

'It's my daughter's dog,' I replied.

'Oh, yer found it then?' Jackson commented.

'Yes.'

'Where?'

I said nothing and tried to come up with a suitable answer.

'Wouldn't have been out Dural way by any chance?'

Again, I said nothing.

'Oh, by the way,' Jackson continued, 'you'll be relieved to know that Granston will no longer be bothering you. He's dead.'

'A cop friend of mine in charge of the case contacted me.'

I feigned surprise but none too convincingly.

'How did he die, car accident?' I asked.

'He was shot,' Jackson replied.

'Shot wow. Do you know who did it?'

'Oh, yes, the father of one of Granston's victims, a girl he raped, and then killed her fiancée. His name is Simpson, a regular prison visitor, you may have met him.'

I understood now what Simpson had meant. I'd had a rough idea but now had the full story. He had handed himself in.

'He visited Granston a couple of times wanted to face him, try and forgive. When he realised Granston had escaped, his good intentions went out the window.

Very messy. Granston was lying in a pool of blood, and someone had inscribed the letters HIV in it, the blood that is; very considerate of them. They must've known Granston quite well to have been aware of his alleged illness.'

The Police officer stared at me.

I remained expressionless as I listened.

'Is the girl Granston raped still alive?'

'No, she killed herself, took an overdose six months later.'

I nodded and understood the motivation of Simpson and why it had been so strong.

'You weren't anywhere near the Dural area last night, were you?' Jackson asked casually.

I looked back at the Police Sergeant. 'No.'

'I didn't think yer would have been. Anyway, just thought I'd let yer know about Granston. Nice dog. Looks like a pit bull terrier.'

'Really?' I replied. 'I don't know much about dogs.'

'Stay out of trouble.' Jackson made for the door. 'I hope things work out for yer.'

I felt the sincerity of the man and acknowledged him with a nod.

'I will, and sorry again about your partner.'

'Yeah,' Jackson replied thoughtfully.

He left; I heard him go down the stairs and out of my life.

'Come on, mate. Let's take you home.'

I left my flat to walk to Sally's just after one o'clock and arrived outside her house three quarters of an hour later. I felt a flush of pleasure at the thought of reuniting my daughter with her beloved Bozo. I pushed open the gate and heard a sound from within which made my heart sink and Bozo's ears prick up.

I knocked cautiously on the front door, stepped back onto the pavement, and closed the gate.

The door opened and Sally stood framed in the doorway. At her side, the dark muzzle of an almost identical dog to the one on my leash thrust vigorously to get through to me.

Both dogs growled furiously at the sight of each other and Bozo, the real Bozo, rushed at the gate. I stepped further back and pulled "my dog" away from the fence.

Clare appeared in the background.

'Who is it?' she enquired.

'It's your father,' Sally replied, 'and he's got a dog just like Bozo.'

Clare came and stood at the gate.

Sally dragged Bozo back into the house. 'I'll be back in a minute.'

Clare put her hand through the railings and felt the dog's square powerful head.

'He's just like Bozo,' she said and stroked the wet muzzle that furiously licked her hand.

'Yeah, I thought it was Bozo.'

'He came back yesterday evening. Someone found him and brought him back. He'd been staying with them.'

'That's great,' I replied, 'and, how are you?' 'I resisted the temptation to lift her up and squeeze her.

'Good thank you.'

'We'll go to the zoo like I promised, okay?'

Clare put her finger on the gate and traced the railing as she spoke.

'How old is your dog? What's his name?'

'Oh, I don't know. I only got him yesterday,' I answered.

Sally came out through the front door. Bozo's bark could be heard faintly from the back garden.

'I thought this was Bozo,' I said as Sally took in his appearance. 'I wanted to make her
happy.'

'Well, we had a call yesterday and some people brought him back. They had been looking after him and hadn't seen the ads and informed the RSPCA, well whatever, probably knew all the time but felt guilty. He's home now and Clare's happy.'

'How is she?' I asked.

'She's fine, we'll know soon.'

I felt my heart sink as my mind conjured up images of Clare in hospital wasting away. I quickly dismissed them.

'Well, looks like I made another goof up.'

Sally leaned across the gate and stroked the Bozo look alike who stared intently through the railings.

'You'll have no problems with Granston anymore.'

'I know,' Sally said. 'Detective Jackson told me.'

'How's your dad?'

'He's good. He's making a recovery.'

'When do you think it's best to see him?' I asked.

'When you like really, I saw him yesterday and he seemed very chirpy. I'm going again today this afternoon. I'm taking Clare.'

I smiled. I would have loved to have gone with them but didn't ask.

'Well, I was saying to Clare about going to the zoo some time; maybe next Saturday?'

'Yes, why not. That would be nice wouldn't it Clare?'

Clare bent down and stroked "my" dog's head with her face close to the metal gate and squealed as the dog's nose pushed through the railings and his tongue licked her face.

I looked down at my daughter. 'She likes dogs.'

'Yes,' Sally answered. 'Do you want to go to the zoo with Daddy?' Sally asked.

Clare nodded her approval.

There was an awkward silence.

'Well, I'll leave you to your Sunday. Looks like I'm lumbered with a dog.'

'Where did you get him?' Sally remarked.

'Don't ask,' I replied.

Sally gave me a puzzled look, 'right.'

'Come on, mate.' I tugged on the leash and pulled him away.

'See you soon, Clare.'

I looked at Sally and then away from her dark eyes. I searched for some sign of emotion, some indication that she still felt something for me but if it was there, I failed to recognise it.

'Well, take care and I'll be in touch.' I said awkwardly.

'Bye, daddy.' Clare's childish voice wished me farewell and lifted my spirits a notch. I sensed a new mood of hope that perhaps my relationship with the little girl I desperately loved was not beyond redemption. I walked away from the house and back towards Marrickville, my new companion on a leash at my side.

That evening I sat watching television when the phone rang.

It was Rochester.

'Hello old mate,' a cheery voice said. 'It's me.'

'Where are you?' I asked.

'I'm on my way over to visit you,' Rochester replied. 'Put the kettle on. I'll be there in ten minutes.'

'Okay, mate. It'll be great to see you.'

'Oh, by the way, I've got someone with me who wants to see you. If you don't want to see

her, she'll understand. Would you mind?'

'I'd love to see her. You mean Satchiko?'

'I do,' the voice on the other end of the receiver answered.

'No, that would be great. You'll have to excuse the flat. Anyway, I'll tell you all about it

when I see you.'

'Okay, mate, we'll see you soon.'

I replaced the receiver, stood up and walked into the kitchen to put some water in the kettle. The dog had followed me.

'We're going to have company, mate. I suppose I'd better think of a name for you. How about Fido?'

The dog barked.

'Quiet, you horrible mutt. You'll have us both thrown out on the street. Come 'ere you monster.'

Fido wagged his tail and approached me; I bent down and roughed his ears.

'You're a bit of a responsibility old mate, I'll try and find a good home for you, someone who'll treat you well. In the meantime, looks like you and me are stuck with each other. One thing, okay? Now you listen to this. No fighting! Is that clear? It just gets you into a heap of trouble.'

Fido snuffled, pricked up his ears and gave me, his new master, a sloppy lick on my face as if to signify his agreement.

By Nik Forster

Kiyoshi and the Grumpy Ghost

Feral Cat

Salo: Canine Outlaw

Ayumi Girl of the Borneo Forest

www.ingramcontent.com/pod-product-compliance
Lightning Source LLC
Chambersburg PA
CBHW072058020426
42334CB00017B/1555